GARDENERS

ON THE GO

❧

Twenty terrific tours
around Puget Sound and

S E A T T L

Thank you, Jane, so much for your enthusiasm and support. I do hope you're able to get to "test drive" these tours in person as a gardener on the go!

*Cheers-
Stephanie Feeney*

By Stephanie Feeney

Author of
The Northwest Gardeners' Resource Directory

Dedicated to
my dear friend and mentor
Sarah Eppenbach
for the high
standards she sets as an example and
beyond-the-call-of-duty support
she provided to
get this book
on the go

ISBN 0-9639853-9-6

Printed in the United States of America

For information about permission to reproduce selections
from this book write to:
Cedarcroft Press, 59 Strawberry Pt., Bellingham,
Washington 98226
Telephone: (360) 733-4461
FAX: (360) 647-1825
E-MAIL: publisher@cedarcroft-press.com
http://www.cedarcroft-press.com

Table of Contents

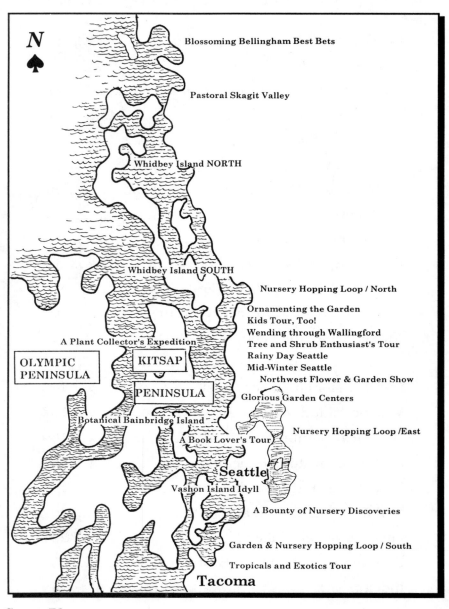

N ♠

Blossoming Bellingham Best Bets

Pastoral Skagit Valley

Whidbey Island NORTH

Whidbey Island SOUTH

Nursery Hopping Loop / North

Ornamenting the Garden
Kids Tour, Too!
Wending through Wallingford
A Plant Collector's Expedition
Tree and Shrub Enthusiast's Tour
Rainy Day Seattle
OLYMPIC
PENINSULA
KITSAP
Mid-Winter Seattle
Northwest Flower & Garden Show

PENINSULA
Glorious Garden Centers

Botanical Bainbridge Island
Nursery Hopping Loop /East

A Book Lover's Tour

Seattle

Vashon Island Idyll

A Bounty of Nursery Discoveries

Garden & Nursery Hopping Loop / South

Tropicals and Exotics Tour

Tacoma

Cover Photos
Front, top to bottom: City People's Garden Store, Seattle; Lucca Statuary, Seattle; Fortner Books, Bainbridge Island
Back: Tease and Riley at work, Swanson's Nursery, Seattle

INTRODUCTORY
NOTES

Author's introduction
How to use the book
Touring tips

Building the itinerary of a memorable day trip is a bit like selecting the complementary elements for a mixed border. Each component is an integral part of the whole, yet each is disparate and unique. A pleasing garden, like a wonderful day of exploration, reflects a considered placement of its elements in artful juxtaposition—but with room for a dash of the unanticipated to create a sense of happy surprise without reducing the harmony of the whole. And both the border and the trip require a framework to give them shape, a theme around which the individual parts may be understood. Just as the physical context of landscape and neighborhood affects a garden, so, too, does historical context help develop the character of the destinations on a tour. And finally, just as garden design requires attention to the cultural needs of the plants, tour planning must incorporate careful consideration of transportation arrangements, opening and closing particulars, where to eat and, for those special occasions, where to spend the night.

AUTHOR'S INTRODUCTION

For over a decade I have had the pleasure of scouring the Pacific Northwest in search of the best resources for gardeners, garden lovers and visitors to this gardening Mecca. In the guise of research for my book *The Northwest Gardeners' Resource Directory,* I have traveled thousands of miles, month after month, in all weather and in all seasons. I have been able to ferret out terrific (though often less visible) small specialty nurseries and to evaluate the strengths (and weaknesses) of the popular big garden centers. I have poked through countless funky junk shops and many elegant garden emporiums. I have attended hours and hours of lectures, workshops, symposiums and classes to glean wisdom and insight from horticultural gurus and down-to-earth, everyday gardeners alike. I have joined virtually every major gardening-related society in the region (and am actively involved in most) and regularly read the newsletters of many I have not joined.

In the course of all that rambling and poking about I often found myself constructing in my mind what I thought of as a great day trip, highlighting my most recent "finds", to share with a crew of like-minded friends. The thought being mother to the deed, I volunteered to lead small groups of intrepid garden tourers from our local horticultural society on day-long explorations that included a nursery or two, a striking little antique shop with a penchant for garden-worthy ornament and perhaps a bookstore that had an excellent horticulture section. I set myself to arranging the car pools, scouting out a great lunch destination (and usually a morning stop for the requisite latte), planning for ferry connections and, of course, making sure all the places we intended to visit would be open to greet our arrival. And it was great fun!

When I was forced to give up this pleasant though time-consuming task there were frequent pleas to put together another season of tours. It occurred to me that I could do so in the form of this guide.

I hope these day-trips bring you as much pleasure as I have had creating them. Some of my happiest hours have been those spent in the company of my gardening friends, reveling in both the horticultural and culinary bounty of the Pacific Northwest--the thrill of a day of garden discoveries coupled with the enjoyment of delicious food shared with delightful companions. It is my hope that *Gardeners On The Go: Seattle* will be the catalyst for many similar days for you and your friends and that you will be inspired to create and embark upon many similar expeditions in the years ahead.

And for those of you who may have followed the course of the *Northwest Gardeners' Resource Directory* for the last nine years, I can report that my husband Larry remains unfailingly supportive of the time I spend away from home researching and the time I *am* at home writing. He understands how enthused I am about this work, and has, in fact, caught the bug himself and now manages our small publishing house, Cedarcroft Press. He works with me on the production of the manuscript right up to the moment we send it off to the printer. Needless to say, I am indebted to him for his encouragement, for his hard work and his excitement about *Gardeners on the Go*.

How to Use this Book

Gardeners on the Go: Seattle is organized around twenty **themes** that set the stage for a day of exploration. Eleven of the itineraries are within the Seattle area and nine take you further afield around Puget Sound. Each is meant to be a day trip although some are *very ambitious* and will require close attention to time if your intent is to make the entire circuit. Remember that these excursions are meant to be fun, so if you get diverted (and believe me, there are plenty of distractions along the way) then why not consider breaking the experience into a couple of half-day tours instead?

Itinerary Highlights provide a quick snapshot of the destinations, emphasizing something distinctive about each place.

The Itinerary in Brief and **Map** two-page spread give a quick synopsis of what you can expect on the tour with a geographic locator map directly opposite to help you visualize where you will be traveling in relation to downtown Seattle. Maps are provided as general guides and work with the Driving Directions (see below).

Tour Timing lists a number of factors that you'll want to consider in putting the day of exploration on the calendar. For instance, on most of the tours there are a few days of the week that one or more of the destination close. Part of the fun and challenge of putting the itineraries together was to maximize the visiting options my readers would have in planning forays.

Some of the suggestions tie a day trip into something of gardening significance that may induce you to plan a two-day excursion or modify the tour to accommodate a special event such as Bainbridge Island's big Tour of Private Gardens in July or the one in Bellingham annually in June.

At the time of writing the opening/closing days and event dates for

1998 are correct. However, everything in the world of gardening is subject to change, so a call in advance to confirm details is always wise planning policy.

Tour Tips pass along lessons gained from my own personal experience to help maximize the pleasure and success of your trip.

Setting the Scene provides some historical background for the areas where you'll be traveling. As the heading suggests, this material is meant to evoke a sense of place and the people who shaped it—and something of what influences those who live there now. I have further given a brief **Community Profile** of many of the towns and neighborhoods you'll visit.

Driving Directions appear above the destination profiles to provide enough detail to help you navigate from destination to destination. Mid-town Seattle on I-5 is used as the **starting point** to avoid confusing everyone by trying to write directions to cover every contingency. My selected route is the one I have deemed the quickest path that is also straight forward. I have provided the **Driving distance** and **Estimated driving time** to help in your planning. These figures cannot foresee road work detours and traffic jams. If the excursion requires that you take a ferry, see the information on "Taking the Ferry" below.

Always pack along detailed street maps, too, and if you get lost, don't be shy -- ask directions to get back *on the go.*

Destination Profiles start with street address (including the mailing address if different from the street address), telephone, Web site information and opening times.

Symbols have been used to help you check the following at a glance:

❖ open year round

☂ some type of shelter from the rain (a shop, greenhouse, etc.)

📖 gardening books for sale

☆ gardening related gifts for sale

✳ display garden

RR restroom available

Lunch suggestions have been made from my personal experience while researching each of the tours. I have tried to include one that is a particularly special, fancy place for days when lingering a little longer, perhaps over a glass of wine and an elegant meal, is an important part of the excursion. At the other end of the spectrum, and for many of us no less special, are picnic recommendations, with a site or two and usually a shop near-by that can supply the fixings. Then there is at least one suggestion between these two extremes, often a Bistro, Northwest Brew Pub or small town café. Details, including address, hours and price range are provided in.. ☞

Further Resources provides the details on the highlighted Lunch suggestions and adds a few options to provide more choice.

Food Symbols give a price range and opening information:
$ inexpensive, entrees mostly under $5
$$ moderate, entrees mostly $5-$9
$$$ expensive, entrees mostly over $9
B Breakfast (Brunch is also noted)
L Lunch
D Dinner

Picnics My mother was an "any excuse for a picnic" kind of person. She was also a creative cook with a spirit of adventure, and one who delighted in the juxtaposition of a rustic setting and a civilized "table". Even when there wasn't an actual table, there was the family Pendleton blanket to spread out, cloth napkins, lemon scented wash cloths packed in sandwich bags – that kind of thing.

Lodging More and more small inns and bed and breakfast establishments are opening every year, and many of them feature a garden—which in turn generally means a host(ess) who is a gardener, too! I have attempted to find comfortable, special lodgings with an emphasis on those with style and character, pleasant ambiance and enthusiastic owners and staff who offer a warm welcome. Many have gardens. I also urge you to look through the travel guides I have listed in this section as the ones I personally turn to in planning trips in this area. You will need to check when making reservations about house policies concerning pets, children, smoking and the like. Many Bed and Breakfasts have a two-night minimum stay required on week-ends or in peak season.
$ inexpensive, under $80/night for lodging for two
$$ moderate, $80-$125/night for lodging for two
$$$ expensive, more than $125/night for lodging for two
Many places of accomodation have Web sites these days (if I have known of their address I have listed it). Often there are photos and detailed descriptions that help you find just the right place.

Camping There are more than 80 Washington State Parks with campgrounds and over 500 U.S. Forest Service campgrounds in Washington. Each offers some form of reservation system covering a number (*but not all*) of their facilities.

U.S. Forest Service Campgrounds reservations (800) 280-CAMP
Washington State Parks reservations: (800) 452-5687, up to eleven months in advance, with the best time to call Wednesdays through Fridays after 1 p.m. Call early–September through April the lines are virtually clear. Information center: (800) 233-0321. They also maintain an excellent Web site, where, for instance, you can find out about the yurts, cabins and historic homes available to rent (with photos). www.parks.wa.gov/

For More Information Listings of the local Chamber of Commerce and/or Visitor Bureau are provided to help you gather additional trip planning materials or to provide helpful information should you have questions. The offices I visited during my research were universally staffed with helpful folks anxious to please. They stock a gazillion brochures from area businesses, from B & B's and other lodging options to event fliers, restaurants and local service providers. While I was browsing through a huge photo album featuring pictures of all the near-by B & B's in La Conner, the volunteer was talking to a potential visitor calling from Germany. As they spoke, the volunteer was standing at the brochure rack compiling a handful of pieces to send off in the next mail. One of the most valuable planning tools you can get from them is their free Visitor Guide publication, filled with useful information, photos, historical background and fascinating facts.

More Resources for Gardeners Additional opportunities of interest to a gardener in the tour vicinity. If a destination on the official itinerary happens to be closed then you can look here for other options to fill in the day or induce you to make this a two-day excursion. In this section I also list books that supplement the tour with pertinent information.

Further Touring Tips
GENERAL TOURING KIT
- good maps (essential); I use the **Thomas Guides**, which, though expensive, are extremely valuable tools as very detailed street locators. For a more general area map I use the **Washington Atlas and Gazetteer**.
- small cooler for drinks, snack (when you are too obsessed to stop for lunch), picnic (especially salads) and a good place to safely store fresh produce, fruit, seafood and pasta picked up en route from

roadside farmstands.
- waterproof shoes (even on a nice day where there is the chance of heavy dew, irrigation or a change in the weather)
- current ferry schedule
- parking change (I keep a roll of quarters in the glove box)
- picnic blanket
- protective tarp, sheet, newspaper or such on which to set plants and, for a hot day when cars heat quickly, a flagon of water for the poor beasts!
- gardening reference books

DELUXE FANATIC'S TOURING KIT adds:
- note taking materials
- camera
- 3-ring binder with tabbed divider for each tour including a zip lock bag for collected business cards, brochures, menus, maps, etc.

GOOD BOOKS / TRAVEL GUIDES

Access Seattle, (1997, HarperPerennial). The Access series of travel books are just fabulous – visually exciting and informative, easy and fun to read, well-researched and well-written.

Garden Touring In the Pacific Northwest (1993, Alaska Northwest Books), Jan Kowalczewski Whitner. An insightful guide to public gardens in Oregon, Washington and British Columbia.

Garden Tourist, (1998, Garden Tourist Press), Lois Rosenfeld. Updated annually and supported by a Web site for current updates, this is a useful guide to garden tours, garden open days and special events for every state in the U.S. and beyond.

Seeing Seattle (1994, University of Washington Press) by Roger Sale. I like this walkabout approach to getting to know Seattle. The length of time for each walk and bus connections are provided, a nice detail for out-of-towners.

Washington Handbook, Don Pitcher, (Moon Travel Handbooks), a masterful piece of research and writing covering the entire state in rich detail. A staple in my own library for savvy travel information and thoughtfully considered historical coverage.

Washington State Parks, a Complete Recreation Guide (The Mountaineers) Marge and Ted Mueller have written a number of excellent books focusing on outdoor recreation in western Washington. They are thoroughly researched, well written and supported by terrific maps and photos.

TAKING THE BUS

If you are going to be in Seattle without a car, many of the places featured in *Gardeners on the Go* are readily reached by Seattle's Metro

system of buses. Buses link to the ferry at Pier 52 and there is a wide free zone in the downtown Seattle area. The 24-hour rider information number is (206) 553-3000; they have an excellent Web site to help you plan in advance: http://transit.metrokc.gov.
Consider an all-day pass for the week-ends with unlimited travel (available from bus drivers) for $1.70.

TAKING THE FERRY / Washington State Ferry System

For schedule information: (800) 84-FERRY;   (206) 464-6400
www.wsdot.wa.gov/ferries/
Request a free copy of the Ferry System's 14-page color brochure for the full skinny on ferry travel (including schedule and fares for the entire system).   Here's a synopsis: Fares can be paid in cash, in-state checks or travelers checks (no credit cards accepted). On some routes the fare paid on the mainland covers the round-trip (example: the San Juans and Vashon Island). Otherwise there is a driver/vehicle fee both ways (Bainbridge, Whidbey and Kingston). An example of what to expect (as of this writing): a passenger fare on the Bainbridge Island run is $3.50 (half fare for passengers over 65 years of age), collected westbound only (and free to walk-on passengers on the return trip). Vehicles/drivers pay both ways, in the neighborhood of $6 to $7 each way, depending on peak or non-peak season. Ferries run frequently. If you are unfamiliar with using the Washington ferry system, then familiarize yourself with the schedule for the route you are taking so you'll be able to add the necessity of the wait in line and the crossing time into your plans. The system serves thousands of commuters and vacationers daily. Especially in summer at peak times for week-end travel (westward Friday afternoons and Saturday mornings and eastward Sunday afternoon and evenings) travel may require a long wait, so build this into your plans.

SEATTLE TRAVEL NOTES
LODGING / Seattle and around Puget Sound
Three Capitol Hill Bed and Breakfast/Inns provide excellent access to destinations of interest to Gardeners on the Go (Volunteer Park, Washington Park Arboretum, Capitol Hill shops/restaurants, downtown, the Seattle Convention Center, decent I-5 access....)
Gaslight Inn/Howell Street Suites: 1727 15th Ave., Seattle, WA 98122; (206) 325-3654. www.gaslightinn.com $$-$$$. Side-by-side turn-of-the-century homes have been elegantly fashioned into one of the most appealing big city Inns I have found. The tasteful decor is at once crisply professional and invitingly homey, the location on Capitol Hill places guests near excellent restaurants, Volunteer Park and downtown but provides the amenities of a splendid urban garden,

pool, library, crackling fire and graciously comfortable rooms all of which provide the happy dilemma of staying put or venturing out! **Roberta's Bed and Breakfast**: 1147 16th Ave. E, Seattle, WA 98112; (206) 329-3326. $$. The most dreamy of sweets magically appeared upon my arrival at Roberta's – the kind of treat you linger over with a cup of tea, easy conversation and suddenly realize an hour has slipped by and you've only just met. This Capitol Hill classic provides a relaxing, comfy nest with well-appointed rooms, garden surrounding the house, convenient location, welcoming hostess. **Salisbury House**: 750 16th Ave. E, Seattle, WA 98112; (206) 328-8682. $$. Built in 1908, nestled into a quiet residential neighborhood of tree-lined streets and handsome historic homes, Salisbury House is a welcome haven for travelers seeking gracious hospitality, a lovely room to call one's own, a garden to remind one of home and an ideal location for Gardener's on the Go exploring Seattle.

One of my favorite ways to travel is to seek out a place I can feel at home settling in to as a comfy home base. I like the option of being able to eat/cook in or nip out to a restaurant. I like having the amenities of home like a washer/dryer and iron, and I like to have a secure place to leave my car. An option I have used for years is: **Pacific Guest Suites**: 411 108th Ave. NE, Bellevue, WA 98004-5515; (800) 962-6620, (425) 454-7888. (Three day minimum stay required, reservations secured up to 30 days in advance). This company manages residential properties in condominiums and apartments throughout the Puget Sound area (Seattle, Bellevue, Redmond, Kirkland, Issaquah, Renton and Mukilteo). My favorite place to stay has been the Newmark Tower, which overlooks Pike Place Market in the heart of downtown Seattle. I can pop out early for the freshest of pastries and be back by the time the coffee has perked, read the morning paper and look out over the skyline of an awakening city as commuter ferries scurried across Elliott Bay delivering commuters from island homes to city jobs. The facilities are reasonably priced, especially when I have traveled with friends sharing a two-bedroom place. Many of the accommodations come with amenities of a pool, health clubs or tennis courts, have landscaped grounds and are generally well-located for convenience to shopping, restaurants, theaters, parks, etc. Several of the properties invite children and some even allow pets. There is a broad range from classy up-town to suburban low-rise to appeal to a variety of needs and desires.

Bed and Breakfast Association of Seattle: P.O. Box 31772, Seattle, WA 98103-1772; (206) 547-1020, 10 a.m.-7 p.m. PST; or visit the web site: http://uspan.com/sbba This organization can send you

a brochure profiling their member establishments, many of which
would be ideal for Gardeners on the Go visiting Seattle.
Pacific Reservation Service: (206) 784-0539

Books to help you find lodging:
Best Places to Kiss in the Northwest (1997, Beginning Press),
Paula Begoun. The emphasis here, as the title suggests, is romanctic
destinations, covering lodgings, restaurants, parks and scenic drives
(including "Romantic Warnings" where needed). Everything from
extravagant penthouses to affordable seaside cabins are covered,
rated with up to four "lips" (for the really *hot* spots).
Northwest Best Places (1998), *Northwest Cheap Sleeps* (1995) and
Seattle Best Places (1996), Stephanie Irving with Nancy Leson on
the Seattle book (Sasquatch Books), updated every three years. The
Best Places series has endured as the standard reference in travel
planning for this region since 1975. Restaurant and lodging reviews
(rated by stars) prevail though the books point out notable shopping,
events, parks, kid friendly options, historical places of interest and
some itinerary suggestions.
Washington State Division of Tourism (800) 544-1800. Included
among the publications you can request is the *Washington State
Lodging and Travel Guide* (offering a comprehensive listing of
accommodations and camping options) along with lots of other travel
planning information.

Airport Access
If you are a Gardener on the Go with a (long) lay-over in Seattle at
Sea-Tac airport, you might consider taking a shuttle into town. The
Gray Line Airport Express leaves every 15 minutes from 5 a.m. to
midnight and stops at seven downtown hotels. The trip to/from the
airport (barring traffic jams) is 50 minutes.

Our Web Site: www.cedarcroft-press.com/

GLORIOUS
GARDEN
CENTERS

────────────── Itinerary Highlights ──────────────
mega-nursery and garden emporium with pizzazz
long-established nursery with a loyal following
beloved neighborhood nursery catering to urban gardeners
old-fashioned garden center matures with grace, elegance

Only a brief time ago it was to the garden center that we all trooped in search of our every gardening need, from vegetable starts to the trowel we needed to dig them in, from the bonnets to protect us from the blazing sun to the rubber boots to protect us from the damp and cold. Over the past decade Northwest gardening has gone topsy-turvy with a proliferation of small specialty nurseries and shops featuring gardening goods. Mail-order sources present the consumer with a vast array of choice. Yet, true to form, our faithful old friends have kept abreast of the latest trends – eye-popping perennials, more pest-resistant fruit trees and better tasting tomatillos. And there remains that great exhilaration of wandering the labyrinth of a quality garden center, a fruitful, comforting return to our roots.

🍂 **THE ITINERARY IN BRIEF** 🍂

❶ Molbak's

Molbak's is the Nordstrom's of the nursery trade (or is Nordstrom's the Molbak's of the clothing trade?) In any event, the name is synonymous with top quality merchandise, an emphasis on knowledgeable and friendly service, classy digs and a flare for theater. They are the largest single-outlet garden center in the United States, with an estimated 1 million people visiting annually!

❷ Furney's Nursery

Furney's has a fiercely loyal following for their professional service and a solid selection of well-grown plants. This long-established Northwest garden center draws me back again and again with an excellent selection of trees and shrubs – sometimes for varieties I haven't found elsewhere and often for a more reasonably priced, larger and better shaped version of ones I have.

Lunch Two nice Asian restaurants, an innovative and classy vegetarian café or a picnic in the park.

❸ City People's Garden Store

With the warm and fuzzy feel of a sophisticated country mercantile, this urban nursery miraculously packs in an amazing array of home and garden goodies. This is the kind of place one drifts through at a leisurely pace, lingering among the beautiful displays, whether in the gift shop poring over the book nook, in the bright airy nursery wing pondering an enviable selection of herbs or out in the sales yard padding up and down well- stocked aisles of appealing ornamentals.

❹ Swanson's Nursery

One of the top stops in Seattle for any dedicated plant hunter, this elegant favorite not only keeps abreast of the fast-paced horticultural scene in the Northwest, but leads the pack, displaying their seductive savvy and secret sources!

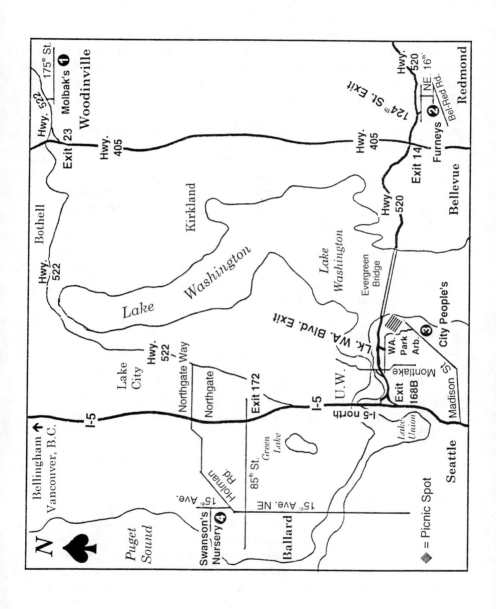

Tour Timing and Tips

🍎 Garden Centers are notorious for going wild at holiday time. Think of them for a Halloween field trip with the kids and at Christmas not only for conifers (live or cut) but poinsettias -- **Molbak's**, for instance throws a festive bash each year from mid- to late November that dazzles visitors with a dramatic display of 30 striking varieties -- 5,500 cheery poinsettias (representing about 10% of what the greenhouse grows).

🍎 Of special note for families is **Molbak's** *Floral Fairyland*, a live performance of a classic from children's literature (as an example, in 1998 it is Hans Christian Anderson's "The Nightingale"). True gifts to the community, these plays are extravagant productions with delightful sets and elegant costuming. They are offered Thursday-Sunday in October, evening and day times with special American Sign Language performances offered as well. (425) 483-5000.

🍎 **Swanson's** offers a serious sale – one I have made the 200 mile round trip to attend! If you plan your visit to coincide with the annual fall 50% off sale, come early and come prepared to spend a good couple of hours examining the extensive offerings.

Setting the Scene

Molbak's is a venerable leader in the retail gardening world of the Pacific Northwest. Their main retail facility of 100,000 square feet, plus three acres of nursery stock, is located on a 15-acre site in Woodinville, 20 miles northeast of Seattle, 10 miles north of Bellevue. Molbak's grows 90% of the plants it offers, with a majority grown on their 40-acre farm and in a state-of-the-art greenhouse complex in the Redmond Valley east of Woodinville.

The story of the nursery begins in 1948 when Egon Molbak arrived in Washington from Denmark on an international horticultural exchange program, intended as a year-long commitment. After three months he returned to Denmark to retrieve his wife, Laina, for a permanent move to the Northwest. For a period he worked for others, but the discovery of a greenhouse for sale in Woodinville (then far out in the country) gave birth in 1956 to their own wholesale cut flower business. As Americans developed a passion for fresh flowers, indoor, garden and landscape plants and all the accouterments that support this interest, Molbak's had the vision to be at the head of the line offering a very broad range of quality plants and genuine service. In 1966 the retail nursery opened in Woodinville.

Furney's Nursery: Originating at their Des Moines site, south of Seattle, in 1940, the nursery began as a peach orchard. Everett Furney was the farmer of the family (edibles) and wife Edith was the gardener (flowers). In fact her green thumb produced such appealing results that friends began to beg pieces of this camellia or that azalea. Her propagation prowess suggested the enterprise might develop into a business, and so it did. In the mid-1970's, their son Robert took over and through his business acumen the nursery grew to three locations (of which two remain). The company also invested in land in the fertile Oregon fields around Gresham, where they now maintain 175 acres for Furney-grown plants (largely the woody ornamentals).

City People's Garden Store is the second of four City People's opened by Judith Gille. In 1979 the Capitol Hill Mercantile came to life and set the standard and general style that additional outlets have emulated. While each store is unique, there is a consistent philosophy of snugly fitting into an urban neighborhood with old-fashioned values and the ambiance of the well-stocked, has-everything neighborhood general store. The Madison Street City People's opened in 1988 with an emphasis on gardening needs. In 1991 the Fremont District welcomed City People's like a long lost relative. In 1998 a new neighborhood home and garden shop opens on Sand Point Way, again a welcome addition for resident gardeners and homeowners alike.

Swanson's Nursery actually dates back to 1888, but in Minnesota not Washington. That year August Swanson, who had paid his way to America from Sweden with the money he earned from a booklet he wrote on horticulture, founded Swanson's Land of Flowers. He met and married his wife, Selma, who had her own flower business. After a stint in California they came to Seattle in 1924 and started a new nursery business on ten acres in the Crown Hill neighborhood. Three generations of the Swanson family spent the next 50 years building the business into the full-service nursery that has won the hearts and respect of so many area gardeners over the years. A favorite story from the early years involves teenage son, Ted, who would load up his bicycle and deliver flowers to downtown Seattle. He later was able to take the trolley and sell his flowers to florists, door to door.

In 1976 Ted and his wife Frances retired and sold the business to the current owner, Wally Kerwin. He has retained the family nursery atmosphere and country ambiance while expanding the full selection of choice plants.

DRIVING DIRECTIONS:
From mid-town Seattle drive north on I-5 to Hwy. 520 exit 168B toward Bellevue/Kirkland. This takes you over the Evergreen Floating Bridge. Take the exit for "I-405 North/I-405 South" toward Everett keeping left at the fork in the ramp. Merge onto I-405 northbound. Drive 8 miles to the Hwy. 522 East/522 West exit 23 towards Monroe/Wenatchee and keep right at the fork in the ramp. Merge onto Hwy. 522 east and take the exit for Woodinville/Redmond. Turn right onto 131st Ave. NE and then left at NE 175th St. Molbak's is .5 mile on the right.
Insider's Tip: Molbak's offers verbal directions from various areas in Seattle via a voice mail message: (425) 483-5000 ext. 400.
Driving distance: 20 miles; *Estimated driving time:* 30 minutes.

Molbak's

13625 NE 175th St., Woodinville, WA 98072-8558; (425) 483-5000. Open year round daily 9 a.m.-6 p.m., Fridays until 9 p.m. See the "Resources" notes at the end of the chapter for addresses of additional Molbak's outlets.
Insider Tip: Request their quarterly newsletter featuring a calendar of special events, classes, sales and, of course, gardening ideas.
❖ ☂ 📖 ☆ ✱ RR
Molbak's is a nursery built for superlatives: grand, colossal, expansive and vibrant, for instance. Altogether the company grows over 2,225 different plant varieties themselves (400 bedding plant varieties, 900 foliage plant varieties, 60,000 poinsettias -- approximately two million pots of their major plants every year. Of the perennials and annuals they offer, that amounts to about 95% grown in-house). They carry over 2,500 seed varieties, from the best known and respected seed houses to many rarities from obscure sources. That speaks well for the sleuthing abilities of their skilled buyer! For navigating the 15-acre site this nursery occupies you'll appreciate the handy map available at the entrance to plot your exploration of the complex of greenhouses, shops and outdoor sales yards, not to mention the aviary/conservatory and user friendly Information Booths. The staff of trained horticulturists brings a wide breadth of experience, with encouragement from the management to work abroad to bring back fresh ideas. Summer horticultural interns from overseas are hired to work at Molbak's on the same principal.

If I sound enthusiastic about Molbak's I am. I have shopped here for over a decade, from the beginning of my new life in Washington as I was developing my interest in gardening. While they have been on the retail scene since 1956, they have never gone dormant, nor have they lost their sense of adventure. I haven't a clue what it is like at corporate headquarters, but as a customer I get the feeling that someone is having a lot of fun building on their grand success. From the wild new rooftop nursery at University Village to the extravagant and theatrical display gardens they are famous for conjuring up at the Northwest Flower and Garden Show, I can count on them to pull off their plans with panache.

DRIVING DIRECTIONS:
Return to Hwy. 522 by turning left from Molbak's onto NE 175th St. At the traffic signal at 131st turn right and follow the signs for Hwy. 522 west. From Hwy. 522 take the I-405 south exit towards Bellevue/Renton. Drive 8 miles then take the Hwy. 520 East/Hwy. 520 West exit #14 towards Redmond/Seattle keeping left at the fork in the ramp. Merge onto Hwy. 520 East. Take the 124th Ave. NE exit. Turn left onto Northrup Way, which becomes NE 20th St. Turn right onto 132nd Ave. NE and then right onto NE 16th St.
Driving distance: 15 miles; *Estimated driving time:* 25 minutes.

❖ Furney's Nursery

13427 NE 16th, Bellevue, WA 98005; (425) 747-8282. Open 10 a.m.-4 p.m. See the "Resources" notes at the end of the chapter for the address of Furney's Des Moines store.
❖ ☂ 📖 ☆ RR

Furney's Nursery holds a warm place in the hearts of home gardeners and landscape professionals alike– not a nursery built on fanfare and spectacle, but rather on its solid reputation for great plants well grown. Specimen-sized trees have long been a hallmark here and of recent years there has been a branching out into more uncommon varieties of old standards. They have begun to assemble plant vignettes, mixing compatible small trees or shrubs with ornamental grasses, perennials and garden statuary to help their customers visualize handsome combinations. I find it very helpful to see plants in juxtaposition in the same way I appreciate seeing clever clothing ensembles displayed at The Gap or Eddie Bauer. The Furney's staff is knowledgeable and anxious to help.

DRIVING DIRECTIONS:
Turn right from Furney's parking lot going west on NE 16th St. Turn left onto 132nd Ave. NE. Turn left onto NE 20th St., which becomes Northrup Way. (If you are famished stop at the suggested restaurants near this intersection, otherwise proceed another 10 minutes to Café Flora or an Arboretum picnic, both adjacent to your next destination.) At 124th Ave. turn right and take the Hwy. 520 West on-ramp toward Seattle. Hwy. 520 takes you over the Evergreen Floating Bridge. Take the Lk. Washington Blvd. exit. Turn left onto Lk. Washington Blvd. E. and follow it through the Washington Park Arboretum. At the traffic signal on E. Madison St. turn

right. Watch for the Nursery and (just beyond) Café Flora on the left. *Driving distance:* 9 miles; *Estimated driving time:* 20 minutes.

Lunch: If the lure of Chinese Dim Sum or Japanese Sushi appeals, two excellent restaurants lie directly along your route to the next destination (also offering take-out--I suggest the Arboretum for a picnic spot). Another wonderful choice is the classic **Café Flora**, located a few steps from City People's Garden Store.

❊ City People's Garden Store

2939 E. Madison, Seattle, WA 98112; (206) 324-0737. Open year-round, Monday-Saturday 9 a.m.-6 p.m., Sunday 11 a.m.-5 p.m. See the "Resources" notes at the end of the chapter for addresses of additional City People's.

❖ 🌱 📖 ☆ RR

City People's Garden Store keeps the potentially diverse needs of its clientele in mind: for example, materials are sold in bulk to conveniently meet the needs of an apartment dweller with a 15 square foot balcony garden as well as the home owner tending a 5,000 square foot backyard paradise. Trees and shrubs suitable to urban settings are offered alongside water plants perfect for containerized water features. Houseplants and a flower shop cater to city folks with green thumbs and generous hearts. Even in the most wretched of weather a stroll through the covered plant house is a joy. Smaller sized seasonal stars and special plants are set out on row after row of wooden tables in a bright and cheery indoor space that feels like a protected outdoor room. Plants displayed here are sinfully tempting!

The nursery maintains a strong organic commitment, with a well trained staff of enthusiasts who expertly answer questions ranging from the safe use of effective alternatives to pesticides to the benefits of composting to an explanation of Integrated Pest Management. Plastic plant pots are accepted for recycling the last week-end of the month (gosh, *another* good excuse to make a stop at City People's!) And while this is first and foremost a gardener's garden center, with an emphasis on the practical, I dearly love to wander the gift shop where I have been known to lose myself among racks of enchanting cards (a major weakness), shelves laden with horticulturally related books (another addiction) and countertops displaying botanical what-nots for gardens of character.

Driving Directions:

Retrace your route through the Washington Park Arboretum–from E. Madison St. turn left at the traffic signal onto Lk. Washington Blvd. E. Turn right at the traffic signal onto Montlake Blvd. E. At the next traffic signal you are allowed to make a U-turn to follow signs for Hwy. 520 toward Seattle. Turn right onto the ramp for Hwy. 520 and follow it to the exit for I-5 North/Roanoke St. toward Vancouver, B.C. Merge onto I-5 north. Take the N. 85th St. exit #172 toward Aurora Ave. N. Travel west on N. 85th St. to 15th Ave. NW. Turn right. Move into the left lane (at this point 15th Ave. NW becomes Holman Rd.) and at the blinking yellow signal move into the left turn lane. Turn left. The street you have jogged onto remains 15th Ave. NW. Drive about .75 mile, the nursery is on the left. *Driving distance:* 11 miles; *Estimated driving time:* 25 minutes

▨ Swanson's Nursery

9701 15th Ave. NW, Seattle, WA 98117; (206) 782-2543. Open spring and summer, daily 9:30 a.m.-6 p.m.; fall and winter, daily 9:30 a.m.-5 p.m.

 ❖ ⍑ 📖 ☆ ✳ RR

I know out-of-town gardeners who wouldn't even consider a trip to Seattle without a stop at Swanson's. And the lure of a visit with the trusty resident Golden Retrievers (pictured "hard at work" on the back cover) has nothing to do with this staunch devotion! These are folks who just consider regular trips to this nursery a natural element in the rhythm of the gardening year.

What makes this destination so popular? Swanson's has faithfully catered to gardeners of all persuasions for nearly 75 years with the best of the best. So when I am after the most common of petunias which I use year after year in urns at the front gate, I can find ones with just the right color, healthy and happy, then scoot over to the perennials department and find intriguing rarities I have seen no place else. And after lingering over a stunning new mildew-resistant phlox or scrutinizing a sturdy, no-stake required English delphinium, I am invariably drawn to the beautiful display garden, lushly planted with a heartstopping selection of ornamental grasses, irresistible perennials and a smashing mix of woody ornamentals. From here it is time to sit awhile and weigh the many temptations at hand. This, thankfully, can be accomplished quite pleasantly with a visit to **Festivities**, the on-site bistro, for a comforting pot of tea and a tangy lemon bar—or something more substantial.

DRIVING DIRECTIONS, END OF THE TOUR:
Retrace your route back to I-5: turn right from the nursery onto 15th Ave. At the intersection with Holman Rd., turn right. This is 15th Ave. NW. At the traffic signal turn left onto NW 85th St. Drive about 3 miles. At I-5 take the southbound ramp to Seattle (about 4 miles).

FURTHER RESOURCES

Food

These two side-by-side restaurants are on the route from Furney's to City People's Garden Store near the intersection of NE 20th and the freeway entrance for Hwy. 520. They are set back from the street, across a wooden footbridge traversing a pleasant waterway garden of bamboo and moisture-loving plants. They both offer take-out so you could plan a picnic at the Arboretum. Ask the restaurant to FAX you their menu in advance!

Bingo Ya Japanese Restaurant: 13238 NE 20th St., Bellevue, WA 98005; (425) 644-6462. $, L,D. Open Monday-Saturday. Pick up a take-out Bento Box style lunch of Teriyaki or Tempura or stay to relax over Sushi, Donburi or a curried dish served over rice.

Ming Place: 13200 NE 20th, Bellevue, WA 98005; (425) 643-3888. $,L,D week-end brunch. Dim Sum is served every day. There's an extensive menu of Hong Kong and Szechwan style Chinese dishes. Seafood is a specialty.

Café Flora: 2901 E. Madison St., Seattle, WA 98112; (206) 325-9100. $$, L,D. Closed Mondays, brunch week-ends. Vegetarian by philosophy, adventurous by nature, this ultra popular restaurant often requires a reservation. Tables in the glass-enclosed courtyard encircle an ornate fountain, and there is a tiny patio garden tucked in the back, open in summer. And be sure to save room for dessert!

Festivities Café and Catering: 9701 15th Ave. NW, Seattle, WA 98117; (206) 789-1163. $,B,L early D. Open daily 9:30 a.m.-5 p.m. Located at Swanson's Nursery, they make well-crafted Torta Rustica, Quiche and Polenta Pie, tasty soups, salads, sandwiches and wickedly wonderful sweets.

LODGING

See the "Seattle Travel Notes" for Seattle accommodation ideas.

FURTHER RESOURCES FOR GARDENERS

City People's has three additional locations:
- **Capitol Hill**: 500 15th E., Seattle; (206) 324-9510 ;
- **Fremont**: 3517 Fremont N., Seattle; (206) 632-1200;
- **Sand Point**: 5400 San Point Way NE, Seattle; new in spring of 1998

Furney's second location:
21215 Pacific Hwy. S., Des Moines, WA; (206) 878-8761. Larger garden/gift center; the original Furney's location.

Molbak's has two other locations:
- **Seattle Garden Center**, Pike Place Market, Seattle; (206) 448-0431;
- **Molbak's at University Village**, new fall, of 1998

Smith and Hawken: 12200 Northrup Way, Bellevue, WA 98005; (425) 881-6775. Up-scale home and garden shop offering durable, attractive work duds, high quality imported tools, handsome teak garden benches and other essential details for the elegantly accessorized garden.

A BOUNTY
OF NURSERY
DISCOVERIES

———————————— Itinerary Highlights ————————————
Earlington classic oozes character, packs pizazzy plants
Magnolia stalwart blossoms under new ownership
"Center of the Universe" Fremont's brilliant botanical star
tiny courtyard nursery wisely uses limited space

"Psssst ... have you heard so-and-so just bought such-and-such nursery and gad-zooks have they ever made changes!!" So it goes for a nursery sleuth in search of those horticultural gems that represent the aspirations of bright and innovative (and optimistic) plant lovers who throw their sun hats into the retail ring. It is their dream to provide what is unusual, what is uncommon, what is better grown, better looking or just more appealing to the burgeoning masses of adventurous gardeners. As much as one might think there is only so much room in the nursery trade to meet the needs of the plant-buying public, **Gardeners on the Go** *are restless, voracious and demanding explorers at heart – anxious for an opportunity to unearth a treasure!*

🦃 **THE ITINERARY IN BRIEF** 🦃

❶ Minter's Earlington Greenhouse & Nursery

The original glass greenhouses here, dating back to 1938, provide an intriguing sense of history. Conservation conscious "plant fanatics" (who also happened to have been loyal customers) took over ownership of this classic Renton/Skyway area neighborhood nursery in 1996. Meandering through the four-plus-acre labyrinth one is imbued with that tingly feeling of exploration and discovery.

❷ Magnolia Garden Center

This community garden center has experienced a burst of expansion and evolution as energetic new owners have brought their creative ideas and ambitious plans for more and varied plants, plant environments (courtyard and water garden) and services for their Magnolia neighbors. Plant-loving enthusiasts who are not already Magnolia buffs will find this an appealing destination for discovery.

Lunch Magnolia village offers a number of inviting small ethnic eateries, one of Seattle's best restaurants and picnic places with striking views of the Seattle skyline and Puget Sound.

❸ Fremont Gardens

Snugged into a tight wedge of property along busy Leary Way on the fringes of Fremont is one of the best little nurseries in Seattle. Every square inch provides a jam-packed display of heart-stopping perennials, trees and shrubs perfect for small urban gardens, graceful ornamental grasses, "I've-never-seen-this-before" vines, heady herbs, unusual must-have annuals and hard working ground covers.

❹ City People's Mercantile

The City People's Mercantile nursery graces a lightwell cum courtyard on the ground level of a turn-of-the-century Fremont building. This traditionally-styled mercantile houses an utterly delightful (maybe the world's smallest?) indoor/outdoor plant nursery. Because of the space limitations (small plot urban gardeners take note), there is very careful consideration given to what is on offer here – with choice and unusual plants the rule.

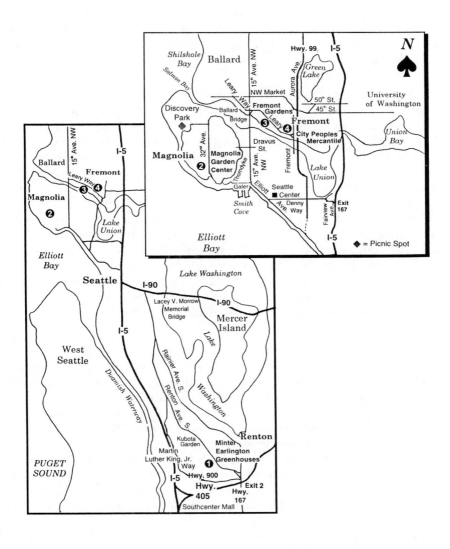

TOUR TIMING ANd TIps

❧ All nurseries listed in this chapter are open year-round, so you can expect to find the best of each season to greet your arrival. During the most active gardening season (April-September) all these nurseries (at the time I write) are open seven days a week. As with most nurseries, a call in the heart of winter is in order to check on hours.

❧ Nursery hopping does have a number of prime times that may influence your calendar. Well in advance of your day of exploration, call each nursery listed and ask if they have a newsletter or maintain a mailing list. What you will get will be *advance notice* of sales, events, classes and special shipments, discount coupons, free advice from experts and notification of any changes in hours, opening days and special services – free.

❧ Arriving with a "wish list" of specific plants or types of plants you are looking for provides an excellent opportunity to engage the nursery staff in conversation. They know their stock (including what may be on order and arriving tomorrow). Most are willing to make an extra effort to seek out and obtain uncommon plants for you or, alternatively, suggest others sources to try, or (sigh!) tell you the sought-after treasure is simply not available in the trade.

SETTING THE SCENE

In the early days of the nursery trade in the Northwest a gardener's ambitions might well be satisfied by the neighborhood vendor and a handful of favorite seed catalogs. As gardening has grown as a pastime through the 1980's and the 90's, the demand for a wider selection of plants induced some wholesale growers to move into or add a retail operation, beckoned others to open garden centers and finally inspired a flood of small specialty nurseries to meet the ever more sophisticated demand of collectors in search of rarer plants and the very "best" varieties of old favorites. In the state of Washington there are now nearly 7,000 registered retail nurseries! That's a lot of petunias, Penelope!

With the proliferation of new nurseries, there is a wonderful sense of discovery in ferreting them out and venturing into unfamiliar territory. Generally it is that *first* journey to an undiscovered spot that seems most like an adventurous expedition and once the route is no longer an unknown, repeat visits come easily. That's when you graduate from intrepid explorer to knowledgeable expedition leader, assembling gardening friends with whom you'd like to share your pleasure of "the chase".

COMMUNITY PROFILES

Earlington: This unincorporated Township is located in the Skyway district, directly west of Renton. Before the Lacey Morrow (Mercer Island) Floating Bridge was built, this area provided a link in the route from Seattle to Spokane. The west-facing hills here housed many, many wholesale greenhouse growers who took advantage of the exceptional light and favorable air circulation. The earliest mention I could find for the area was in 1917. Minter's Earlington Greenhouse and Nursery is the last vestige of the former horticultural enclave that served a tight-knit residential community and a broader landscape design and gardening community throughout the Seattle area.

Magnolia: This bluff-top neighborhood north of downtown Seattle should in actuality be called Madrona instead of Magnolia. George Davidson of the U.S. Coast and Geodetic Survey is credited with the mistaken arboreal identity, thinking the native Madronas were Magnolias. The local Garden Club is redressing the situation by encouraging the planting of more magnolias.

The cozy community of Magnolia has a village ambiance with a number of good restaurants and the ubiquitous coffee stops. Situated along a high bluff above the northern reaches of Elliott Bay you'll find one of Seattle's most breathtaking view drives, looking south to the impressive city skyline, west across Puget Sound to the Olympic Coast Range and east to the Cascade Mountain Range. At the northwestern end of this hillside community is 535-acre Discovery Park, the largest park in Seattle and a legacy of the Olmsted Brothers' visionary 20-mile string of gems stretching from Seward Park in the south to Discovery Park in the north.

Fremont: The self-proclaimed "Republic of Fremont" has adopted an official motto, "Freedom to be Peculiar" and illustrates its point with a 53-foot high Russian rocket at the corner of 35th and Evanston Ave. (declared "The Center of the Universe"). Is it any wonder a major route into this up-beat funky neighborhood arrives via the world's most active drawbridge!? Fremont was settled along the waterfront of what is now a busy ship canal linking Puget Sound and Lakes Union and Washington. This all seems a far cry from the rollicking mill town first recorded as the Denny-Hoyt Addition in 1888.

DRIVING DIRECTIONS
On I-5 drive south to Hwy. 405, the Renton exit, and follow it east past
Southcenter Mall to the Rainier Valley Freeway 167. Take exit #2 onto
Hwy. 167 and follow it north to Renton Ave. S. Turn left and drive about .5
mile. *Driving distance:* 17 miles; *Estimated driving time*: 35 minutes

❇ Minter's Earlington Greenhouse

13043 Renton Ave. S, Seattle, WA 98178; (206) 255-7744. Open year-round,
May-September, Monday-Friday 9:30 a.m.-7 p.m., Saturday 10 a.m.-5 p.m.;
winter hours Monday-Saturday 9:30 a.m.-6 p.m.

❖ ☂ 📖 RR

My introduction to this southend nursery was through previous
owners, Tomi and Tosh Mano. They were carrying on the family
tradition dating back to 1938 of providing a well-rounded garden
center that also offered starts of unusual Asian vegetables in spring.
After their many years in the business they decided to retire and close
the nursery, the last of many greenhouse operations that had lined
the route along Renton Ave. South. Then along came familiar
customer and landscape designer Paul Farrington who was
determined not to see this favored growing site turned into another
condominium project. With partner Ron Minter they have saved the
historic nursery and have added more unique and challenging fare to
the nursery's palette, with a specialty of "overlooked exotics for the
Northwest". What draws me to Minter's is the enthusiasm the
knowledgeable owners and staff exude for introducing plants
heretofore unavailable or very difficult to find like *Brugmansias,
Abutilon, Tibouchina, Lantana* and *Cestrum.* They continue to grow
the old favorites, too, but look for the best varieties and cultivars.
They are plant people to the bone, which visitors to the nursery
immediately pick up on as the lure of well-organized tables of perky
perennials and unique annuals (like Paul's grandmother's antique
hollyhocks) inspire further inspection. They also feature displays of
appealing trees, shrubs and vines. I love the character of the old
greenhouses and appreciate the respect for the business' heritage in
plans for refurbishment and expansion as Ron and Paul make their
own mark on their 4.7-acre site.

DRIVING DIRECTIONS:
From the nursery turn right onto Renton Ave. S., and at the curve as you
go down the hill turn right onto SW Victoria St. Turn right on Rainier Ave.
S then right onto Sunset Blvd. W, (Hwy. 900). This road becomes Martin
Luther King Jr. Way and meets I-5 after 3 miles. Take the northbound
ramp toward Seattle, and exit at the Mercer St./Fairview Ave exit (from
the left lane), turning right onto Fairview Ave. Turn left onto Valley St. and

another left onto Broad St. Turn right onto Denny Way and then right again on Elliott Ave. W, which becomes 15th Ave. W. Watch on the right for the sign for the Magnolia Bridge and follow the bridge onto W. Galer St., which becomes Magnolia Blvd. And then Clise Pl. W. Turn with a slight right onto Unnamed Rd., which becomes 32nd Ave. W. The nursery is on the left at W. Smith Rd.

Driving distance: 17 miles; *Estimated driving time:* 35 minutes

⚙ Magnolia Garden Center

3213 W. Smith St., Seattle, WA 98199; (206) 284-1161. Open in spring Monday-Saturday 9 a.m.-6 p.m., otherwise 9:30-a.m.-6 p.m. and year round on Sunday 10 a.m.-5 p.m.

❖ ⫟ 📖 ☆ RR

As with our previous destination, Magnolia Garden Center has served the avid gardeners in this community for many years but is now in the hands of new owners Margaret and Chuck Flaherty. They are anxious to balance their desire to continue serving a loyal neighborhood clientele with the need to express their ambition for a wider selection of choice trees and shrubs for urban settings, the best perennials they can hunt up for northwest gardening, a new selection of water-loving plants and more unusual annuals. Here, for instance, you will find trees and tree peonies from China, located through a source they have cultivated in Canada. With the building of the new structure (in 1998) to house gifts, books and gardening sundries there is also the addition of easy access ramps and a courtyard garden for contemplation and inspiration. Stop by to encourage their enterprise!

Lunch: If you are in the mood for a picnic, visit **Celebrations To Go**, for freshly baked soups and sandwiches. (See a list of picnic spots at the end of this chapter). On the other hand, why not take advantage of the opportunity to treat yourself to a special lunch at **Szmania's**, one of Seattle's top-rated restaurants, noted for ambiance, tasteful decor, the theater of an open kitchen and chef Ludgar Szmania's great talent in marrying dishes and techniques from his German homeland with Northwest culinary influences.

DRIVING DIRECTIONS
Leave Magnolia village turning right onto 32nd Ave. W., left onto Clise Pl. W, which becomes Magnolia Blvd. W, which becomes W. Galer St. Turn left at Thorndyke Ave. W., and at the intersection with W. Hayes St. turn right to stay on Thorndyke Ave. Turn left on 20th Ave. W, right onto Dravus St. and then left onto 15th Ave. N.W. Take the first exit after crossing the Ballard Bridge on the right, with a right turn onto NW Leary Way. Fremont Gardens is on your right after .9 mile, at the corner of NW 40th St. *Driving distance:* 4.3 miles; *Estimated driving time:* 12 minutes

❈ Fremont Gardens

4001 Leary Way NW, Seattle, WA 98107; (206) 781-8283. Open Tuesday-Saturday, 10 a.m.-6 p.m., Sunday noon-5 p.m.

❖ ↑ ⊞ ☆ RR

I get such a kick out of how many fabulous plants can be packed into this diminutive, wedge-shaped nursery site (there are those among us who will feel right at home!) There is even a stairway to the roof, packed with plants (for sale and on display). Every flat surface has been taken advantage of. What draws me back time and again is the talented trio of plant lovers who have a special gift for seeking out truly unusual and uncommon plants. Northwestern plant enthusiasts are spoiled to beat the band with the great number of small new nurseries catering to those of us in search of new varieties and top performers. Here you'll find hard working pros who not only know their plants and diligently seek out excellent sources, but are noted for building a loyal customer base through knowledgeable advice and genuine service. The inviting shop has a nice mix of the practical what-nots we need to practice our passion, like stainless steel garden tools, to the embellishments that appeal to the heart, like a romantic weathered Moroccan lantern. They carry the latest botanical periodicals from Britain and exotically fragrant Chinese sacred lilies. All books in their well-conceived library are discounted 15%, all the time, and they have a marvelous schedule of classes and workshops, offered days and evenings, too.

DRIVING DIRECTIONS:

Turn right onto Leary Way NW and drive east. Leary Way becomes 36th St. As 36th bends to the right, it becomes Fremont Pl. N. At this intersection there is a statue of Lenin. Turn (what else but) hard left at this point (which actually keeps you on 36th St.) City People's is on the next corner, on the right, at the intersection with Fremont Ave. N. *Driving distance:* 1 mile; *Estimated driving time:* 5 minutes

❈ City People's Mercantile

3517 Fremont Ave. N, Seattle, WA 98103; (206) 632-6143. Open Monday-Friday 9 a.m.-7 p.m., Saturday 9 a.m.-6 p.m., Sunday 10 a.m.-6 p.m.

❖ ↑ ⊞ ☆ RR

Here you will come upon a wonderful hidden gem. The nifty nursery and appealing garden center represent but another perfect element in what makes this a favorite one-stop-browse-and-shop for a bit of this and a bit of that, from housewares to hardware, garments to garden gear. Would that we were all blessed with such a charming, old fashioned yet contemporary neighborhood mercantile! As with many of the businesses in Fremont, City People's is appropriately ensconced in a historic building dating back to the early 1900s. Originally a furniture store, it has been used continuously as a hardware store of one sort or another since the 1930s. City People's Mercantile opened here in 1991, then expanded the gardening department to the lower level in 1995. A highlight is the tiny courtyard nursery for outdoor plants. The feel is very European to me – using every square inch of this lightwell space wisely and cleverly. In addition to the outdoor selection there are houseplants offered in the adjacent space. Within the garden center there is everything from soup to nuts: organic fertilizers and pest controls, soil and compost, weather vanes, garden furniture, books and magazines, fountain supplies and equipment, tools, gloves, footwear, pots large and small, and, yes, seed and feeders for birds and nuts for squirrels.

Driving Directions, End of the Tour
To reach I-5, follow N. 36th. St. to Stone Way N. Turn left. At N. 50th St. and turn right. At I-5 take the southbound on-ramp for Seattle (or the northbound ramp if headed in that direction).
Driving distance: 2.5 miles; *Estimated driving time:* 15 minutes

FURTHER RESOURCES
Food
Magnolia is blessed with many wonderful places to dine with a wide range of ethnic cuisines represented, a well-loved village pub, a top notch three-star restaurant, bakeries and, at last count, seven coffeehouses. Here is a sampling:

Caffé Appassionato: 3217 W. McGraw St, Seattle, WA 98199; (206) 281-8040. $, L,D daily. This attractive Italianesque coffeehouse roasts its own beans on site, offering marvelous espresso drinks that couldn't be richer. Pastries and panini are also particularly praiseworthy.

Celebrations To Go: 2434 32nd St. W, Seattle, WA 98199; (206) 286-8755. $, 9 a.m.-6:30 p.m. Monday-Friday, 9 a.m.-3 p.m. Saturday.

Kinnaree: 3311 W. McGraw St., Seattle, WA 98199; (206) 285-4460. $$, L Tuesday-Saturday, D daily. This popular, unassuming spot is one of my favorite Thai restaurants in Seattle.

Magnolia Thriftway: 3830 34th W, Seattle, WA 98199; (206) 283-2710. The deli here can supply all the fixings for an impromptu picnic, from a sandwich and chips to a freshly roasted chicken.

Szmania's: 3321 W. McGraw St., Seattle, WA 98199; (206) 284-7305. $$, L Tuesday-Friday, D Tuesday-Sunday. This handsome, open-kitchen restaurant (pronounced smahn-ya), tucked along the quiet main street of Magnolia village at 34th Ave. W, has deservedly garnered awards from regional restaurant reviewers. This is my choice for a memorable, let's-linger-a-little-longer lunch with their inspired menu featuring the Northwest's best ingredients married with dazzling preparations. On a cool day, the fireplace will undoubtedly provide additional appeal!

Picnic Places:

Discovery Park, at the far northwestern reaches of the Magnolia neighborhood, provides many opportunities for a woodland, bluff or beachfront picnic. If yours is a relaxed sunny day, perhaps splitting the itinerary into two days, consider a picnic on the beach near the picturesque West Point Lighthouse, built in 1881. It is located at the far western tip of Discovery Park.

Magnolia Park, along W. Magnolia Blvd. (via the Magnolia Bridge and Galer St.) provides captivating views of Puget Sound and a quiet refuge among the Madrona trees for a special picnic.

Lodging

See "Seattle Travel Notes" for accommodation suggestions.

For More Information

Discovery Park Visitor Information Center: 3801 West Government Way, Seattle, WA 98199; (206) 386-4236. Guided nature walks offered Saturday afternoons.

Specialty Nursery Association: 1220 NE 90th, Seattle, WA 98115. Send a self-addressed stamped envelope with two first class stamps for copies of their "Nursery Guides". There are two information-packed, annually updated editions -- one covers western Washington generally north of Tacoma to Lynden, and the other covers the Olympic Peninsula and the area around and south of Tacoma.

More Resources for Gardeners

Kubota Garden, P.O. Box 12646, Seattle, WA 98111-4646; Garden (206) 684-4584, Foundation 725-5060. Located at Renton Ave. S. and 55th Ave. S., this 20-acre American-Japanese garden was created originally by Fujitaro Kubota in 1927. It is open daily, dawn to dusk, there is no entry fee and free tours are offered every 4th Saturday and Sunday at 10 a.m. Specimen trees, the use of water, and their traditional pine pruning classes are special features.

Magnolia's Bookstore: 3206 W McGraw St., Seattle, WA 98199; (206) 283-1062. This is a cozy neighborhood book shop that happens to have a very appealing gardening book selection. Literary Gardeners on the Go will be sorely tempted to nip in for some serious browsing!

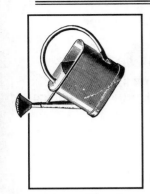

RAINY DAY SEATTLE

Itinerary Highlights
---

explore a two-and-a-half-acre tropical rain forest—indoors
discover a stylish garden shop on Queen Anne Hill
enter the festive Pike Place Market spirit
hunt treasure at Seattle's most intriguing seed source
brighten your day with a fresh Hawaiian bouquet
poke around a gardening paraphernalia Mecca

❧

With an average of 150 days of measurable rain in Seattle in a typical year, this could well prove to be the most popular Tour in the book! Even a dyed-in-the-wool gardener may pray for such days to relish the satisfaction that the garden watering is someone else's chore for the day, and enjoy the excuse to nip into haunts often reserved for inclement weather. Blessed with numerous diversions, the Gardener on the Go revels in opportunities to expand botanical horizons, stock up on inspiration, plot next season's garden and replace worn and weary tools. Gardeners get out, even in the rain!

THE ITINERARY IN BRIEF

❶ Woodland Park Zoo / Rain Forest Exhibit

Can you imagine a better way to escape a drafty, drizzly, dark day than to go to the tropics? Fanciful birds fly free and fantastical foliage flaunts its tropical heritage.

Lunch Opportunities abound to warm up with ethnic cuisine!

❷ Ravenna Gardens, Queen Anne Hill

Here you will cosset yourself within an imaginatively designed shop, pondering distinctive wares that gardeners and non-gardeners alike find appealing as home and garden accessories.

❸ Pike Place Market

An Historic District and *bone fide* farmer's market that dates back to 1907, this colorful potpourri of shops and vendors occupies a magnificent setting on a bluff above the picturesque harbor and Elliott Bay, just a few blocks from the heart of bustling downtown Seattle.

❹ Molbak's Seattle Garden Center

This shop offers an *extensive* selection of seeds and plants appropriate to its Pike Place Market location (eg. best and uncommon vegetables, herbs, bulbs and perennials.)

❺ The Enchanted Garden

If the Rain Forest exhibit left you with a lingering desire to invite some exotic tropicals into your Northwest home (or to enliven your hotel room), this tiny shop specializes in orchids, cacti, succulents and flowering tropicals. Also find dazzling flowers and foliage flown in fresh weekly from Hawaii.

❻ The Complete Gardener

This downtown gardening wares shop has got a lot to offer, not the least of which is an admirable array of top quality hoses and related paraphernalia. Great for gift shopping, browsing, stocking up and dream making.

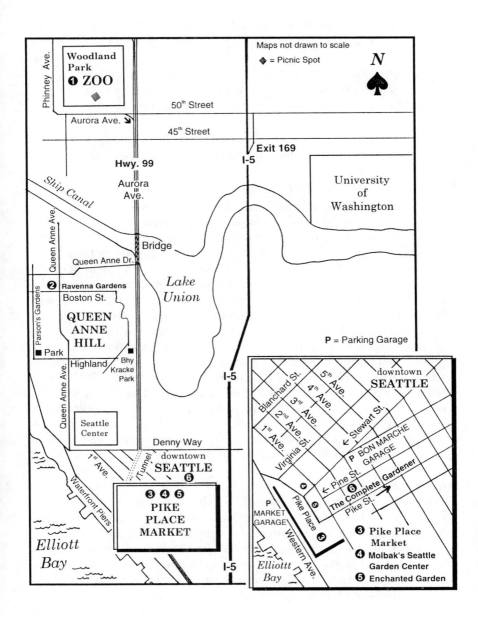

Woodland Park
❶ ZOO

Phinney Ave.

50th Street

Aurora Ave. ↘

45th Street

Maps not drawn to scale

◈ = Picnic Spot

N

Hwy. 99

Aurora Ave.

Ship Canal

Queen Anne Ave.

Bridge

Queen Anne Dr.

❷ Ravenna Gardens
Boston St.

QUEEN ANNE HILL

Parson's Gardens

■ Park

Highland

Bhy Kracke Park

Queen Anne Ave.

Seattle Center

1st Ave.

Waterfront Piers

Tunnel

Denny Way

downtown
SEATTLE
❻

❸ ❹ ❺
PIKE PLACE MARKET

Elliott Bay

Exit 169
I-5

University
of
Washington

Lake Union

I-5

P = Parking Garage

I-5

Blanchard St.

5th Ave.
4th Ave.
3rd Ave.
2nd Ave.
1st Ave.

Ave. St.

Virginia

Stewart St.

downtown
SEATTLE

P BON MARCHE GARAGE

← Pine St.

The Complete Gardener

Pike St.

P
MARKET
GARAGE

Pike Place

Western Ave.

Elliottt Bay

I-5

❸ **Pike Place Market**

❹ **Molbak's Seattle Garden Center**

❺ **Enchanted Garden**

TOUR TIPS AND TIMING

❧ All the destinations on this itinerary are open year-round, daily.

❧ While the destinations are all indoors, dress comfortably and remember comfortable footwear.

❧ This tour readily adapts to a half day outing and makes an impressive itinerary to entertain out of town guests on a rainy day. It also makes a good choice for children accompanying adults.

❧ If you often rely on credit cards remember that parking and street food temptations at Pike Place Market generally require cash.

SETTING THE SCENE

Phinney Ridge / Woodland Park Zoological Gardens:
Woodland Park and the Zoo are located on 92 acres of Seattle's Phinney Ridge neighborhood. Purchased from Guy Phinney in 1899 for use as a city park, in 1903 the famed Olmsted Brothers firm (designers of New York City's Central Park) was given the task of drafting a full-fledged zoological garden plan. The property is noted for magnificent trees: stands of *Fagus sylvatica* (European beeches), *Ulmus minor var. Vulgaris* (English elms), *Robinia pseudoacacia* (Black locusts) and many other rare and distinguished varieties of herbaceous plants, trees and shrubs throughout the extensive grounds, including many native to this area.

The Zoo was revolutionary in its approach in the early 1970's to integrate animals on exhibit and their natural habitat. They were among the first of such institutions to hire a full-time horticulturist and to work with a visionary Landscape Design firm (Jones and Jones) in *simulating* environments using a diverse number of species of plants that grow well in Seattle.

Queen Anne Hill:
The highest and steepest of central Seattle's hills, Queen Anne rises 456 feet above downtown to the north of the Seattle Center. This area takes its name from the architectural style favored by early timber barons who built here in the late 1800's for the view afforded of town. The commercial district tends to cling to the main street, Queen Anne Avenue N, running north and south through the area, surrounded by neighborhoods with a number of intriguing public pocket parks, tucked off in unexpected niches (see "Additional Resources" section at the end of this chapter).

Pike Place Market:

Nearly a century ago, in mid-August, 1907, a handful of farmers drove their wagons brimming with fresh produce up Western Avenue from the waterfront to Pike Street, and designated their destination as "Produce Row." A crowd of customers awaited their arrival, anxious to beat the high prices commanded elsewhere for fruit and vegetables. The following Saturday 70 wagons offered their products, selling everything they brought within a few hours. A three-block-long byway connecting this intersection with First Avenue was later called Pike Place, honoring John Pike, the architect for the University of Washington's first campus in Seattle. The popularity of the farmers' market continued through the 1930s. I have heard many stories of my Grandmother making her weekly trek by trolley, returning with her hand cart bearing bags of potatoes, beets and carrots, apples and pears, ling cod and red salmon. Then came World War II and the internment of the Japanese Americans, who formed the core of the Market's farmers; the loss of farmland in the region to industrial use; the deterioration of First Avenue with the proliferation of peep shows and the move of families to the suburbs. The Market went through a decline that lasted until the 1960s. At that time, demolition seemed certain. Activists organized an Initiative campaign in 1971, which brought resounding public support and resulted in designating the Market a historical district, thus preserving its character, mandate and future. Now on the National Register of Historic Places, the Market is managed by the Pike Place Market Preservation and Development Authority.

Today the Pike Place Market is a much loved symbol of the spirit of Seattle. It is a true melting pot of nationalities, ages and economic classes. It caters to the full spectrum of ages from the very young (with a day care center) to the elderly citizens (with a senior center) and its fabric is woven from the down-and-outers to the very wealthy and everything in between. At its heart it continues to provide area farmers, fishmongers, butchers, flower growers, artists and a host of other small businesses an outlet for the very best they have to offer. The atmosphere here is lively, colorful and a wild sensory stimulant – *especially* on a rainy day in Seattle!

DRIVING DIRECTIONS:

From I-5 northbound take exit 169 onto N. 50th St., drive west. You'll drive under Aurora Ave. to Phinney Ave. N. Turn right. Look for the Zoo's West Entrance Gate. There is a parking lot (fee charged) or park free on the street (2 hour limit). The Rain Forest Exhibit is nearest this gate. *Driving distance:* 6 miles; *Estimated driving time:* 15 minutes.

❊ Woodland Park Zoo / Rain Forest Exhibit

5500 Phinney Ave. N., Seattle, WA 98103; (206) 684-4040. Open 9:30 a.m.-6 p.m. (until 4 p.m. October 31-March 14.) Web site: www.zoo.org

❖ ↑ ▣ ☆ ✳ RR

Most of us will never have the experience of visiting an actual tropical rain forest, yet we are increasingly aware of their importance in our daily lives whether through controversies over the use of endangered wood in our garden furniture or in the enormous potential plants from the tropics play in pharmaceutical product development. The Woodland Park Zoo Rain Forest Exhibit provides a wealth of information that entertains and enlightens visitors. It offers a unique opportunity for gardeners to observe plants we may only have read about but have never seen, to learn about tropical plant inter-relationships and to come away with inspiration to simulate a bold vignette in an appropriate garden spot at home.

This exhibit was opened in 1992 and covers 2¾ acres. It displays nearly 700 plant species (both temperate and tropical), contains over 50 birds, 33 species of animals, and was awarded Best Exhibit of the Year in 1994 by the American Association of Zoos and Aquariums. Especially interesting are plants of economic importance (vanilla, chocolate, coffee, black pepper), carnivorous plants, endangered orchids and over 20 species of tropical palms. This lush, diverse exhibit takes visitors from the forest floor of the understory on up to the tree canopy along a circular ramp, past 25 animal enclosures.

Lunch: If your visit has captured your imagination and time has flown by, two near-by lunch possibilities are: the **Rain Forest Café**, adjacent to the Exhibit, appeals to youngsters (fast food vendors, food court style) or plan a picnic. *On weekends* find the highly respected **Santa Fe Café** nearby at 5901 Phinney Avenue N., for innovative southwest cuisine. Otherwise press on, as there are many lunch stop options on Queen Anne Hill.

DRIVING DIRECTIONS:
Travel south on Phinney Ave. N. (back the direction you came from), turning left onto N. 50th St. At the Aurora Ave. (Highway 99) intersection keep right and enter carefully onto this busy by-pass traveling south. Take the first right turn after crossing the Aurora Bridge, onto Queen Anne Dr., follow the signs to Queen Anne Ave., turn left to Boston St. Find a place to park (check posted time limits).
Driving distance: 2.5 miles; Estimated driving time: 15 minutes

✾ Ravenna Gardens

Queen Anne Avenue N., Seattle, WA 98119; (206) 283-7091. Open Monday-Saturday 10 a.m.-7 p.m., Sunday 10 a.m.-6 p.m., year-round.

❖ ♈ 📖 ☆

This is the newest botanically-themed shop from Gillian and Jack Mathews (originators of Made in Washington and Ravenna Gardens at University Village). Gardeners love the masterful wand the Mathews employ in conjuring their clever shops. There are two elements at work here that make this a destination that builds a loyal following. The ambiance is relaxed with pleasant background music and a rustic/sophisticated decor that suggests ideas to try in one's own garden. The other element is the careful balance of merchandise from the practical (a wonderful selection of seeds and bulbs, basic but quality tools and potting soil) to the ethereal (garden-related bath products, beautiful cards and paper goods). There is a distinguished selection of annuals, perennials, trees, shrubs and vines available from early spring to mid-fall in an annex to the shop across the street. Not only is it evident we are in the company of dedicated gardeners, but ones who have made their reputation on seeking out the unique, the well-crafted, the whimsical and the truly useful for our own garden plots and homey nests.

Lunch: The Queen Anne neighborhood is represented by a strong contingent of good ethnic restaurants. In close proximity find: East Indian, Thai, an Asian Grill that features Vietnamese cuisine and sushi, and an excellent Italian restaurant. Most establishments post menus outside to give you a culinary preview of what's offered within.

Driving Directions

Driving south on Queen Anne Ave. N. you'll descend a rather steep hill emerging into lower Queen Anne. Continue on to the stop light at Denny Way. Turn left and then right on First Ave. The Pike Place Market runs between Virginia St. and Union St., just to the west of 1st Ave. *Driving distance:* 3.5 miles; *Estimated driving time:* 15 minutes.

Tour Tip:

Parking around the **Pike Place Market** can be a pain because the area is congested with slow moving traffic trying to nab a parking meter. Why waste time circling the busy streets then have to fret over a parking ticket or tow? I avoid the pressure of the clock ticking and park in one of many parking lots/garages. There are approximately nine parking lots and garages in the vicinity. Those along First Ave. are the most expensive. Try the **Bon Marche Garage** at 3rd and Stewart, reasonably priced and 3 blocks from the Pike Place Market (west on Stewart) and 1¾ blocks (north) from The Complete Gardener.

✠ Pike Place Market

Insider's Tip: There is an information booth at the "entrance" to the Market near the intersection of First Ave. S and Pike. You can leave packages here, on a space available basis, and retrieve them later, pick up a Market Map, ask questions and buy books about the Market. (206) 682-7453.

The Market arcades are open year-round Monday-Saturday , 9 a.m. to 6 p.m. and also Sunday, early May through December, 11 a.m.-5 p.m. There are many eateries and some other businesses that are open earlier and close later than the official Public Market, however. Gardeners on the Go will probably want to check out: **Read All About It**, an excellent newsstand for gardening magazines, national and international; **Market Spice**, an institution here since 1911 selling dried spices and herbs, coffee and tea, in bulk and pre-packaged (and, yes, the home of the famous tea bearing the establishment's name, often the selection for the complimentary tea of the day); **Tenzing Momo & Co.**, an herbal apothecary with several hundred varieties of medicinal, aromatic and culinary herbs and the *many* vendors who display voluptuous bunches of fresh cut flowers and generous bundles of fragrant herbs.

✠ Molbak's Seattle Garden Center

1600 Pike Place, Seattle, WA 98101; (206) 448-0431. Open January-March 15 and July 15-December 3, daily 9 a.m.-5:30 p.m., Sunday 10 a.m.-5 p.m.; March 15-July 15, daily 9 a.m.-5:30 p.m.

❖ ☂ 📖 ☆

This great little nursery cum garden center is jam-packed with a wide variety of garden goods, from indoor and garden plants, bulbs, mushroom growing kits, pots, tools, a terrific bonsai section (including an elegant assortment of quality tools) to a well-stocked book section. The mega-selection of seeds is awe-inspiring! It may be the largest anywhere in the region. Many packets come from abroad, with text in their own language (Japanese, Chinese, French), so one must turn to the photographic and iconic clues. This is just one more example of how this shop is imbued with the magical spirit of its Market locale. And as such, it especially features what is "fresh," what is in season (throughout the year). So in spring this is a terrific stop for vegetable starts (including the seeds) and herbs. Lots! You'll find plenty of inspiration all around from the farm-to-market vendors' colorful stands. Maybe you'll see something they are selling that you'd like to try growing yourself. Look for these plants or seeds at SGC. And the same is true for bulbs and the wonderful bouquets of fresh flowers. This is an excellent source for quality tools, bulk amendments, fertilizers, cover crops, and organic pest/disease controls, too.

The Enchanted Garden

1524 Pike Place Market, Seattle, WA 98101; (206) 625-1205. Open daily year-round.

❖ ☂

The Enchanted Garden is a flower and plant shop specializing in exotic flowers and foliage, with several shipments a week fresh from Hawaii. Here you will also find unusual plants of the tropics from *Aeranthos* to *Xiphioides* and from those voracious carnivores to the most fragile of orchids. The new owner, Jessie Lyle, has also begun carrying the most stunning of local seasonal foliage from flowering branches in winter to wildflowers in summer. Additionally she looks to local artisans for some *very* creative botanically-inspired ironwork (hooks and garden stakes that emulate nature's fine details). Since this is a rainy day tour, why not pick up a flamboyant, fragrant bouquet to brighten your spirits for the *rest* of the week!

WALKING DIRECTIONS:
Leave the Market going east (toward downtown) on Pine St. two blocks. Look for the Complete Gardener on the south side, mid-block.

❖ The Complete Gardener

205 Pine Street, Seattle, WA 98101; (206) 623-7818. Open year-round Monday-Saturday, 9:30 a.m.-7 p.m., Sunday 11 a.m.-6 p.m.

❖ ☂ 📖 ☆

This makes a handy downtown location for gardeners in pursuit of a special book or in search of gardening gear—from bibs to boots to bonnets. Jean Harrington has packed an amazing diversity of goodies into this shop, from the Hall's line of quality English greenhouses she's very keen to tell you about to the seeds you're buying it for! On my last visit I was charmed by a number of intriguing indoor water gardens, finding their "music" soothing and restful. They take up very little space (or time) for the great pleasure they bring. If you are planning to purchase a bouquet of flowers before you leave the market, look here for an unusual vase – there is a large collection of them to choose from. With an insider's connection to Canada, Jean brings unusual products not readily found south of the border.

FURTHER RESOURCES
Food
Rain Forest Café at the West Gate, Woodland Park Zoo, with a half dozen fast food outlets—the likes of Burger King and Pizza Hut. Open year-round, though various operators' hours vary. Indoor and outdoor seating.
Santa Fe Café: 5901 Phinney Avenue N., Seattle, (206) 783-9755; $$, L (weekends), D (weekdays). This innovative restaurant was a pioneer in

introducing Northwesterners to Southwesterners' cuisine.
Raga Cuisine of India: 7 W. Boston Street, Seattle, (206) 281-8877; $$, L,D
(daily). The Bellevue sister restaurant has been a favorite haunt of mine for
years. Although both put on the ubiquitous buffet, and it is quite good, my
preference is to go straight to the a la carte menu because it is here that the
chef's skill in coaxing subtleties from aggressive spices really shines.
Ristorante Buongusto: 2232 Queen Anne Avenue N, (206) 284-9040. $$, L
(Tuesday-Friday), D daily. A rainy day begs for a special lunch and the
atmosphere in this comfortably converted house is cheery and inviting. The
food is authentic southern Italian and reliably wonderful.
Teacup: 2207 Queen Anne Avenue N, Seattle 98109, (206) 283-5931; $, tea
and a selection of sweets daily in this tiny shop offering over 100 teas!
For a **coffee break** find **Starbucks, Tullys** and **Café Lado** close at hand.

LodGING
See "Seattle Travel Notes" in the Introdcution for lodging suggestions.

MORE RESOURCES FOR GARdENERS
There are two pocket parks on Queen Anne Hill that I find particularly
exciting discoveries. Have a peek, returning on a sunnier or drier day and
include a walk in this pleasant neighborhood.
Parsons Garden Park, 700 W. Highland Dr. (at 7th Avenue W), Seattle;
(206) 684-4075. To reach this romantic spot, turn west onto W. Highland
Drive from Queen Anne Ave. N. (watch for the street as you descend/ascend
the steep hill connecting upper and lower Queen Anne.) Tucked in behind
mature streetside trees and shrubbery, this family garden was a gift to the
Parks of Seattle in 1956 from the children of the Reginald Parsons. Planted
imaginatively and well-maintained, the garden is a popular wedding site.
One of Seattle's most commanding viewpoints, officially Marshall Park but
popularly named for Arts supporter Betty Bowen, is located kitty-corner
across the street.
Bhy Kracke Park, 1200 5th Ave. N., Seattle; (206) 684-4075. (Also called
Comstock Pl. Park.) To reach this charming hillside "secret garden" turn east
from Queen Anne Ave. N. onto Boston St., then turn south (right) on Bigelow
Ave. Watch for Comstock Place on the left and proceed past the "Dead End"
sign. There are a couple of benches and a picnic table on a grassy landing and
the garden proceeds down the steep hill in a series of switchbacks. The 1.4-
acre site was the conception of Walter "Bhy" Kracke, a bank accountant, world
traveler and ardent gardener.
M. Coy Books, 117 Pine Street, Seattle, WA 98101; (206) 623-5354. Open
daily. The small independent book seller is a rare and endangered species, so
use them or lose them! We are lucky Michael Coy happens to have a soft spot
in his heart for gardening-related literature and has made an excellent
selection bound to tempt his patrons.

MID-
WINTER
SEATTLE

Itinerary Highlights

hard-to-find house and garden hardware and fixtures
mid-city Molbak's -- innovative retractable roof greenhouse
sophisticated garden inspiration for urban settings
browse thousands of gardening books, magazines, catalogs
a winter garden designed to strutt its stuff "off-season"
the warmth, fragrance, foliage and flowers of the tropics

In spite of our garden-friendly climate, there is a period mid-winter when the ground is decidedly soggy, the sky indisputably leaden, the air unforgivingly chilly and the resolute spirit of the Northwest gardener doggedly determined not to go dormant. This is a day destined for poking through cheery shops, digging through a gold mine of gardening literature, relishing a brisk garden visit and finally retreating into the enveloping humidity of a tropical conservatory. This is my personal prescription for a mid-winter tonic, providing a beneficial botanical buck-you-uppo.

University Village

❧ hot beverage (coffee, tea, hot chocolate, hot cider) and requisite sustenance in the form of a decadent pastry

❶ **Restoration Hardware**: handsome details for the home and garden especially house numbers; gate, door and drawer hardware; outdoor lighting fixtures and garden books/accessories

❷ **Molbak's**: an urban sanctuary created by one of this region's most respected and beloved nurseries

❸ **Ravenna Gardens**: snazzy, gazebo-esque space specializing in stylish and innovative container gardening creations for urban gardeners, unique garden art and structures, tools, books

❹ **Blue Canoe**: elegant details for home and garden, one-of-a kind indoor and outdoor furniture, rustic to urbane bird houses

Lunch A broad spectrum from which to choose at University Village

Center for Urban Horticulture

Gardeners flock to this educational facility for valuable gardening ideas (display gardens, interesting plantings and educational demonstration plots), class, lecture and event opportunities, and...

❺ Elisabeth C. Miller Horticultural Library

Gardeners on the Go of every persuasion will feel at home here. Whether researching a perplexing question on pruning or browsing the British magazine "New, Rare and Unusual Plants: A Journal for Plant Enthusiasts," a knowledgeable and friendly staff is on hand and anxious to make your visit pleasant and profitable.

❻ Washington Park Arboretum / Joseph A. Witt

Winter Garden

Find inspiration to carry you through the season, with a botanical focus on bark, berry, foliage, flower and form. Plants that flaunt their finery in winter months are featured in this seasonal garden.

❼ Volunteer Park Conservatory

Envelop yourself in the pleasantly warm humidity of a tropical paradise, the delicate fragrance of rare orchids, bold foliage and the startling beauty of flowering cacti and fleshy succulents.

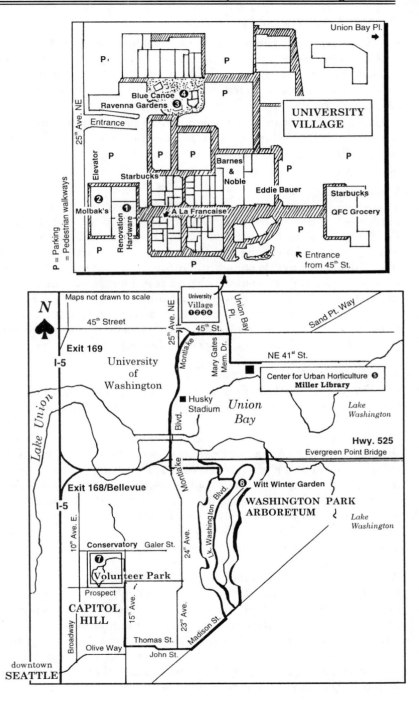

Tour Timing and Tips

❧ Please put aside the temptation to curl up with the cat, a good book and a crackling fire, and set out on the exciting path of a mid-winter adventure. There are many delightful diversions here that will quicken the pulse and spark the imagination of the Gardener on the Go whose green thumb twitches in every season.

❧ Everything on this tour is open daily, year-round (except holidays) but for the Miller Library, which is open on Saturdays, 9 a.m.-3 p.m. (except July/August) but never on Sunday.

Setting the Scene

University Village

This shopping complex, east of the University of Washington, is bordered by NE 45th St., NE 46th St., 25th Ave. NE and Union Bay Pl. An aggressive and imaginative revitalization of an aging commercial site has brought not only a bevy of big name anchor stores (like **Eddie Bauer**, **Barnes and Noble**, a spiffed up **QFC** and the first outlet for Robert Redford's **Sundance**) but many small, independent shops selling everything from freshly made pasta to upscale fashions for tots. Outdoor café seating spills out from appealing restaurants, fountains provide restful water music and several life-sized bronze castings of endearing animals appeal to all.

Elisabeth C. Miller Library

In 1984, Pendelton Miller endowed this library as a gift to honor his wife, local horticultural luminary, Elisabeth Carey Miller (1914-1994). This is the only public horticultural library west of Denver and north of San Francisco. Like the most extravagant of Chinese banquets, there is more choice than one can imagine: nearly 8,000 books, over 300 newsletter and journal titles, over 1,000 seed and nursery catalogs from around the world, a rare book room, every imaginable gardening and related periodical (national and international), and now a computer set-up with many topical CDs (landscape design programs, plant finders, etc.) and Internet access (complete with well-researched bookmarks and help available to get you on-line).

Washington Park Arboretum

Washington Park was set aside for a botanical garden and arboretum in 1924. In 1930 the Arboretum and Botanical Garden Society of the State of Washington (later the Arboretum Foundation) was formed. Largely through their efforts and those of many other civic groups (notably the Seattle Garden Club) an agreement was forged between the University and the City. The first Master Plan was drawn up by James F. Dawson of the noted Olmsted Brothers architectural landscape firm from Brookline, Massachusetts, who designed many parks throughout the country. (An architect partner and Frederick Olmsted, Sr. founded the profession of landscape architecture in 1857.) Work at WPA was begun in 1936 when 11,000 azaleas, 700 flowering cherries and 150 eastern dogwoods were planted along Azalea Way, a key element in the Arboretum design scheme. Today there are over 40,000 trees, shrubs and vines, native and exotic, representing 4,768 different species and cultivated varieties spread throughout the grounds.

The 200-acre Arboretum is located on the shores of Lake Washington, 1 mile south of the University of Washington and a 10 minute drive northeast of downtown Seattle. The UW Center for Urban Horticulture owns and manages the plant collections and manages the associated public programs. The land is owned by the City of Seattle, responsible for the infrastructure, turf, native plant areas, the Japanese Garden and the Waterfront Trail. While in actuality a city park, and thus a superb place for recreation, a primary purpose of the Arboretum is to *educate*. In addition it is charged with the role of conservator, with some 130 different plants now on the endangered species lists, collected from around the world, along with a commitment to the conservation of local native plants.

Volunteer Park Conservatory

Set along the north side of Volunteer Park on Capitol Hill, the Conservatory is a grand reminder of the master plan conceived for the Park by the Olmsted Brothers architectural landscape design firm in 1904. Construction of this Victorian style iron, swamp cypress and glass conservatory (now five glass houses) began in 1912. The early years were splendid times with donations of rare specimens and extraordinary collections. By the Depression, however, the humidity had taken its toll and left the building in dangerous disrepair. It wasn't until the 1980s that funds became available to begin the half-million dollar restoration. The one remaining original ornamental glass piece, the peacock, was recently restored to once again strut its stuff in splendor. A second major piece of public art, "Homage to Man" by stained glass craftsman Richard Spaulding, seen in the vestibule, has received loving restorative work by the artist.

Driving Directions:

Travel north on I-5. Take the 45th St. exit #169 and head east, through the University District, down a steep hill, and at the stop light turn left. Slip into the first turn lane to the left and carefully cross into University Village. *Driving distance:* 5 miles; *Estimated driving time: 15 minutes.*

University Village

There are a number of excellent places for a wake-up cup, be it coffee, tea, hot chocolate or mulled cider. Here are some suggestions: **Starbucks**: there are two Starbucks within University Village. I head for the one in QFC because they have considerately lit a fire to greet me on this wintry day and offer comfortable couches to plunk down into. **Cinnabuns** is conveniently located adjacent, an irresistible fragrance of my youth wafting through the air. The other Starbucks franchise (also very pleasant) is located at the northwest corner of the central building (the one that also houses Barnes and Noble and Eddie Bauer). **A La Francaise**: This is also a top contender because the pastries here are brilliant and the ambiance transports you to a tiny Parisian bakery. Hearty souls retreat to outside seating on brisk but tolerable winter days, others jockey for the limited seating within.

The following four destinations are located at University Village. I have arranged this exploration to begin at the southwestern corner of the complex and proceed clockwise.

Hours for these destinations conform to general Mall Hours: Monday-Saturday 10 a.m. to 7 p.m., Sunday 10 a.m. to 6 p.m.

Restoration Hardware

University Village; (206) 522-2775, (800) 762-1005

Many will greet this store as a familiar friend (perhaps through their long-established mail-order catalog). Gardeners on the look-out for home and garden hardware and details will find unusual hinges and handles for the front gate or new potting shed door, eye catching street numbers, handsome garden motif drawer pulls, and Mission-style lighting fixtures for indoors and out. While not an extensive selection, there is always an attractive display of quality tools, glossy gardening books, a fountain or two, sturdy benches and practical what-nots like goat skin gloves and bag balm (the wonder potion used by farmers to soothe the tender udders of milk cows and by gardeners to soothe hands chapped from the ravages of their labors of love).

❖ Molbak's

Open September 1998, University Village
As I write, construction crews are furiously working to create a second urban interpretation of the famed Woodinville nursery giant. Just as the charming Molbak's Seattle Garden Center reflects the character of its home in the Pike Place Market, the new Molbak's at University Village exudes the upbeat, upscale and trendy persona of its Village neighbors, and is even located in a rather unique position atop the structure housing Banana Republic, Restoration Hardware and Pottery Barn (with access by car from 25th St. on the west and from the lower level by stairs to the south and on the north side by stair or elevator). The central retail space will be airy and bright with a 21' ceiling and decor inspired by Monet's French garden and home, Giverney. With more than 40 years of experience in the nursery business in the Northwest, Molbak's has wisely decided to incorporate a retractable-roofed greenhouse structure to house plants -- a natural approach to our on-again-off-again weather. An unheated 2,500 square foot terrace will offer a (literally and probably figuratively) cool display of perennials and statuary.

❖ Ravenna Gardens

University Village; (206) 729-7388
❖ ☂ 📖 ☆

This enchanting garden shop is a perfect destination any day, but seems particularly cheery on a blustery day because the wizards who deck this shop out have tons of talent and terrific taste. It is one of the most inviting places I know of to poke around in search of something special for "The Garden" (I am always giving the nicest gifts to this garden of mine). I am impressed by the collection of distinctive hand-crafted garden art and equally artful garden structures (potting benches, trellises, arbors, chairs), and the good range of periodicals and well-chosen books. Down-to-earth good sense has gone into the selection of seeds, organic fertilizers, useful tools and widgets that get-in-there-and-do-it gardeners truly appreciate. A specialty here is the attention given creative container plantings, perfect for patios and small urban gardens for the "I haven't any time to garden" gardener. Astute, avid (and busy urban) gardeners obviously own this shop!

❖ Blue Canoe

2592 NE University Mall, Seattle, WA 98105; (206) 528-1776
Open May 1998
❖ ☂ 📖 ☆

This stylish home and garden gift, decor and accessories shop began life on Capitol Hill's East Pine St., but moves in May 1998 to

University Village where its stylish wares will immediately look right at home. If the pleasure of the chase is part of the fun you have in searching out special and unique decorative details, then this shop will provide fertile ground for the hunt! Owner Rändi Severson has a penchant for sleuthing out one-of-a-kind pieces that, as she colorfully remarks, "pop my hood!" What has caught my own attention? A recent collection she offered of reproduction old French finials, my favorite being a chubby, seductive dove. The ornately designed bird houses (for any homeless Victorian birds you may have wandering about) are utterly spellbinding, in an era when I think we are becoming overwhelmed with entirely too many poorly crafted specimens. And I find the replicas of classical architectural details (pieces of columns and capitals) whimsical and the gracefully arched antique ironwork picturesque.

Hungry? Let's have lunch:
Within University Village there are many excellent dining options from an elegant, let's-linger-over-lunch at **Piatti** to the heavenly oh-so-French café ambiance at **A La Francaise** and quite a potpourri of choice in between. There are tables set along the bricked central concourse beautifully planted with trees (*Acer palmatums, Katsuras, Magnolia grandiflora* 'Samuel Sommers' and 'Southern Butterfly', *Viburnum davidii* and Pieris 'Forest Flame' for example). Pick up picnic fare at **Briazz, QFC, Urban Bar-B-Que** or **Pasta and Company**. And top it off with a truffle from **The Confectionery**.

DRIVING DIRECTIONS:
Use the exit on the eastern boundary of University Village to avoid crossing the traffic on 45th St. Turn right on Union Bay Pl. and continue straight at the traffic light. The street becomes Mary Gates Memorial Dr. for a few blocks and then 41st St. NE as it passes by the Center for Urban Horticulture. Parking is free in a choice of three adjacent lots.
Driving distance: .75 miles; Estimated driving time: 5 minutes

❊ Center for Urban Horticulture (CUH)

Union Bay Campus, University of Washington, 3501 NE 41st St., Seattle; (206) 685-8033; mailing address: P.O. Box 354115, Seattle, WA 98195-4115. Office open Monday-Friday, 8 a.m.-5 p.m., grounds open dawn to dusk daily
❖ ✳ RR

Under the auspices of the University of Washington College of Forest Resources, this educational program was the first in the country to embrace the study of horticulture (plants and ecosystems) specifically in the demanding urban landscape. The CUH offers academic programs, research studies, a broad range of public education opportunities, a newsletter and special events. One of my all-time favorite spots to visit in the entire region is the superb **McVay**

Courtyard Garden (designed by the imminent Seattle landscape architect Iain Robertson) and the Seattle Garden Club-sponsored **Entry Shade Garden**. Within the scale of most residential gardens, one finds a sophisticated planting of small trees, ornamental grasses, handsome shrubs and an appealing tapestry of ground covers. The dynamic use of a graceful curved path delineating the two raised beds adds immensely to the charm of the garden, which is appealing in every season, but my favorite time to visit is in winter.

TOUR TIP:

❧ Planting plans of the McVay Courtyard and Shade Garden are available, free, at the CUH information desk(enter at the southeast corner of the building surrounding the courtyard) or at the Library.

Elisabeth C. Miller Horticultural Library

Located at the CUH, Merrill Hall, with the same addresses as listed above; (206) 543-0415. Open Monday-Friday 9 a.m.-5 p.m., Monday evenings until 8 and Saturday 9 a.m.-3 p.m. (except July and August).

Insider Tips:

❧ The staff here are wizards at answering even the most obscure gardening questions. They are anxious to help you (don't be shy!)

❧ Submit gardening questions via e-mail (hortlib@u.washington.edu) or visit their Web site (http://weber.u.washington.edu/~hortlib/)

❧ there are just so many tempting gardening books to buy that the expense can be daunting. Visit the library to give your intended book purchases a once-over to decide if the expense is justified.

❖ ☂ 🕮 RR available in Merrill Hall

The breadth of gardening, horticulture and botany books and publications to be found in this library is so vast it would be *easy* to spend an entire day (a month? a year?) here—believe me, I know from personal experience! One of my favorite pastimes is to scout out the periodicals section. Subscriptions are a costly part of my gardening literature budget, so I look forward to an opportunity to peruse periodicals I don't have funds to receive myself. Another area that absorbs my interest for hours is the vast collection of specialist newsletters and journals from across the country and around the world. It was here I discovered the Holly Society, the Primrose Society and the Scottish Rock Garden Society, and where I have found answers to questions on daylilies, irises and delphiniums from the communiqués of the true fanatics who band together in their love of a particular type of plant. Another priceless resource is the exceptional collection of nursery and seed catalogs. There is generally a basket of outdated copies available to take home, too. Finally, the computer station offers instruction about and access to the Internet, with many well-researched sites available with a simple click on Bookmarks. The

CD selection allows you to test drive landscape design programs to decide which one might work best for you (*before* you invest) and to access the extensive RHS Plant Finder.

TOUR TIMING:

Note that the Volunteer Park Conservatory (the destination after the Arboretum) closes at 4 p.m. in winter so plan accordingly.

DRIVING DIRECTIONS:

Leave the Center for Urban Horticulture by turning left onto 41st St. NE and proceed to the stop light. Turn left onto 45th St. NE and follow as it curves to the left onto Montlake Blvd. Pass Husky Stadium, cross the Montlake Bridge and then turn left at the second traffic light onto Lake Washington Blvd. Follow the signs to the Arboretum. At the stop sign and "Y" turn left following signs to the Graham Visitors Center.
Driving distance: 3.5 miles; *Estimated driving time:* 15 minutes.

Washington Park Arboretum – Joseph A. Witt Winter Garden

2300 Arboretum Drive E, Seattle 98112-2300; Graham Visitors Center, (206) 543-8800. Open year round, 8 a.m. until sunset

❖ ✻ RR available in the Graham Visitor Center

While a majority of visitors to the Arboretum in winter months may view its delights from the warmth of their heated automobiles, intrepid aficionados make their way to the J.A. Witt Winter Garden which highlights the trees, shrubs, ground covers and perennials that save *their* display for this quieter season. **Joseph A. Witt** (1920-1984) received his BS and MS from Washington State University studying plant physiology. He was very active in the Association of American of Botanical Gardens and Arboreta, a member of many horticultural organizations and served as a highly respected Curator of the Washington Park Arboretum.

Located near the Graham Visitor Center where you can park, check the plant stand for the Arboretum's botanical highlights of the day, and pick up a plant list and Arboretum map from the Information Desk. One of the most startlingly beautiful plants featured in the Winter Garden is the *Rubus biflorus* var. *quinqueflorus*. This bramble (yes, bramble) is prized for the ornamental value in winter of its stark, powdery white (and very thorny) stems. Arching gracefully to 12', they are indeed eye-catching. They pair stunningly with the red-twigged Dogwood (*Cornus stolonifera*). If you long for something to fill a shady moist spot at its worst in winter, look to *Stachyurus praecox* (known only by its botanical name) for the soft yellow racemes that dangle elegantly from mahogany barked stems in late March and early April. Another dazzler to seek out on your Witt Winter Garden tour is *Acer griseum* (Paperbark maple) for the riveting sight of the flaking cinnamon-brown bark along the trunk.

TOUR TIPS:

🌢 Free Arboretum Guided Walks are led by experienced volunteers featuring an aspect of the Arboretum of particular seasonal interest. Tours are free, 1-2 p.m., week-ends, from the Graham Visitor Center (except December, holidays and Husky home football game Saturdays).

🌢 60-90 minute guided walks through the Arboretum are available (for a fee and for a minimum of fifteen participants), seven days a week between 10 a.m. and 3 p.m., year-round. Call for a reservation, (206) 543-8800, with three weeks notice required.

DRIVING DIRECTIONS:

Leave the Graham Visitor's Center through the Arboretum along Arboretum Dr., E. Keep your eye peeled for the *Hamamelis* (witch hazel) and *Ilex* (holly) Collections on either side of the Drive, at their prime in mid-winter. At the stop sign turn left onto Lake Washington Blvd. E. At the stop light turn right onto E. Madison St. Proceed to the traffic light at E. John St. and turn right (this street becomes E. Thomas. At the stop sign at 15th Ave., turn right and follow right on through the tempting neighborhood of appealing shops and restaurants to E. Galer (an entrance into Volunteer Park). Turn left and park near the Conservatory. *Driving distance:* 1.5 miles; *Estimated driving time:* 10 minutes.

❇ Volunteer Park Conservatory

1402 East Galer St., Seattle 98112; (206) 684-4743. Open daily 9 a.m.-5 p.m., winter 10 a.m.-4 p.m., including holidays

❖ ☂ ✳

The enveloping warmth of these tropical glass houses on a bone-chilling day is an incomparable luxury. With an extraordinary display of orchids to greet your entry (the Conservatory is home to the Anna Clise Orchid Collection, begun in 1919), late fall and early winter are considered their finest period of bloom. In late winter and early spring come for the delicate blossoms of the large cacti and succulent collection. A koi pond is ensconced amid the lush company of temperate ferns and a sago palm overstory. For their wonderful textural complements visit the westernmost wing for the bromeliads (an exceptionally fine collection) and the staghorn ferns.

DRIVING DIRECTIONS, END OF THE TOUR:

Leave the Conservatory along the western drive to Prospect St. Turn right and proceed to 10th Ave. E. Turn right and drive to the traffic light at Roanoke St. and follow signs for I-5 south (to downtown Seattle). *Driving distance:* 3 miles; *Estimated driving time:* 15 minutes.

Further resources
Food

Both the **Starbucks** locations at University Village (QFC and western location) feature numerous coffee concoctions, tea, hot chocolate, juices, pastries, and, at lunch, sandwiches; $, B,L,D. Open daily.

Starbucks, University Village western location; $, B,L,D. Open daily.

Tully's Coffee, NE 45th and Union Bay Place NE. $, B,L,D. Open daily.

A La Francaise, University Village along the central plaza, (206) 524-9300. $, B, L, D. Open daily. With a well deserved reputation as one of the best bakeries in Seattle, you can anticipate delectable pastries (every bit as good as they look), and at lunch baguette sandwiches, freshly made soups, individual pizzas, and filled croissants.

Asia Grille, (206) 517-2877, open daily. $$, L,D. The influences for the inventive menu come from Thai, Chinese, Japanese, Northwest and even Mexican cuisines. A trio of taco shells are filled with zesty Chinese stir fry combinations, a grilled ahi sandwich is married with a chipotle mayonnaise.

Piatti, (206) 524-9088. $$, L,D. Open daily. This colorful, up-beat and lively restaurant is one of my favorite places to meet friends for a special meal in Seattle. There is a wood-burning oven, mesquite charcoal grill, and rotisserie from which come flavorful, imaginative and generous dishes, beautifully presented. On a cold day ask for a seat by the cheering fireplace.

Lodging

See "Seattle Travel Notes" in the Introduction for suggestions.

More Resources for Gardeners

Visit the **Arboretum Foundation Gift Shop**, Graham Visitor's Center, for an excellent book shop devoted to gardening, botany, natural science and the Arboretum. There is an especially good selection of books and educational nature games of interest to children. Open daily 10 a.m. to 4 p.m., January weekdays and holidays noon to 4 p.m.

Trees of Seattle, Arthur Lee Jacobson (1989, Sasquatch Books, 432 pages., color photos). An extraordinary reference and resource in all seasons. The text describes 750 varieties of trees that grow in Seattle, many are rare. Addresses along public streets or in public parks of outstanding individual trees are provided so you can see mature specimens in their context!

Winter Ornamentals by Dan Hinkley (1993, Sasquatch Books, 104 pages, color photos) This knowledgeable horticulturist writes with authority and such enthusiasm that the prospect of NOT growing these miraculous plants in our gardens would seem rather foolish!

The Woody Plant Collection in the Washington Park Arboretum, *compiled by Tracy Omar, WPA's registrar and assistant curator* (updated 1994). This catalog lists 10,000 plants and explains where to find them. Botanical and common names are provided (Arboretum map included).

Center for Urban Horticulture, P.O. Box 354115, Seattle, WA 98195-4115; (206) 685-8033. Request a free copy of the quarterly newsletter "Urban Horticulture" for a complete listing of the classes, lectures, and special events sponsored by the CUH (with additional listings for Arboretum and Northwest Horticultural Society programs).

NORTHWEST FLOWER AND GARDEN SHOW

──────────── Highlights ────────────

five acres on two floors of the Seattle Convention Center
thirty breath-taking display gardens in full bloom
fifty plant and garden societies, horticultural schools
three hundred commercial booths
one hundred free seminars and demonstrations
renowned Orchid Show, one of largest in the world

While the Pacific Northwest is blessed with a mild climate, we find the march of the seasons nonetheless requires all but the most ardent of year-round gardeners to cool their heels through the holiday seasons, roughly Thanksgiving through President's Day. And just as we begin to weary of counting the subtle shades of browns, grays and greens, our senses are shaken into a full alert by the magical appearance, overnight, of magnolias and roses in full bloom, heady jasmine-clad arbors and brilliant masses of hyacinths, luscious lettuce and frilly fennel. Annually, in February, we of the Northwest catapult ourselves from calm to chaos as the Northwest Flower and Garden Show opens its doors to invite us into it's hypnotic realm.

Annually in February (February 17-21, 1999 on the theme, *Gardens for the New Century*), Washington State Convention Center, Seattle. Office: Northwest Flower and Garden Show, 1515 NW 51st St., Seattle 98107; (206) 789-5333. Detailed brochures are available in December before the Show. *Insider Tips*: Arrive at the Convention Center early (with a ticket pre-purchased at a reduced rate), or, better yet, in the evening. *Avoid weekends and mid-day* at the Show or you'll be fighting the crowds. Take the shuttle bus from the parking lot at Northgate Mall for $2.

If you have ANY soil coursing through your veins where mere mortals run on blood, you will find it impossible to escape the fever to get out and garden after meandering under the influence of the heavenly scent of cherry trees, past luxuriant perennial borders, amid dazzling beds of spring bulbs—all in ravishing full bloom! Never mind that this is a trick played on us all by the clever nursery people who have learned to manipulate old Mother Nature to perform on a perfectly unnatural schedule for our edification and entertainment. The show acts as a catalyst to move us from the dream world of winter "gardening" to the high energy phase required of early spring.

This is the third largest Flower and Garden Show in the U.S., an accomplishment achieved in only a decade (whereas the Philadelphia Show has been in existence for over one hundred years!) In 1998 the Show drew 85,811 visitors over five days.

Three hundred commercial exhibitors bring everything from tools and supplies to greenhouses and exotic garden sculptures to sell; every imaginable plant society, club and foundation vies for our membership support and dozens of noncommercial public garden and horticultural organizations bring representatives anxious to answer questions and disseminate armloads of free literature. Each year 30 large and small nurseries and horticultural organizations pull out the stops in designing and miraculously bringing to flower dazzling display gardens and major exhibits. Five days of seminars and demonstrations, generously sponsored by *Sunset* Magazine, compete for one's time at the show with extensive offerings from recognized experts of regional, national and international repute. Amateur (I use that word loosely!) floral designers compete, providing elegant displays of enormous talent and over 100 children's gardens demonstrate the skills and imaginations of our youngest gardeners. Twenty-four popular Vignette Gardens, pocket versions of the grander displays on the main show floor, are designed and installed by horticultural organizations. Recently added were Miniature Garden dioramas, along with Window Box and Front Door Planting Design Vignettes. One of the world's largest Orchid Shows draws thousands of enthusiasts and those who are anxious for an opportunity to see so many exquisite flowers, close up.

TROPICALS & EXOTICS TOUR

―――――――――――――― Itinerary Highlights ――――――――――――――
the call of the jungle: hardy bananas and palms
lunch along the shores of Commencement Bay
a Victorian-style Glass Conservatory
extensive and irresistible collection of indoor plants

―――――――――――――――――― ❧ ――――――――――――――――――

Whether a passing flirtation or an enduring passion, Northwest gardens are taking on bold, tropical accents with the inclusion of Musa Basjoo (a variety of banana hardy enough to survive zone 7 winters), Hedychium 'Tara' (a peachy-toned ginger) and Trachycarpus fortunei (a windmill palm willing to forgive even an arctic blast). Is it tongue in cheek or a serious case of zonal denial? Or is it the urge to punctuate our soft gray-green environment with splashy color and outlandish foliage that inspires this dynamic and exciting botanical expression? For those who would be artists in this medium there are plant sources and inspirational resources readily at hand. For those content to pack along a smile and simply bask in the aura of the tropics, let's go!

THE ITINERARY IN BRIEF

TOUR NOTE:

The number of destinations on this itinerary reflects the distances covered rather than the lack of local resources available to the tropical plant aficionado. Check out the "Further Resources" section at the end of the chapter and conjure additional tours (in all seasons!)

Brunch – Jungle Fever does not open until 11 a.m. on Sunday. Consider fortifying your expeditionary forces with brunch (served 9 a.m. to 2 p.m. on Sundays) at Tacoma's **Shenanigans** (see details at the end of this chapter).

❶ Jungle Fever Exotics

This unique Northwest source for hardy varieties of the lush, dramatic plants of the tropics can't help but make you smile, and perhaps shake your head in disbelief. It is great fun to explore -- don't forget your monocle and pith helmet!

Lunch Picnic at Point Defiance Park or on the waterfront at one of the pocket parks along Ruston Way. There are a number of good restaurants along this promenade/drive, as well.

❷ W.W. Seymour Botanical Conservatory

One of the West Coast's three remaining Victorian-style glass conservatories, chock-a-block with tropical flora that impress visitors with striking foliage, bold stature and exquisitely delicate or flamboyantly colored flowers.

❸ Molbak's

With an international reputation, this 15-acre nursery houses one of the area's finest collections of indoor and tender collector plants. Housed within a massive glass greenhouse, the extensive selection offers a staggering variety of beautifully grown plants from the most familiar to utter rarities.

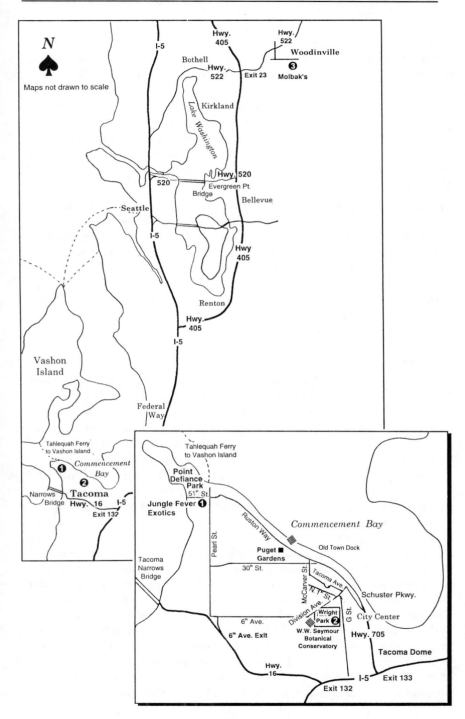

TOUR TIMING ANd TIPS

🙠 I recommend you select a sunny day for your introduction to this visual feast, perhaps in late spring so that any temptation that makes its way home with you will have the summer to strut its stuff!

🙠 If your day of exploration dawns blustery and cold, it may be a good time to see how the cast of botanical characters at Jungle Fever holds up to this abuse. W.W. Seymour Botanical Conservatory and Molbak's are indoor locations, very inviting on a nasty Northwest day.

SETTING THE SCENE

The so-called **"Mediterranean Climate"** of the Pacific Northwest, with its characteristic dry summer and wet winter cycles, supports a range of plants that are native to regions of similar climates, though they are located south of the equator. The mountainous regions of Chile, the Cape Province of South Africa and western Australia toughen temperate flora, yielding many plants that can make a transition to our coastal mountain-influenced terrain. Likewise, many plants successfully make their way here from favorable regions in Mexico, Korea, Japan, China, Nepal and New Zealand.

COMMUNITY PROFILES

Tacoma: Tacoma is the second largest city in Washington State, with a population of 176,664 (1990 census). It is located 32 miles south of Seattle on Commencement Bay, an arm of Puget Sound. The natural deepwater harbor here has developed into one of the busiest ports in the U.S. While the community was laid out in 1868, it wasn't until 1884 that it incorporated. From the early days, Tacoma served as a service and industrial hub focusing on timber, fishing, boat building, and manufacturing. Today Tacoma is emerging as a cultural and historical center. A keen awareness of the value of preservation has saved many of the elegant historical buildings -- a primary example being the grand Union Station, which features spectacular works of native son and art glass master, Dale Chihuly. The innovative new Washington State History Museum adjoins this complex, sensitively marrying the old with the new. A scenic waterfront drive along Ruston Way borders Commencement Bay where the Metropolitan Park District of Tacoma has developed a two-mile promenade of walkways and four pocket parks. You'll find free parking, picnic tables and open grassy areas, beach access and many pieces of public art. A historic fireboat and the 1873 Old Town dock share this stretch with a number of excellent million-dollar-view restaurants. The Bay is busy with pleasure boats, commerce, sea birds and other wild life.

Point Defiance Park. Within the 698-acre Park visitors can walk along trails through old growth forest or meander through a number of specialty gardens (focusing on roses, dahlias, irises, herbs, native plants and rhododendrons) and a Japanese Garden. The Park is open daily, except Thanksgiving and Christmas, dawn to dusk, (253) 591-5337. Within the Park are the **Zoo and Aquarium**, known for sensitivity to animal habitat. Exhibits are very naturalistic, representing the countries that border on the Pacific Ocean from Arctic Tundra to the Discovery Reef of the South Pacific.

Wright Park, located near the Tacoma city center, is a public park and arboretum of some 700 trees representing 100 species from four continents planted on 27.2 acres. Thirty three of the registered Washington State Champion Trees (see the "Tree Interest Tour — "Further Resources" listing for further details) are located here. The **W.W. Seymour Botanical Conservatory** is situated along the G Street, northern boundary of the Park. It is one of three remaining Victorian-style Conservatories on the west coast.

Woodinville: The first settlers were the Woodin family, who arrived in 1871. They established a store, post office, school and Sunday school in their home. In 1910-11, Seattle lumber baron, Frederick Stimson and his wife Cecile moved to their 206-acre country estate, Hollywood Farm, a dairy and agricultural demonstration project. Mrs. Stimson ran a large greenhouse from which she sold flowers around the world. Today, the manor house and carriage house remain on what are the grounds of the Chateau Ste. Michelle Winery, secluded in a grove of trees. The Winery maintains manicured gardens, an arboretum, experimental vineyards and trout ponds. In the summer music and arts events are held in the amphitheater and picnickers are welcome (I recommend you avoid the weekends at the height of the summer season when this is a very popular destination).

Today the community of Woodinville has a population of 26,000. It is located on what is locally termed the "Eastside" (referring to the eastern side of Lake Washington) a 25 minute drive from Seattle. Residents have prided themselves on the town's country charm and urban proximity for years. The area is home to the largest single outlet garden center in the country (Molbak's), a number of wineries (including Chateau Ste. Michelle, the largest winery in Washington), microbreweries, a flourishing high technology industry and hoards of happy joggers, cyclists, equestrians and hot air balloon hobbyists.

DRIVING DIRECTIONS:
Drive south 38 miles on I-5, take exit 132 for Hwy. 16 west to the 6th Ave. exit, following signs for the Vashon Ferry. From the middle lane turn left at the stop light onto 6th Ave. then right on Pearl St. At about mile 3 you will definitely know you are at 51st. St. as Jungle Fever waxes whimsical along the streetscape on the left.
Driving distance: 41 miles; *Estimated driving time:* 1 hour

Sunday Brunch first option: from I-5 take exit 133 sign-posted for the Tacoma Dome and Hwy. 705 west. Follow signs for the Point Defiance Zoo as this route takes you onto Stadium Way, which becomes Schuster Pkwy. and then Ruston Way. The waterfront restaurant, Shenanigans, is 5 miles from I-5. After brunch continue south on Ruston Way, which becomes 51st St. At Pearl St. you'll see palms waving their welcome.

Jungle Fever Exotics:

5050 N. Pearl St., Tacoma, WA 98407; (253) 759-1669. Open summer, Monday-Saturday, 10 a.m.-6 p.m., Sunday 11 a.m.-5 p.m.; winter hours vary so call ahead. Located 3 blocks north of the Point Defiance Park entrance.
❖ 📖 ☆

The tropical craze has hit Northwest gardeners with a whoosh. Perhaps our monsoon reputation has gone to our heads! Everybody has been abuzz about this crazy nursery down in Tacoma that offers hardy and nearly hardy (needing winter protection) garden exotics — things like palms and bananas, giant *Gunneras* and passionflower vines. My personal introduction to Jungle Fever was a visit with Linda Cochran on Bainbridge Island. Her exuberant, convivial and expertly maintained private garden accomplishes a masterful presentation of a large plant palette, which highlights the liberal use of so-called tropical exotics (*Gunnera*, cannas, bananas, palms, voodoo lilies and outsized ornamental grasses). I felt I really must visit the nursery mentioned as Linda's local source, so I chose one of the most brutal days in mid-January with temperatures hovering around 20F and a stiff breeze blowing off Puget Sound. I felt this would be the ultimate test of fire (ice?) to prove the claims made about this daring nursery. I was stunned and impressed with their display of audacious plants, even under the most demanding of circumstances! My kind of place. And every visit brings a fresh wave of appreciation. If you have adventurous botanical blood coursing through your veins, if you lust for a bit of the Pacific Islands in the Pacific Northwest, then here's your ticket. You will also find unique, locally-crafted garden art (functional and ornamental) among the jungle of plants, which also include lots of rare and unusual perennials, many broadleaf evergreens, ornamental grasses, aquatic plants, herbs, ferns, hardy varieties of fruits, and conservatory and cool (as in temperature "cool") greenhouse plants from *abutilons* to *zantedeschia.*

Lunch: I hope you have selected a gloriously sunny day for your tour, because picnic destinations abound. With 698-acre Point Defiance Park only three blocks from Jungle Fever at 54th and Pearl St., this would make a logical spot to consider. They offer full picnic facilities (including shelters, grills, tables, etc.) Another option is to head west along 51st to Commencement Bay where the road becomes Ruston Way. Along the waterfront there are many opportunities to park and spread out a picnic on a grassy knoll or at a picnic table.

DRIVING DIRECTIONS:
If you are continuing on from Point Defiance Park, return on Pearl St. to 51st (the intersection where Jungle Fever is located). Turn west, toward the water, and proceed down the hill, winding to the right. Go through the tunnel and continue on Ruston Way along the waterfront. If you have chosen to stop for lunch along Commencement Bay, drive north on Ruston Way (along the waterfront in the direction of the Tacoma city center). At Commencement Park and the Old Town Dock turn right onto McCarver St. Topping the hill, at the blinking light, turn left onto Tacoma Ave. At N. 1st St. turn right two blocks to Wright Park, at Division Ave. Turn left and circle the Park clockwise onto G St. to the Conservatory. *Driving distance:* 5 miles; *Estimated driving time:* 15 minutes

❊ W.W. Seymour Botanical Conservatory

316 S. G St., Tacoma, WA 98407; (253) 591-5330. Open daily, (except Thanksgiving and Christmas) 10 a.m.-4:30 p.m. Gift shop open 11 a.m.-4 p.m. Admission is free. Web site: www.tacomaparks.com/gardens.html
Insider's Tip: The gift shop offers plants propagated from the collection so be sure to give the selection your best plant hunter's attention in search of a rare or uncommon treasure.
❖ ⚘ 📖 ☆ ✳ RR (in Wright Park)
This handsome Victorian-style Conservatory was dedicated in 1908, the gift of William W. Seymour, a wealthy Tacoman who made his money in timber, utilities and land speculation. The Seymour Conservatory is one of only three examples of glass houses from this era remaining on the West Coast (the other two being the Seattle Volunteer Park Conservatory and the Conservatory of Flowers at San Francisco's Golden Gate Park. *see below). The Seymour Conservatory is elegantly capped with a 12-sided windowed dome and clad with more than 4,000 panes of glass. It is now owned and managed by the Metropolitan Park District of Tacoma and is listed on the city, state and national historic registers. There is no current

record of the number of plants housed here, but it is estimated to feature some 200 species of tropical exotics, including the likes of cacti and succulents, bromeliads, orchids, palms, ferns and vines. Seasonal displays (spring bulbs, Easter lilies, a Haloween pumpkin patch, Christmas poinsettias) are staged through the volunteer efforts of local garden clubs and the Conservatory's Foundation.

❧ A sad note is that the **Conservatory of Flowers** at San Francisco's Golden Gate Park, assembled in 1877, suffered severe damage in a winter storm in 1995. Now empty, covered in sail cloth and awaiting the long and expensive process of restoration, it will be well into the 21st Century before there is any hope of re-opening. The losses to the collection have been staggering, as well. If this topic interests you, there is an excellent story with photos on The Bay Area Gardener Web site: www.gardens.com/ Look for it under "Articles".

DRIVING DIRECTIONS:
Return on G St. to Division Ave. Turn right. At Stadium Way turn right and watch for (and take) the Hwy. 705 freeway entrance on the left, then follow the signs for I-5. Take I-5 north toward Seattle. At about mile 30 you will pass Southcenter Mall. Take the Hwy. 405, Burien/Renton exit and follow north, past Bellevue and Kirkland to exit #23, Hwy. 522 for Woodinville. Take the first exit on the right. At the stop sign turn right. At the traffic light on NE175th turn left. Molbak's is on the right after .5 mile. *Driving distance:* 48 miles; *Estimated driving time:* 1 hour 10 minutes

❋ Molbak's

13625 NE 175th St., Woodinville, WA 98072-8558; (425) 483-5000. Open daily, year round, 9 a.m.-6 p.m., Fridays open until 9 p.m. (closing hours vary seasonally). To arrange a tour (about one hour long) for your group of 10 to 20 people, call (425) 481-4557, ext. 349 at least 4 weeks prior to your visit.

❖ ☂ ▥ ☆ ✳ RR

It is interesting to see how many of this area's most respected gardening "gurus" make regular forays to the indoor plant section at Molbak's in search of the uncommon, flamboyant and the bizarre. There are aisles and aisles of top quality indoor plant favorites from begonias to philodendrons, anthiriums to ferns that establish Molbak's as a premier source for tropical and exotic plants, many of which will grow beautifully on the patio or planted out in the garden from spring to fall. I always make a beeline for the "Collector's Foliage" table (usually tucked near the back of the foliage plant greenhouse). Here I find the likes of Bat Wing *Passifloras, Daturas* and *Brugmansias, Mandevilla, Clerodendrum thomsoniaes* (including the heavenly variegated form) and *Solanum jasminoides.* The majority of plants found in this section are small starts, very reasonably priced (and easy to pack if you have come from afar.) I also have a growing collection of cacti and succulents, never a particular interest of mine until my introduction recently at an Odd Plant Show and Sale held in Seattle annually. Now I find a snoop through this section imperative.

DRIVING DIRECTIONS, END OF THE TOUR:

From Molbak's, turn left onto NE175th, then at 132nd St. (Hwy. 202) turn right and continue on over Hwy. 522 where you will immediately turn left to the on-ramp for Hwy. 522 west. Stay in the right lane and follow signs for Hwy. 405/Bellevue. Heading south on Hwy. 405 follow signs for Seattle via Hwy. 520, the Evergreen Point Bridge.

Driving distance: 20 miles; *Estimated driving time:* 25 minutes

FURTHER RESOURCES

Food

Picnic fare: if you are convenient to downtown Seattle and wondering where to pick up something interesting for an al fresco lunch, I suggest you make an early foray (say 8:30 a.m.) to the Pike Place Market to select from the offerings of Three Girls Bakery (622-1045), Cucina Fresca (448-4758), Piroshky-Piroshki (441-6068), or De Laurenti's (622-0141).

Anthony's Homeport: Opens its doors in 1998. Adjacent to the Vashon Island ferry dock, located at the western end of Pearl St., this restaurant will continue the lead of the Ballard flagship Anthony's with a specialty in fresh seafood. With a waterside location on the western boundary of Point Defiance Park need I remark that the view is superlative?

C.I. Shenanigans: 3017 Ruston Way, Tacoma, WA 98402; (253) 752-8811. L, D Mon.-Sat.; Brunch, D Sun. (brunch is served 9 a.m.-2 p.m.) This waterfront restaurant offers a sumptuous Sunday Brunch where tables laden with fresh seafood (like shrimp in the shell and mussels), baked goods, omelets to your order, roast meats and a huge selection of fresh fruits.

LODGING

See the "Seattle Travel Notes" for accommodation suggestions.

FOR MORE INFORMATION

Chateau Ste. Michelle: (425) 488-1133. Ticketmaster handles tickets for their events, (206) 292-2787.

Cascade Cactus and Succulent Society: (206) 325-9383

Metropolitan Park District of Tacoma: administration office, 4702 S. 19th St., Tacoma, WA 98405; (253) 305-1000.

Pacific Northwest Palm and Exotic Plant Society: 10310 Hollybank Dr., Richmond, B.C. V7E 4S5

MORE RESOURCES FOR GARDENERS

Baker and Chantry: 18611 132 Ave. NE, (mail: P.O. Box 554), Woodinville, WA 98072; (425) 483-0345. For orchid enthusiasts, whether as a novice or an accomplished grower, do make the time to discover this unique place. You will always find breathtaking orchids in bloom.

Bamboo Gardens of Washington: 5016 192nd Pl. NE, Redmond, WA 98053-4602; (425) 868-5166. One of this region's most complete sources for bamboo and bamboo products. (See "Nursery Loop East" for more details).

Enchanted Garden: 1524 Pike Pl., Seattle, WA 98101; (206) 625-1205. Located at Pike Place market, this flower shop specializes in fresh tropical foliage and cut flowers, orchids, cacti and tropical houseplants. (See the "Rainy Day Tour" for more details.)

Flower World: 9322 196th St. SE, Snohomish, WA 98296; (425) 481-7565. It is possible to lose oneself literally for hours in the indoor plant houses here! Many plants have reached a mature size so the feeling is truly jungle-like. (See the "Loop North" Tour for more details.)

Indoor Sun Shoppe: 911 NE 45th, Seattle, WA 98105; (206) 634-3727. As the name implies, houseplants reign supreme in this shop featuring an extravagant collection of tropicals and exotics. This is a great source for carnivorous plants, cacti and orchids and probably the best source of all for indoor lighting equipment, including high intensity and natural spectrum lighting to counteract the gloomy weather of a Northwest winter.

Little and Lewis Water Garden: (206) 842-8327. Open by appointment, this garden of exotics is the botanical gallery setting for the sculpture of David Little and George Lewis. (See "Bainbridge Island" Tour).

Moorhaven Water Gardens: 3006 York Rd., Everett, WA 98204; (425) 743-6888. One of this area's most respected water garden nurseries, set in a forested residential neighborhood, Moorhaven also includes aviaries (pining for a peacock or a partridge?), an *extensive* selection of koi, goldfish, tadpoles and other aquatic beasts, and pond equipment, supplies and advice.

Oasis Water Garden: 404 S. Brandon, Seattle, WA 98108; (206) 767-9776. Here you will find over 50 varieties of hardy and tropical water lilies and lotus, over a hundred web-footed water and bog loving plants, koi and goldfish and pond equipment and supplies.

The Odd Plant Show and Sale: Held annually the second week-end of September at Sky Nursery, the plants are grown and shown by members of the Cascade Cactus and Succulent Society, the NW Chapt. of the American Bamboo Society and the PNW Carnivorous Plant Society (joined by others).

Volunteer Park Conservatory: 1400 E. Galer St., Seattle, WA 98112; (206) 684-4743. This Victorian-style iron and glass conservatory composed of five glass houses. The orchid collection is breathtaking as are the many other exhibits, including the cactus and succulent house, the bromeliads and the palm house. (See the "Mid-Winter Seattle" Tour for more details.)

Woodland Park Zoo: 5500 Phinney Ave. N, Seattle, WA 98103; (206) 684-4040, Zoo information, 684-4800 (TDD 684-4026). Plant people love the commitment of the WPZ to the importance of the horticultural context. (See the "Rainy Day Seattle" Tour for more details.)

BOOK LOVER'S TOUR

Itinerary Highlights
---

read and ride—start the day with a ferry trip!
out-of-print garden books in a cozy Island shop
European style bistro, picnic or Northwest brew pub lunch
horticultural heaven for nature and garden book lovers
an entire library specializing in gardening and related journals, books
and catalogs
University bookstore boasts serious gardening selection

❧

We are fortunate here in the Northwest to have an abundance of fine authors, publishers, book sellers and libraries dedicated to the subject we hold so dear! How many different kinds of gardening books and magazines are there to quench the thirst of gardeners of every persuasion in search of inspiration, education and entertainment? Heaven only knows, but if you love books as much as I do, then you probably will rate a day dedicated to haunting the stacks of our region's abundance of botanical books right next to getting to spend a whole day just reading them!

THE ITINERARY IN BRIEF

Ferry across Elliott Bay to Bainbridge Island

❶ Fortner Books

A compelling draw to this warm and cheery book shop is their collection of antique, out-of-print and used books. Lucky for us, gardening books are a specialty.

LUNCH A snazzy European influenced bistro, a genuine Northwest brew pub overlooking the boat harbor or a heavenly picnic in a waterfront park (or on the water, ferrying back to Seattle) – Winslow offers a pleasing selection for famished visitors.

Ferry back to the Seattle waterfront

❷ Flora and Fauna Books

Located in Seattle's historic Pioneer Square district, this is Mecca to the literary gardener and natural history buff. A quintessential book shop, in a charming building packed to the gills with new, used, rare and out-of-print books for gardeners, birders and naturalists. Proprietor David Hutchinson's frequent journeys to Britain yield hard-to-obtain books from across the pond.

❸ Elisabeth C. Miller Horticultural Library

Under one very pleasant roof, the public is invited to peruse an enviable collection devoted exclusively to horticultural topics

❹ University Book Store

Located adjacent to the University of Washington campus you'll find a most popular book emporium -- local affection for this destination is legion and long standing. Loyal customers make a pilgrimage here from across town and across the state because they relish the selection, the atmosphere and the quality of the service.

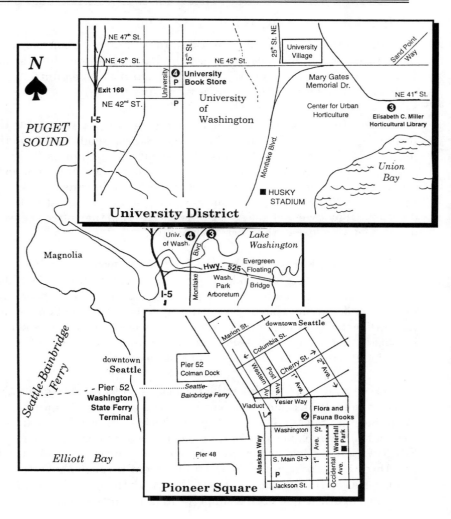

University District

Pioneer Square

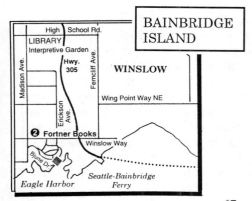

BAINBRIDGE ISLAND

67

Tour Timing and Tips

🌨 Plan this tour for a weekday or a Saturday. Fortner Books does not open until noon on Sunday and Flora and Fauna Books and the Miller Library are closed on Sunday. The Miller Library is open until 3 p.m. on Saturdays (closed that day in July and August).

🌨 To save the cost of a vehicle on the ferry, park in a garage near the ferry terminal. The walk into Winslow on Bainbridge Island from the ferry dock, a distance of 5 blocks, takes about 15-20 minutes. Take advantage of Early Bird Specials at downtown garages and park up to 10 hours for between $5 and $7.50. This generally means "checking in" before 9:30 a.m. I suggest you try the Republic Garage at S. Jackson St. just west of 1st Ave. S. As I write this they offer the best deal – and are close to the Ferry Terminal.

🌨 **Taking the Ferry**: The Bainbridge Island Ferry leaves from Pier 52, the Colman Dock, on Alaskan Way between Marion and Columbia Streets. Schedules change with the seasons, so plan ahead by calling to confirm departure times. As a gateway to the Olympic Peninsula, the traffic back-ups here in the summer, especially on a weekend can be frustrating. (Another reason to go as a walk-on passenger) See more Ferry information at the end of this chapter.

🌨 Have you discovered the audio tape edition of *The Writer in the Garden* yet? Professional readers bring you writings of 44 authors, including Vita Sackville-West, Beverley Nichols, Henry Mitchell, Gertrude Jekyll, Nancy Mitford, Louise Beebee Wilder, E.B. White, Edith Wharton, Eleanor Perenyi, Colette and Andrew Marvel. You'll find three hours of inspiration and amusement through the letters, poems, essays and book excerpts within this anthology. (Find source information at the end of this chapterand in the Introduction.)

Setting the Scene

Not many places on earth invite you to start your day of adventure enjoying a pleasant voyage by ferry en route to a picturesque island village and a charming little book shop. Seattle is blessed with a stunning setting, nestled between snow-capped mountain ranges (the Cascades to the east and the Olympics to the west) and the protected inland passages of Puget Sound. This island-studded waterway teems with activity, to the delight of visitors and residents alike. Seattle is a busy and successful port, attracting shipping from around the Pacific Rim and the world. Elliott Bay, the body of water at the foot of the central downtown business district, provides safe anchorage for large container ships awaiting their turn to unload at the vast near-by docklands. From the Seattle waterfront the Washington State Ferry System provides routes to and from Bainbridge Island and the city of Bremerton, and a passenger only ferry to Vashon Island. Pleasure boats, working fishing boats, tourism-related craft and ferry services connecting to Victoria on Vancouver Island, B. C. use this Bay. There is plenty of room, though, for Orca whales, seals and sea birds that may be seen from the decks of passing boats. And the view of the sophisticated Seattle cityscape from the deck of a ferry takes your breath away as it rises dramatically up steep hills from the waterfront piers.

COMMUNITY / DISTRICT PROFILES

Winslow, Bainbridge Island: The tiny town of Winslow is nonetheless the largest community on the Island. Originally called Madrone, the name Winslow became official in 1903. In the early 1950s the first Winslow ferry terminal was constructed and in 1970 the existing ferry terminal was built. A staggering 44% of the Island's population commutes to Seattle each day, with an additional 7% commuting off-Island elsewhere. (See the "Bainbridge Island" Tour for more details about the history of this town and the Island).

Pioneer Square: It was on the shoreline of the present day Pioneer Square district that the first permanent Seattle settlers disembarked in 1852. From the beginning, early entrepreneurs envisioned a great city, despite the steep forested terrain and cumbersome tidal mudflats. In the early years a busy mill provided timber for homes and businesses. The completion of the railroad in 1889 brought a flood of new residents, but shortly afterwards a catastrophic fire burned the fledgling city to the ground. The many elegant brick buildings that remain today were constructed in response to that fire. The Klondike Gold Rush of 1897 sealed Seattle's destiny as a commercial and residential hub. In the 1960s there was a bureaucratic move to level what is now the Pioneer Square area for parking, as it had become largely a hang-out for the homeless and the buildings were deteriorating. Seattlites rallied to preserve this historical district, successfully saving 40 blocks of vintage architecture under strict restoration rules. While the neighborhood is still a popular "home" to the homeless it simultaneously, and not without some discomfort, has developed as an upscale urban housing and commercial precinct.

University District: Typical of the commercial and residential neighborhoods adjacent to other major universities, you will find the goods and services that support a population of 50,000 students and staff and a neighborhood of 35,000 permanent residents. The eclectic mix of inexpensive eateries (many of which specialize in ethnic cuisine), an art film theater, penny-wise clothing shops, import emporiums and used book stores meld with the stately turn-of-the-century mansions on Greek row, the tree-lined boulevards and hoards of football fans, be-decked in purple and gold surging to or from a home game of the beloved Huskies.

DRIVING DIRECTIONS:

This trip begins at the Washington State Ferry Terminal, Pier 52 on the Seattle waterfront. On I-5 from the north take the 4th Ave. S. exit #164. At 4th Ave. S. turn right, and then left onto Royal Brougham, move to the center lane, following signs to the ferry terminal. This route will take you along the elevated Alaskan Way Viaduct. Watch for Jackson St. on the right if you are going to park in the Republic Garage. The Ferry Terminal is well marked.

TOUR TIPS

Fortner Books opens at 10 a.m. As the ferry crossing takes 35 minutes, look for a departure around 9:30 a.m. from Seattle. For early birds who arrive comfortably before this ferry (say an hour), with a craving for some of the best lattes Seattle has to offer there's: **Torrefazione Italia Coffees** (624-5773), on the brick plaza of Occidental St., between Main St. and S. Jackson St., my personal vote for latte heaven, serving in exquisite hand painted Italian cups, offering seating on the tree-lined plaza or inside the handsome shop. Pastries and the morning paper are available as well. This is five blocks from the ferry terminal.
A La Francaise Bakery (624-0322) Fabulous selection of freshly made, European-style pastries, and espresso (of course!)

Early in Winslow? Try **Café Nola**, for a delectable bite. You can cradle a frothy bowl of coffee and pretend you are in Paris.

❊ Fortner Books

210 Winslow Way, Bainbridge Island, WA 98110; (206) 842-6577, (800) 842-6577. Open Monday-Saturday 10 a.m.-6 p.m., Sunday, noon-5 p.m.
E-mail fortnrbk@interloc.com
❖ ☂ 📖

Nancy and Robert Fortner have created an appealing little shop that makes you wish you could pack it all up and take it home as your personal library. The ambiance exudes a warm welcome, with Otis, the Terrier, snuggled up on the crocheted throw on a Stickley chair, the twitter of finches and a cockatiel accompanying the classical music or jazz wafting through the room. And then there are the beautifully displayed books. A loving hand has been at work here. Out-of-print books you have had a dickens of a time finding are right there, and in excellent condition, as the standards here are very high. It is evident that serious attention has been paid to assembling a superlative collection of gardening books, from the latest releases from Timber Press to tried and true favorites to books from local luminary, Ann Lovejoy. You are likely to find yourself cross-legged on the carpet in this comfortable nook trying to decide which books to make your own on *this* visit!

Lunch: Café Nola is a European café (which means they take their pastries seriously, their extraordinary coffee is served in bowls as in France and the menu, though small, is innovative). As an alternative, a walk to the boat harbor takes you to Harbor Public House, a Northwest brew pub with a welcoming fire in cool weather, a sunny deck with a view on a bright day—and great food. Or consider a picnic from the creative selection at the Town and Country Market deli counter, with the likes of crab cakes with red pepper aioli and tortellini. Picnic at tables provided on the lower level or in the park along the waterfront (exiting the Market turn left, through the Tot Lot Park, continuing to the left and following the trail across from the Community Center). Another option is to picnic on the ferry route back to Seattle.

Ferry to Seattle

With three additional destinations to reach it would be prudent to pace your time in Winslow to catch a mid-day ferry (as I write there is a 12:20 that would be a good choice).

WALKING DIRECTIONS:
The next destination is Flora and Fauna Books, which is located on First Ave. S at S. Washington St. This is three blocks east of the Ferry Terminal where you have disembarked.

🏵 Flora and Fauna Books

121 First Ave., Seattle, WA 98104; (206) 623-4727. Open Monday-Saturday, 10 a.m.-6 p.m. Also at Northwest Flower and Garden Show, etc.

❖ ♈ 📖

I think many people miss this valuable resource because it is tucked down a stairway. What a pity, as this is an exceptional shop. For it's depth and breadth of well-selected contemporary, used, rare and out-of-print books, it is difficult to visit its equal on the west coast. Here you will find the most focused of monographs—scholarly works dealing in depth with a specific genus—alongside books for fresh-out-

of-the-box beginners in search of *something* that will help answer a
novice's questions in a language they can understand. An added
bonus at Flora and Fauna is the knowledgeable staff, who field
queries from across the country from sleuths on the hunt for a
particular book or are looking for advice on what book will meet their
particular needs.

Owner David Hutchinson, active in Audubon, offers an exceptional
selection of ornithological and natural history books, audio tapes and
CDs and a small collection of botanical and historical prints as well.

Tour Tip
While in Pioneer Square, visit **Waterfall Park**, at the corner of S.
Main St. and 2nd St. S, a privately owned and maintained pocket
park commemorating the birthplace of the United Parcel Service.
There are places to sit and marvel at the ingenious use of stone in
creating a monumental waterfall on a tiny, urban, corner site. There
are lovely plantings of small trees with seasonal flowering
ornamentals and annuals.

Driving Directions
From Pioneer Square you need to make your way to I-5 north. Drive
north (toward downtown) on First Ave. S to Cherry St. Turn right and go
up hill, under I-5, and at the traffic signal at 7th Ave. turn left onto the
freeway entrance ramp. After 3 miles, take the NE 45th /50th St. exit. To
avoid the traffic through the University District on 45th stay in the left lane
for 50th St. Turn right and drive to 15th St. Turn right and then at 45th St.
turn left. Follow 45th St. past the University and down the hill. At the
traffic light turn left (this is still called 45th St.). Take a right turn at the
next street onto Mary Gates Memorial Dr., which turns into NE 41st. The
Center for Urban Horticulture is on your right. There is free parking. The
Miller Library is through the McVay Courtyard, on the right.
Driving distance: 6 miles; *Estimated driving time: 20 minutes*

❊ Elisabeth C. Miller Horticultural Library
3501 NE 41st St. (P.O. Box 354115), Seattle, WA 98195; (206) 543-0415.
Open Monday-Friday 9 a.m.-5 p.m., Monday evening until 8 p.m., Saturday
(except July and August) 9 a.m.-3 p.m. E-mail hortlib@u.washington.edu
Web site: http://weber.u.washington.edu/~hortlib
❖ ☂ ✳

This is indisputably the foremost horticultural library anywhere in
the region—and it is open for you to visit. The library houses a
remarkable collection of nearly 8,000 books (500 in a lending library);
1,000 bound periodicals; 1,000 current nursery and seed catalogs; 300
journals and society publication subscriptions, from around the world;

and a climate-controlled room preserves a collection of 500 old and rare volumes.

The Miller Library was the gift of Pendleton Miller, in 1985, to mark the accomplishments of his wife, Elisabeth, who was very active in the world of horticulture in Seattle and created a distinguished garden at their home in the Highlands. In 1990, Mrs. Miller made expansion of the library possible and today it is supported by a small stipend from the University, and by contributions, donations and grants from individuals and organizations.

All this and a computer station complete with an Internet connect (instruction cheerfully provided) and a dandy assortment of garden and landscape design software for you to test drive (Microsoft's "Complete Gardening", Sunset's "Western Garden" & "Problem Solver", Books That Work's "3D Landscape" & "Garden Encyclopedia", Country Living's "Gardener", Michael Dirr's "Woody Plant Photo-Library", Chris Philips' "RHS Plant Finder" demo version). There is an extensive and current computerized journal index. The helpful and knowledgeable librarians field gardening and related questions with aplomb (including those received by phone and e-mail!) The extensive collection of nursery and seed catalogs is useful for finding ones you want to order yourself. Master Gardeners are available at the Library Mondays 4-8 p.m.

DRIVING DIRECTIONS

Leaving the Center for Urban Horticulture turn left onto NE 41st, then left at NE 45th., follow the right hand lane up the hill, past the University to 15th Ave. NE. At that traffic signal turn left one block, then right and right again into the parking lot for the University Book Store. For patrons parking is free (purchasing or not -- request a sticker from store staff). Validation stamps are accepted at any other attended lot in the University District that has a blue and yellow sign at the entrance -- the closest are at the corner of 15th Ave. N.E. and N.E. 42nd and on the east side of Brooklyn Ave. N.E. between N.E. 42nd and N.E. 43rd , an easy walk to the store.

Driving distance: 1.25 miles; *Estimated driving time:* 5 minutes

❊ University Book Store

4326 University Way NE, Seattle, WA 98105; (206) 634-3400. Open Weekdays 9 a.m.-9 p.m., Saturdays 9 a.m.-6 p.m., Sundays noon-5 p.m. Also at Northwest Flower and Garden Show, etc.
www.bookstore.washington.edu   bookstore@u.washington.edu
Insider's tip: they generously offer many FREE services—toll-free ordering (800) 335-READ; free shipping anywhere in the U.S.; free gift wrap service; free special orders by mail, e-mail or fax; free out-of-print book search service; and free convenient parking.

Currently the largest independent college bookseller in the U.S., the

Book Store's history goes back to 1900 when two enterprising students opened for business in a small cloak room next to the university president's office. From the outset the store was considered a business enterprise and did not rely on student support. The website provides a fascinating history of the relationship to the ASUW and the eventual signing of a trust agreement that clearly identified the store as an independent entity, but one with a close working relationship with the University and an obligation to serve and benefit members of the University community.

A loyal and broad customer base is drawn to the enormous choice offered in any department, very popular bargain book tables and for Gardeners on the Go, their strong commitment to gardening literature. As many of the staff are themselves gardeners, they pay special attention to best current titles and seek a broad representation of horticultural topics for all levels and interests.

DRIVING DIRECTIONS, END OF THE TOUR
To get to I-5, drive west (away from the University campus) on 44th St. to 12th Ave. Turn right one block and then left at the traffic signal onto 45th St. Watch for I-5 on ramp signs directing you to the north or to the south (toward downtown Seattle).
Driving distance: 4.5 miles; *Estimated driving time:* 15 minutes

FURTHER RESOURCES
Food
A La Francaise: 417 First Ave. S, Seattle, WA 98104; (206) 624-0322. $, Open from 6:30 a.m daily.
Torrefazione Italia: 320 Occidental S, Seattle, WA 98104; (206) 624-5847. $, Monday-Friday from 6:30 a.m., Saturday from 8 a.m., Sunday from 9 a.m.
Café Nola: 101 Winslow Way East, Winslow, WA 98110; (206) 842-3822; $$ B, L Tuesday-Saturday 8 a.m.-4 p.m., Sunday 8 a.m.-3 p.m. A favorite with locals for freshly baked pastries, espresso bar, creative European influenced breakfast and lunch menus. Intimate café with some outside seating,.
Harbor Public House: 231 Parfitt Way SW, Winslow, WA 98110; (206) 842-0969; $$, L,D daily. Specials join creative sandwich and burger combinations, excellent Brew Pub selection, picturesque setting with view, dining deck overlooking the pleasure boat harbor and snug fireplace within for cooler days.
Town and Country Thriftway Market: 343 Winslow Way, Winslow, WA 98110; (206) 842-7717. Open daily. This is a well-stocked, up-scale market with a particularly appealing deli department. A delectable picnic could easily be assembled and enjoyed on-site at tables provided on the ground level, at a nearby harborside park or on the ferry back to Seattle.

Lodging

See "Seattle Travel Notes" or for a grand slam two- to three-day get-away refer to the "Bainbridge Island" Tour Lodging listings.

For More Information

Bainbridge Island Chamber of Commerce: (206) 842-3700. In season there is a staffed kiosk at the ferry terminal with visitor information. **Washington State Ferry**, 52, 801 Alaskan Way, Seattle, WA 98104; (800) 84-FERRY (from with-in Washington), (206) 464-6400. Web site: http://www.wsdot.wa.gov/ Also see the "Seattle Travel Notes" for ferry tips.

More Resources for Gardeners

Elliott Bay Book Company, First Ave. S at Main St. in Pioneer Square; (206) 624-6600. Open daily 10 a.m.-11 p.m. One of Seattle's best-loved literary attractions, with a good selection of gardening books and magazines. *The Writer in the Garden*: audio tapes of garden writers, compiled by Jane Garmey, Editor, locally available at A Garden of Distinction, Flora and Fauna Books, Fortner Books and the Lakewold Gardens Shop.

Book loving Gardeners on the Go can check out the following Tours and the "Further Resources for Gardeners" sections for noteworthy book selections: BELLINGHAM Tour—-**R. R. Henderson, Book Seller**, (new and used) and the **International Newstand**, which I think has the broadest selection of national and international gardening periodicals *in the region.*
GLORIOUS GARDEN CENTERS—**Molbak's** has an excellent book department, including lots of periodicals.
NURSERY AND GARDEN LOOP/SOUTH—**Lakewold Garden Shop** for gardening periodicals and books (US, Canadian and British) .
ORNAMENTING THE GARDEN—**A Garden of Distinction** offers a small but tasty array of more uncommon gardening related books, with an emphasis on imagination.
TREE & SHRUB ENTHUSIAST'S and KIDS TOUR, TOO!—**Washington Park Arboretum Gift Shop** has a well-chosen selection and a particularly good array of nature, gardening books and kits and games for children.
VASHON ISLAND IDYLL—**Books by the Way** is an inviting book shop.

For mail order, look to **Calendula Books**, for rare and out-of-print garden books, in Chehalis (360) 740-1784. There are several Northwest publishers who contribute to the field of horticultural literature. Foremost is **Timber Press**, 133 SW 2nd Ave., Suite 450, Portland, Oregon 97204-9744; (503) 227-2878, (800) 327-5680. Visit their excellent Web site at www.timber-press.com They offer an *extensive* catalog of titles covering a broad range of botanical topics for gardeners of all levels and interests. They are noted for their commitment to reprinting titles that have been out-of-print, including a number of British classics.
Sasquatch Books offers a number of Northwest gardening and related titles. 615 Second Ave., Seattle, WA 98104; (800) 775-0817. They offer a catalog and Web site: www.sasquatchbooks.com

AN ECLECTIC LIST / REFERENCE AND RELATED BOOKS

The American Horticultural Society A-Z Encyclopedia of Garden Plants, Christopher Brickell and Judith Zuk , over 15,000 ornamental plants and 6,000 photographs describing many unfamiliar named varieties.

Annuals for Connoisseurs, Wayne Winterrowd (Prentice Hall, 1992) This books provides an excellent guide to exciting, well-performing annuals, most of which can be obtained through diligent sleuthing.

The Collector's Garden, Ken Druse (Clarkson Potter, Publisher, 1996, 248 pages). This book pays tribute to twenty-eight passionate gardeners and collectors with luscious photos and insightful text profiling those whose lives revolve around the search for and conservation of endangered, rare, bizarre and beautiful plants. Heronswood's Dan Hinkley is among those featured.

Dirr's Hardy Trees and Shrubs, Michael Dirr (Timber Press, 1997, 493 pages) shows habit and details of more than 500 species and describes some 700 additional cultivars and varieties. There are 1,660 color plates.

The Garden in Bloom, Ann Lovejoy (Sasquatch Books, 1998) The latest in the "In Bloom..." series from this prolific Bainbridge Island garden writer, is of special interest to Gardeners on the Go for the many insightful references Ann makes to places you will visit on your touring rounds.

North American Landscape Trees, Arthur Lee Jacobson (Ten Speed Press, 1997, 772 pages) An American Horticultural Society winner for Book of the Year in 1997. This comprehensive reference covers some 5,000 landscape trees, providing information on rare and familiar species alike.

Random House books by **Martyn Rix** and **Roger Phillips** are extremely valuable references (especially *Perennials* I & II) and *Shrubs*

Sunset *Western Garden Book* is *always* with me on garden tours!

Winter Ornamentals, Dan Hinkley (Sasquatch Books, 1993). Well written and illustrated insight into top woody plant performers for winter gardens.

The Wise Garden Encyclopedia, this rather obscure reference (originally published in 1936, my edition is from 1970) gets more of a work-out than any other garden reference book I own. It is comprehensive and speaks in terms I can understand, even on complex concepts. Find it in used book stores.

Timber Press offers an unparalleled catalog of horticultural books. Visit their web site www.timber-press.com/ or call (800) 327-5680, (503) 227-3070. I often turn to their series based on *The New RHS Dictionary of Gardening*. I especially use the titles, *Manual of Climbers and Wall Plants*, those dedicated to Bulbs and the one on Ornamental Grasses.

The Northwest Gardeners' Resource Directory provides hundreds of gardening-related resource profiles throughout the Pacific Northwest. There is an extensive chapter on literature that reviews books, journals and magazines of particular interest to gardeners in this region, including those that relate specifically to native plant interest. In addition, among the 18 chapters, the most extensive offers a comprehensive and in-depth look at nurseries in the region (covering western Oregon, Washington and British Columbia). This book is a natural adjunct to *Gardeners on the Go* for the wealth of detailed information it provides on virtually every aspect of the Northwest gardening world.

ORNAMENTING THE GARDEN

————————————— Itinerary Highlights —————————————

hand-picked booty from rural French and Thai markets

snazzy garden nostalgia, fancifully displayed

elegant and affordable Japanese garden elements

imaginative and classical European garden statuary

specialized second-hand store for garden ornament

———————————— ❧ ————————————

Whoever coined the phrase "garden rooms" must have observed how much these horticultural spaces have borrowed from the interior design discipline. Whether selecting furniture with flare for dining al fresco or resting our weary bones, twinkling strings of lights to thread romantically through grape arbors, a classical Italian pot to cleverly whisk into the mixed border the day of a garden tour...gardeners seem compelled to embellish and accessorize the garden as they would their wardrobes or living rooms. And these elements, like the garden design itself, contribute to the artistic expression that gives a garden character, heart and individuality.

❶ A Garden of Distinction

This knocks-your-socks-off shop offers a dazzling selection of garden ornament—exquisite antique classics mingle with unique and distinctive pieces specially hand-crafted for discerning and adventurous garden makers. This is a truly magical place where imagination runs rampant, so expect to dawdle as your fancy is tickled and creative juices flow freely.

❷ Dirty Jane's

These garden gee-gaw buffs are geniuses in the art of salvaging horticultural nostalgia that will bring a flood of memories or just evoke earlier (more innocent?) eras. I dare anyone to enter this shop and resist the inevitable chuckle the engaging displays elicit. This shop has class and pizzazz.

Lunch Close by in this Capitol Hill neighborhood you'll find a *very* special, romantic European-style restaurant. If time permits and the feet are willing, an urbane picnic venue is found adjacent to Freeway Park at the Union Square Plaza. Find a waterfall, flowers and, on Thursdays in summer, classical music, too.

❸ Glenn Richards

Whether you are interested in authentic Asian garden details or are looking for pieces that will help evoke an Eastern nuance in your Northwest garden, the selection at Glenn Richards is extensive, elegant, of high quality and reasonably priced.

❹ Lucca Statuary, *Gardens and Interiors*

Entering the front door at Lucca you will feel transported to a medieval Tuscan town, surrounded by fountains, benches, urns, stately statuary, pedestals, bird baths, planters and cisterns–all artfully displayed.

❺ Home Again

Along with delightful domestic home and garden decor (antique and almost antique), you will find the fruits of their European buyer's talents for acquiring 19th and early 20th century garden and architectural pieces. A nice touch here: the "elegant gifts for dogs, cats and their people."

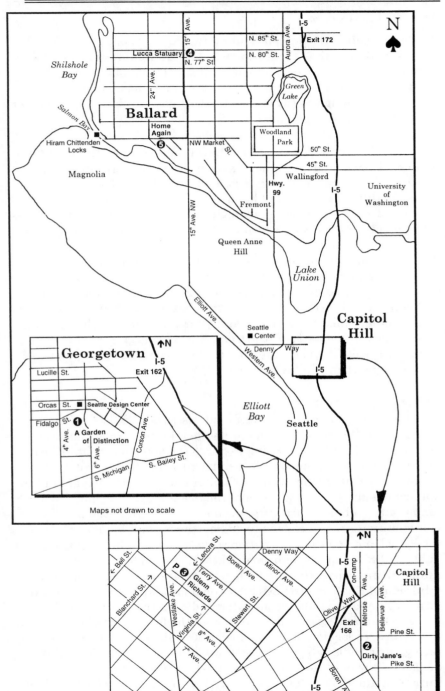

Maps not drawn to scale

TOUR TIMING AND TIPS

🐛 Because all of the destinations on this tour are open year-round, I suggest planning your excursion for a day you would rather not be out in the garden because of the weather (too hot, too cold, too wet, too windy) or the season (too early, too late or just tuckered out). Wednesday through Saturday are the best days to choose for this tour as all the shops are open (as I write).

🐛 Most of the items you will find during this tour are distinctive and unique. They include antiques, "hard won" garage sale/auction/flea market finds (some people are gifted with the knack for zeroing in on the best stuff!), one-of-a-kind hand-crafted items, and classical pieces imported from afar. This rewarding day trip is packed with a fabulous selection of garden accents with individuality and character.

🐛 While you will see many inexpensive pieces to enliven, enrich and enhance a garden setting, others will be an investment which will entail the requisite pacing and pondering. A camera, tape measure and notepad help record vital statistics that may be helpful reminders as you conjure images of what magic your great find can bring to a special spot on the patio, at the front gate or nipped in next to those rampant Rugosas. Just remember that someone else may ponder more quickly than you, so tarry not.

SETTING THE SCENE

This tour travels to distinctly different districts of Seattle: from Georgetown, the industrial and professional interior design area of Seattle's south end near Boeing Field, to the hodgepodge of Pill Hill (medical center); bohemian/college student-populated Broadway to the turn-of-the- century mansions of Capitol Hill; from the fringes of the uptown business district and on to the Scandinavian fishing community and used-furniture precincts of Ballard to the north.

Georgetown: South of downtown Seattle, beyond Pioneer Square, the Kingdome and the International District, there lies a vast tract of industrial warehouses, light manufacturing complexes, a brewery (Rainier), an airport (Boeing Field), a sophisticated aviation museum (Museum of Flight), bustling commercial docklands, the central rail terminal—and the pulse of the interior design trade, the Seattle Design Center. Though only minutes south of the heart of downtown, this is an area locals generally skirt at 60 mph via I-5 and explore only rarely. Few could tell you Georgetown was the first settlement in Seattle. (It was settled on June 22,1851, by Thompson, Maple and Luther Collins). Land in Georgetown was platted in 1890 by Julius

Horton (Seattle's first banker, Dexter Horton's brother) and named after his eldest son, George, who had just graduated from medical school. Though the Duwamish River Valley provided some of the most fertile land for farmers in early Seattle the district is better remembered for the many saloons and breweries that occupied the area until prohibition and for the founding of the Boeing Company here in 1909. The area boasts two unique nurseries, Julius Russo (now offering retail sales) and Oasis Water Gardens (a valuable haunt for water Gardeners on the Go).

Capitol Hill: Rising alongside downtown Seattle to the east of I-5, Capitol Hill houses an eclectic mixture of residents and purposes: an enclave of major medical facilities, three college campuses, a fair representation of well-preserved turn-of-the-century mansions along tree lined streets, two foreign film/art theaters, second-hand shops and the 44.5-acre Volunteer Park featuring the Seattle Asian Art Museum and a Victorian-style Conservatory.

In the late nineteenth century Seattle prospered. Among the city's most enterprising entrepreneurs was James A. Moore, a real estate developer from Colorado. In early 1900 he bought land at the northern end of Capitol Hill (adjacent to and east of Volunteer Park) and sold the expensive lots to the city's well-to-do. Many of the architecturally significant houses they built have been preserved, making this a most pleasant neighborhood for a walk.

Originally known as City Park, the 44.5-acre Volunteer Park was re-named in 1901, to honor those who served in the Spanish-American War of 1898. The plan was developed by the Olmsted Brothers firm, whose founder, Frederick Law Olmsted, Sr. is perhaps most famous for his design of New York's Central Park.

Ballard: In 1852 Ira Wilcox Utter became the first permanent settler to stake his land claim at Salmon Bay in what is today Ballard. By 1890 the population had grown and the town voted to incorporate, making it the first town to do so since Washington had become a state. A primary draw here was the thick old growth forest, which led to a booming logging industry. With a favored harbor on Salmon Bay, commercial fishing, too, became a major industry. Fishermen's Terminal, operated by the Port of Seattle since 1913, is home to one of the largest fishing fleets in the world. A walk around the central business district reflects the Scandinavian heritage of the residents (past and present), from the Nordic Heritage Museum to the lutefisk offered at Scandies. Visitors to this area head for the Hiram M. Chittenden Locks to watch as boats make the passage from the lower waters of Puget Sound to the level of Lake Washington via a maritime "elevator." Fish ladders, complete with underwater glass viewing rooms are a fascination in spring (salmon) and fall (steelhead trout.)

DRIVING DIRECTIONS:
From downtown Seattle, southbound on I-5, take the Michigan St. exit
#162. Turn right onto S. Michigan St. and then right at the turn signal onto
6th Ave. S. The shop is three blocks further, on the left at the corner of
6th and Fidalgo St. (one building south of the Seattle Design Center).
Driving distance: 5.4 miles; *Estimated driving time:* 15 minutes

TOUR TIP:

✍ If you arrive on a weekday before 10 a.m. when your first destination
opens, there is a Georgetown branch of the renowned West Seattle Alki
Bakery at 5700 1st Ave. S, (360) 762-1633. The cinnamon buns alone
are worth this early detour!

✠ A Garden of Distinction:

5819 Sixth Ave. S., Seattle, WA 98108; (206) 763-0517. Open Monday-Friday
10 a.m.-5 p.m., Saturday 11 a.m.-4 p.m., Sundays by appointment or by
chance. E-mail: gardenpots@aol.com   For lots of photos check out the
Web site: members.aol.com/gardenpots/

❖ ☂ 📖 ☆ ✳ RR

My first introduction to A Garden of Distinction was the discovery,
some years ago, of an outdoor sales and storage area for Gail
Chapman's interior design business—and Seattle's first really
extensive selection of BIG pots! I peered through the wrought iron
fencing and lust was in my heart. Since those days, Gail has gone on
to focus on elegant antique and contemporary furnishings for the
garden and the garden room (and her enviable selection of pots and
unusual containers, in all sizes, has only grown more wonderful).
She's the kind of person who hunts and hunts for the unusual, like the
rare 300-year-old Tunisian window grills she discovered. She makes a
trip to France annually to search the village markets in pursuit of
distinctive pieces and often looks to Asia for hand-crafted and unusual
granite lanterns and basins. One of the great finds from Thailand is a
line of graceful and sturdy furniture woven from water hyacinth. The
lines of the pieces are sensuous and inviting (you'll never consider the
brittle stiffness of wicker once you see this miraculous material). Here
you will also find a glorious assortment of books, some of which are not
easily come by, unique potting benches and hand-crafted pieces she
has herself commissioned for careful interpretation from one-of-a-kind
garden antiques that have caught her fancy. What has continued to
impress me here is the very nice balance of budget-conscious
ornaments along with higher value investment pieces.

Several vignettes of "garden room" settings have been created to
offer inspiration and help in envisioning elegant ornamental
compositions. As you are meandering through the oversized arbor,
notice that the overhead stage lighting casts a pattern of leaves at

your feet (or twigs if your visit is in winter.) It is this clever attention to the details of ambiance that especially endears this place to me. Give yourself time for a leisurely visit, there is a lot to see! (You can prepare with a "virtual visit" via their excellent Web site).

DRIVING DIRECTIONS

Leaving the parking lot, turn right onto 6th Ave. At the stop light at S. Michigan St., turn left. S. Michigan St. becomes S. Bailey St. Follow to the I-5 freeway entrance heading north. From I-5 take the Olive Way exit #166 and make a sharp right onto Melrose. Dirty Jane's is on the left in the next block, at Pine St.

Driving distance: 6 miles; *Estimated driving time:* 15 minutes

❊ Dirty Jane's

1530 Melrose Ave., Seattle, WA 98122; (206) 682-9890. Open Monday-Saturday 11 a.m.-7 p.m., Sunday noon-6 p.m. For photos of the shop and merchandise visit the Web site: www.aa.net/dirtyjanes

❖ ♼ 📖 ☆

If you have access to the World Wide Web you can visit Dirty Jane's site in advance to get the flavor of this up-beat, trendy, fun shop. In any event, come with a sense of humor and plop onto their magic carpet as it whisks you back into the fifties. There is genuine talent here not only in the collection on offer to patrons but in the store decor itself, marvelously entertaining. The buyers make trips to Kentucky and Kansas, returning laden with rustic garden tools and funky furniture, from antique watering cans to unusual sprinklers, classic glide bench seats to classy croquet sets. They offer many ornamental turn-of-the-century architectural details for the garden as well, from cast stone cornices to ornate iron gates. ("Some items have been tested for up to a century to guarantee satisfaction."). But wait, there's more! Dirty Jane's is also a floral shop with a dazzling selection of fresh cut flowers as unusual as the other fare you find here. And for your bouquet, a fine assortment of (arrangement) frogs and vintage vases. Candle connoisseurs will appreciate the locally hand-crafted selection for their rich colors and inspired design.

Lunch: I am always on the look-out for those very special, romantic little restaurants where the ambiance soaks in with an instant sense of welcoming comfort and the menu is a striking blend of classical favorites and innovative ideas. Such a place is **Ritz**. Try it! If it is a lovely day, you are in the mood for an urban picnic and you are willing to walk some seven or eight blocks, then head to the Union Square Plaza adjacent to Freeway Park, just west and south of the State Convention Center. Every Thursday noon from June to September music is performed in the plaza, there are umbrellas and tables set out by merchants and a festive, relaxing mood prevails.

DRIVING DIRECTIONS

Go north on Melrose Ave., turn left onto Pine St. then right onto Boren Ave. Turn Left onto Olive Way then right onto Terry Ave. and left onto Lenora St. Turn right down a narrow lane just past the front door of the Glenn Richards shop. There is free parking behind the building.
Driving distance: less than 1 mile; *Estimated driving time:* 4 minutes

Glenn Richards

964 Denny Way, Seattle, WA 98109; (206) 287-1877. Open Tuesday-Saturday 11 a.m.-5 p.m.

❖ ⌐

If you are on the search for a particular style of Japanese lantern, for instance a Yukimi-doro or snow-viewing lantern, you are likely to find an enchanting one at Glenn Richards. The ambiance of the space here is very much the warehouse that it is, which to me enhances the feeling of being on hand as the goods have just arrived from abroad and I have been the first on the scene to discover the treasure trove! I love pacing along the street front, peering into the windows, which display a mouthwatering selection of representative pieces and thus beckon you to explore a little further within. Asian furniture and garden elements imported from Japan, China, India, SE Asia, Indonesia and the Philippines crowd one another for floor space. Their reasonable prices reflect a careful selection of reproduction pieces from traditional Japanese lanterns to stone Pagodas. You will also find iron furniture from India, segments of gorgeous bamboo fencing called sleeve fencing, old and new granite water basins, old stepping stones, and an extensive selection of large jars and pots.

DRIVING DIRECTIONS

Start out by going west on Denny Way. You can follow this route all the way to the waterfront at Western Ave. Turn right (north). Western Ave. becomes Elliott Ave. which becomes 15th Ave. You can watch for Lucca Statuary on the right just past 77th St.
Driving distance: 6 miles; *Estimated driving time:* 20 minutes.

❋ Lucca Statuary, European Garden Ornaments

7716 15th Ave. NW, Seattle, WA 98117; (206) 789-8444. Open Wednesday-Saturday 11 a.m.-5 p.m., Sunday noon-4 p.m.

❖ ⌐ ▣ ☆ RR

Francine Katz and Peter Riches have expended a great deal of effort seeking out quality, weather-resistant statuary, hand-crafted by artisans, with a wide range of custom finishes available. Their 6,000-square-foot showroom is packed with fountains, urns, pedestals, pots and statuary. So much so that it spills out into an adjacent outdoor gallery offering larger pieces for more ambitious sites—your country estate or the palace courtyard, perhaps. Lest you worry that you do not live or garden on this scale, rest assured that there are exquisite smaller pieces as well, from handsome stone bookends to life sized frogs to chubby little cherubs to frolic in your ferny woodland. And -- there is something for every gardener's budget! (You'll see a winsome assemblage of these charming cherubs on the cover of this book, by the way, seated on a classical Lucca cast concrete bench).

DRIVING DIRECTIONS

Return on 15th Ave. NW driving south to the central business district of Ballard. At the traffic signal at NW Market St. turn right and drive to the block between 23rd and 24th Ave. NW. Home Again is on the left. *Driving distance:* 1.5 miles; *Estimated driving time:* 5 minutes

▨ Home Again

2313 NW Market St., Seattle, WA 98107; (206) 789-2621. Open Tuesday-Sunday, 11 a.m.-6 p.m. Web site www.homeagainseattle.com

❖ 🍄 📖 ☆

Susan Goldman and Jim Carey have a special talent for hunting down eclectic, nostalgic and classic (rather than classical) home and garden details. Their great finds help add whimsy, express respect for days gone by, and give expressive form to creative urges when gardeners turn to ornament to supplement their botanical palette. Alongside a nice selection of antique and second-hand garden books you'll find hand-crafted garden plaques and small herb pots, garden tools carefully restored to usefulness and antique watering cans. They generally have on hand those wonderful weathered cement ducks (or deer or flamingoes) of the 50s and tin Litho toys from the 40s. While Jim and Susan are busy scouring the home front for old garden gates and the distinctive work of Northwest artisans, they have a buyer in Europe on the prowl for fancy French plant stands and old terra cotta tiles from England. Prices are very reasonable!

DRIVING DIRECTIONS, END OF THE TOUR

Go east on NW Market St. through downtown Ballard, continuing past 15th Ave NW. NW Market becomes N 46th St. Where Aurora Ave. overpass meets 46th, follow the road to the left along Green Lake Way. At 50th St. turn right and follow to I-5. Take the southbound on-ramp to Seattle
Driving distance: 7 miles; *Estimated driving time:* 20 minutes

FURTHER RESOURCES

Food

Ritz: 720 E. Pike St., Seattle, WA 98122; (206) 329-6448. $$, L (Mon.-Fri.), D, Brunch Sunday (closed for D). My favorite trio is the paté (very traditional), a heavenly spinach salad and their divinely French apple tart.

Six Arms Pub and Brewery: 300 East Pike St., Seattle, WA 98122; (206) 223-1698. $$, L,D Open daily. As one would expect from an establishment that bills itself as a Pub, there is a Ploughman's Lunch and a plentiful menu of ales, lagers and beer on draft. But you will also find many salads, creative burgers and the likes of a grilled ahi tuna steak sandwich with wasabi mayonnaise and pickled ginger-cucumber condiment.

Union Square Plaza: Located in downtown Seattle, on Sixth Ave. between University and Union Streets. To get here from Dirty Jane's follow Melrose St. south two blocks to Pike St. Turn right and go four blocks to the State Trade and Convention Center. Go in the main doors and up the escalator to the Freeway Park level, and exit the building into the Park. One Union Square Plaza is to the right. I have suggested this exciting urban site as a picnic destination because it is within walking distance of Dirty Jane's, offers a setting surrounded by flowers and trees, a noisy waterfall, tables with umbrellas, lots of other places to comfortably settle in and a number of near-by shops providing an excellent array of take-out sandwiches, bagels, Bento Boxes, wraps, salads, smoothies, lattes and juices. On Thursdays, June-September there is a free noontime classical concert.

Lodgings

See "Seattle Travel Notes" in the Introduction for suggestions.

More Resources for Gardeners

AW Pottery: 21031 76th Ave. W., Lynnwood, WA 98036; (425) 778-1227. Open only on Saturdays 10 a.m.-4 p.m., mid-February-October. Retail outlet for a major wholesaler who imports indoor and outdoor pots from Asia, with many seconds for sale, so prices can be very low.

Gargoyles Statuary: 4550 University Way NE, Seattle, WA 98105; (206) 632-4940, (800) 253-9672 Web site www.gargoylesstatuary.com Open Monday-Thursday 11 a.m.-7 p.m., Friday and Saturday 11 a.m.-8 p.m., Sunday noon-6 p.m. Medieval replicas, architectural artifacts, garden plaques and bookends are among ghoulish goodies on offer.

Shortcuts for Accenting Your Garden, Over 500 Easy and Inexpensive Tips, Marianne Binetti (Garden Way Publishing, 202 pages) This is a great idea book from a local garden expert. Marianne is a whiz at articulating clever ways to address problem areas in a garden or create satisfying focal points.

KIDS TOUR, TOO!

Itinerary Highlights
carnivorous plants, colorful toucans and poison-dart frogs
exotic carp, traditional teahouse and a stepping stone bridge
imaginative collection of books and nature kits for kids

Pack up your pith helmet and a tropical-themed picnic and prepare for a whirlwind tour to a Southern Hemisphere Rain Forest. Kids love the transition from the crisp Northwest to the exotic humidity of this tropical habitat, surrounded by fantastical foliage, brilliantly hued flowers and cool carnivorous plants patiently poised to entrap an unsuspecting insect. Spiral up from the forest floor on a rampway to the tree tops far above with face-to-face introductions to elegant ocelots, endangered orchids and exotic free-flying birds.

At the other end of the spectrum, a child's imagination can be sparked by an appreciation of nature's tranquil beauty. Pass through the gates of Seattle's Japanese Garden to an island of serenity -- and discover stimulating elements for exploration, reflection and fanciful daydreams .

❶ Woodland Park Zoological Gardens Tropical Rain Forest

Can you believe that plant over there is a *cocoa* tree (whose fermented and roasted seeds are the source of chocolate)!? And the vine beneath it yields black pepper from it's unripened seeds? This engaging exhibit introduces intriguing examples of the rich diversity of tropical plants on which we depend for medicines, spices and food in our everyday life.

Lunch How about a picnic? Or a great pizza from nearby **Zeek's**?

❷ Seattle's Japanese Garden

The peace and harmony of a Japanese Garden plays a remarkable role in appealing to a child's sense of imagination, wonder and a feeling of well being. Delight comes with the sudden appearance of colorful carp from the murky depths of the pond and from the challenge of negotiating a swift little stream hopping from rock to rock on a naturalistic bridge. There is quiet respect for the simple, fragile beauty of the teahouse and the symbolism that garden elements (water is suggested by the arrangement of sand and pebbles; a large boulder represents a mountain) play in representing the wider world.

❸ Washington Park Arboretum

Be sure to visit the **Arboretum Shop** in the Graham Visitor Center for a particularly wonderful selection of nature books, games and study kits designed for inquiring young minds.

Look-and-learn walks among the plant collections at the Arboretum take curious children, and their inquisitive adult companions, through discussions of far off lands, to investigations of urban forest habitat and perhaps to an exploration of how native people used plants for food, clothing, shelter and medicine.

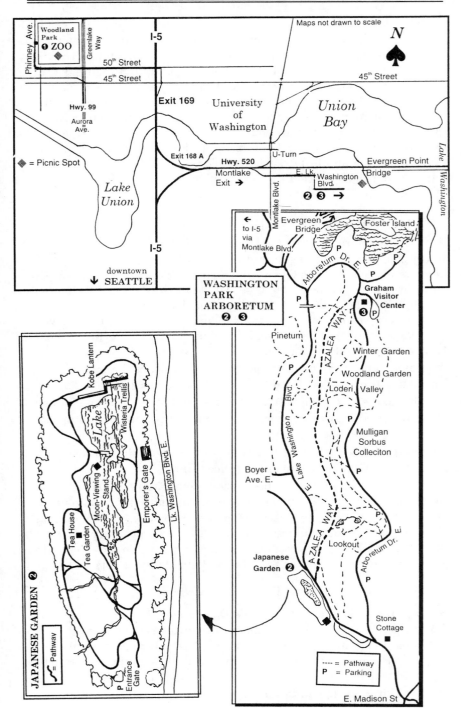

Woodland Park
❶ ZOO

Phinney Ave.

Greenlake Way

I-5

50ᵗʰ Street

45ᵗʰ Street

45ᵗʰ Street

Maps not drawn to scale

N

Hwy. 99

Aurora Ave.

Exit 169

University of Washington

Union Bay

Lake Washington

💐 = Picnic Spot

Exit 168 A

Hwy. 520

U-Turn

Evergreen Point

Lake Union

Montlake Exit →

E. Lk. Washington Blvd.

Bridge

❷ ❸ →

← to I-5 via Montlake Blvd.

Evergreen Bridge

Foster Island

I-5

P

P

downtown
↓ **SEATTLE**

WASHINGTON PARK ARBORETUM
❷ ❸

Graham Visitor Center

❸ P

P

Pinetum

AZALEA WAY

Winter Garden

Woodland Garden

Loderi Valley

Lake Washington Blvd. E.

P

P

Mulligan Sorbus Colleciton

Boyer Ave. E.

P

JAPANESE GARDEN ❷

Kobe Lantern

Lake

Wisteria Trellis

Moon-Viewing Stand

Tea House

Tea Garden

Emporer's Gate

Lk. Washington Blvd. E.

🎵 = Pathway

P Entrance Gate

A ZALEA WAY

Lookout

Arboretum Dr. E.

Japanese Garden **❷**

Stone Cottage

P

----- = Pathway
P = Parking

E. Madison St

89

Tour Timing

In assembling the itineraries for this book I tried to imagine what was possible for a get-up-and-go grown-up gardener to accomplish on a day trip. That was difficult enough! When I began to put together the destinations for the **Kids Tour, Too!** itinerary it was even more difficult to imagine how much to include when I suspect there will be young Gardeners on the Go with a wide range of attention spans, energy levels and just plain interest. Any one of the three suggestions on this tour makes an excellent one-stop choice. Any two of the three make for a rich and full experience. There should be a prize for parents and their energetic children who decide to make this a grand slam three-destination day!

Tour Timing and Tips / Zoo

🐾 The Zoo offers a wide range of educational programs (classes, lectures, Discovery Carts, docent led tours, animal behavior demonstrations and the Open Air Theater). There is a listing at the gates or call in advance (206) 684-4800. For the Tropical Rainforest Exhibit there is a self-guided tour packet that helps prepare chaperones/parents with questions to ask the kids (and the answers) ("Look for a bird that has a long bill. What do you think this bird eats? How would the bird's long bill help it eat?" Etc.)

🐾 Winter and rainy days are perfect times to visit the inviting warmth of the Tropical Rain Forest Exhibit at the Zoo.

🐾 The Zoo requires one adult (21 years or older) chaperone for every 6 children regardless of age, and they must stay with the group throughout the visit.

🐾 There are stroller and wheelchair rentals available for a small fee from the South Gate Visitor Assistance Center.

🐾 If you and the kids are conscientious composters, consider contacting Dr. Doo, the Sultan of Scat on his special Poop Line to order (or find out how to pick up) Zoo Doo and Christmas containers of Holidoo (for a thoughtful and unique gift for a special gardener). Call (206) 625-POOP for an amusing recorded message on how to obtain a place on their ever popular reservation list (I kid you not).

Tour Timing and Tips / Japanese Garden

🐾 **Japanese Garden Children's Day** (celebrated on the traditional Japanese "Boy's Day" date). This multi-cultural celebration features traditional Japanese storytelling, martial arts demonstrations, feeding the koi, hands-on origami and exhibits depicting the activities of children in Japan. In 1998 the date is May 3 from 1-4 p.m.

🐾 The Garden is open March 1 through November, 10 a.m.-dusk.

TOUR TIMING ANd TIPS / ARbORETUM

❧ **Seasonal timing** issues that suggest a visit:
a **spring** tour could highlight propagation and the characteristics and functions of the season's explosion of bloom, especially along Azalea Way and in the Rhododendron Glen
in **summer** explore the insect world or retreat into shade to identify plants that grow better out of the sun's heat especially along the Foster Island trail
in **autumn** look for seeds and berries native peoples harvested for food or medicine and discuss leaf color changes especially in the Woodland Garden's Japanese Maple Collection
in **winter** take advantage of fragrance, bloom and bark interest, especially in the Joseph Witt Winter Garden
❧ There are world renowned and other highly respected collections of plant families at the Arboretum. By taking a particular genus, say *Rhododendrons* in spring/early summer or *Acers* (maples) in the fall you could count the number of different species/cultivars and catalog what makes them differ from one another.
❧ The *Arboretum Bulletin*, a full color quarterly journal of the Arboretum Foundation, dedicated an entire issue to "Children and Gardening". This is a great guidebook to help prepare for a tour of the Arboretum with kids if your goal is to make the experience educational and fun as well as an outdoor adventure. The 1996 issue can be purchased for $5 from the Foundation or the Visitor Center Gift Shop, (206) 325-4510.

SETTING THE SCENE

The **Woodland Park Zoological Gardens**: (see "Rainy Day Seattle" for some historical notes on Phinney Ridge/Woodland Park Zoo.) The 92-acre site features nine major themed exhibits, generally portraying different ecosystems from around the world. The Tropical Rain Forest Exhibit, opened in 1992, was awarded Best Exhibit of the Year in 1994 by the American Association of Zoos and Aquariums.

This zoo has been in the forefront nationally (and internationally) in its approach to ecological awareness in modernizing their displays. Historically zoos (and arboretums, for that matter) presented their collections by taxonomic groupings, segregated by genus and species (so all the bears were in one place, the elephants in another and monkeys were way over there). While convenient for the purposes of maintenance, the exhibit bore no relation to real animal (or plant) habitats. Another popular method of organization has been by continent. So within the African exhibit, for example, animals of the plains were exhibited with those of the mountains with those of the coastal regions. And the plants selected for use in zoos were there as decor rather than representative habitat. Back in the 1970s, through the visionary insights of Zoo Director David Hancocks (working with Grant Jones, senior partner of Jones & Jones landscape architecture firm) embarked upon a revolutionary approach that would demonstrate the relationship between climate and living matter. In the jargon of the profession, they wanted to develop *bioclimatic zones*. Astute gardeners will note local flora that does an excellent job of "feigning foreign flora", so plants that are adapted to living in the Northwest but have an exotic appearance can evoke a southern hemisphere habitat with aplomb.

Seattle's Japanese Garden: The concept for the Japanese Garden began with the Arboretum Special Projects Committee in 1937. It was not until 1957, however, thanks to the efforts of Mrs. Neil Haig, that the garden was to become a reality. In the spirit of international friendship and community cooperation many important relationships developed with Japan. Gifts included two ancient hand-hewn granite lanterns (one weighing five tons) from Seattle's sister city, Kobe and a most generous token of friendship from the City of Tokyo—a beautiful Japanese Tea House. It was constructed in Japan, in the traditional way without nails, dismantled, shipped to Seattle and re-assembled. Sadly it was burned by vandals in 1973 but then re-built in 1981 with the assistance of the Urasenke Foundation of Kyoto and the Arboretum Foundation.

In May 1959 construction was begun on this 3¾-acre "stroll garden", based on designs popular in the Matojabe period of the late 16th- and early 17th-centuries. The principal design was executed by Japanese landscape architect Juki Iida, who was noted for his creation of over 1,000 Japanese Gardens worldwide. He worked with six other eminent landscape professionals on the final design, which consisted of 36 pages of plans. Mr. Iida personally selected the 600 major rocks used in the garden, from the Cascade Mountains near Bandera on the Snoqualmie River and painstakingly directed the handling (to prevent scratches) and placement of each one. Some of the rocks weigh as much as eight tons and most are buried in the Japanese fashion, two thirds underground. Many important stones together with 10 hand-crafted granite lanterns were imported from Japan.

Assistance in the funding, coordination and planting of the Garden was given by the Japanese government, the Cities of Tokyo and Kobe, members of the Japanese Community Service organization and Japanese Gardeners Association, the University of Washington, the City of Seattle and especially one anonymous donor from the Arboretum Foundation who provided the bulk of funds that made the garden a reality. While the City of Seattle Parks Department now manages the Garden, until 1981 it was under the auspices of the University of Washington as part of the Arboretum. Two support groups, the Japanese Garden Society and Unit 86 of the Arboretum Foundation work to maintain and ensure authenticity of the garden.

Washington Park Arboretum: (See "Tree and Shrub Enthusiast's" Tour for a history of the Arboretum). The Arboretum is dedicated to providing environmental, horticultural and conservation education to the whole community, but is particularly active in programs designed for young visitors.

DRIVING DIRECTIONS:
From mid-town Seattle drive north on I-5 to the 45th/50th St. exit #169, keeping left at the fork in the ramp. Turn left onto NE 50th St. traveling west. At the intersection with Greenlake Way N. continue straight and drive alongside Woodland Park. Turn right onto Phinney Ave. N. The West Gate is mid-block on the right.
Driving distance: 6 miles; *Estimated driving time:* 15 minutes.

❖ Woodland Park Zoological Gardens

There are three entrance gates: South—700 N. 50th St.; West—5500 Phinney Ave. N; North—601 N. 59th St. The North Gate is usually closed November to mid-March each year. The West gate provides the best access to the **Tropical Rain Forest Exhibit**. Open 9:30 a.m.-6 p.m. (until 4 p.m. from mid-October to mid-March). Pay parking ($3.50) is available adjacent to each of the gates. There is a fee to enter the Zoo.
Insider Tips: before you visit, check out the Zoo's **Web site**: www.zoo.org (where they often post a downloadable coupon to save $ on your entrance fee). You'll also find a map to download, information on "What's New", special events, details on their overnight camp outs at the Zoo and a snazzy movie of the zoo (with the free downloadable software to run the movie on your computer if you have Windows 95). Animal and **Plant tours** are available by pre-arrangement, (206) 684-4850.

Free parking is available on Phinney Ave. N, near the West Gate but note any time restrictions.

❖ ⚓ 📖 ☆ ✳ RR

A trip to the Zoo is a proven winner with kids. There are nine major exhibits featuring different ecosystems from around the world (African Savannah, Temperate Forest and Family Farm, Northern Trail, Tropical Asia, etc.) I have selected my favorite one for this tour because it provides a rich tapestry of lush plants and awesome animals, amphibians and birds in an exhibit that dramatically shows the interrelationships of the plant world and the animal kingdom and allows spellbinding, face-to-face inspection.

The award-winning Rain Forest exhibit features over 50 different animals, nearly 700 plant species, 25 separate animal enclosures and an open aviary within its (essentially vertical) two and one-half acre ecosystem. It is designed to replicate the earth's three major tropical rain forest areas (good time to get out a world map) in Central/South America (from the Amazon basin, through Central America and into eastern Mexico and the West Indies), southeast Asia (extending from the northeast coast of Australia through Indonesia, Malaysia, the Philippines and into Thailand) and Africa (centered on the Zaire River basin continuing west through Cameroon to Liberia). This exhibit focuses on the fact that tropical forests have a greater diversity of species and more complex relationships than any bio-climatic zone on earth. Their location along the equator results in relatively constant (hot) temperatures, the accompanying humidity of high rainfall and a stable climate that has, in some regions, evolved unimpeded without the temporary aggravations of Ice Ages for more than seventy million years.

One of the primary missions of the Woodland Park Zoological Gardens is conservation. You'll find examples of endangered and imperiled plants, such as orchids and tropical pitcher plants, and the first display you'll meet at the vestibule discusses the topic of ethnobotany (how native peoples use plants for food, shelter, clothing and medicine.) Ironically, there is a re-awakening in the Western world to the medicinal potentials of many tropical plants, just at a time when our society is destroying their environment, endangering their existence and losing the base of knowledge of their traditional uses as well.

The exhibit is organized to introduce visitors to the complex vertical layering of distinct micro-habitats, starting with the forest floor. As you can imagine, light must filter down a long way through the dense foliage of the very tall trees and past a network of vines and plants, including epiphytes, that live *on* other plants. Orchids, for example, are epiphytes and are prominently displayed here (including 18 endangered species).

Watch for clues that show how the plants have adapted to their environment—vines develop mechanisms that allow them to take advantage of the tree trunks and branch structure to climb to light and some trees develop "buttress roots", which, as the name implies, are deep flares at the base that help stabilize the tree in shallow soil and also allow the roots to extend further in search of nutrition.

As you move up the boardwalk ramp to the understory level the trees begin to branch out. More light penetrates to this level and there is much more animal life. Here you encounter the fascinating mini-ecosystem that revolves around *Bromeliads* (of which there are over two thousand species). A thickened cuticle allows for the pooling of water in their rosette, which provides a perfect environment for frogs to lay their eggs (which hatch and become tadpoles). In fact, this mini-ecosystem depending on the Bromeliad involves spiders, insects, mollusks and even crabs. One of the most startling amphibians inhabiting this zone is the poison dart frog (safely displayed behind glass). They are among the most vividly colored creatures on earth. Their brilliant coloring acts as "warning coloration" to alert potential predators that they are poisonous. In fact, some Indians who live in the rain forest where these frogs live use the poison from the frog's skin secretions on their hunting darts.

At the top of the ramp is a forest canopy representative of Southeast Asia, entered through glass doors. Birds fly freely here, which adds to the excitement. Look carefully and you might catch a glimpse of a fairy bluebird or a lesser green broadbill. There are eleven species that make the tree tops their home. There are also many enchanting and colorful flowers (members of the Ginger family and Hibiscus) and the endangered *Vanda coerulea*, a glorious blue-flowering orchid from Burma and Thailand. There are lots of ferns growing on trees and surrounding planted walls, from the bold staghorns to the delicate maidenhairs. You will also find several species of the carnivorous Pitcher Plants (*Nepenthes* species), many of which are endangered.

Lunch: Adjacent to the exhibit is the Zoo's Rain Forest Café, which offers an indoor food court with a variety of fast food concessions (and rest rooms). The near-by North Meadow is a great picnic place. If you have parked near the West Gate, this would be a convenient spot if you need to return to your car for the picnic. **Zeek's** wild pizza combo's kids adore is only a couple of blocks north on Phinney Ave.

DRIVING DIRECTIONS:
From the Zoo retrace your route back to I-5 by traveling south on Phinney Ave. N. Turn left onto N. 50th St. Stay to the left so you do not enter the right hand lane onto Aurora Ave. N. (Hwy. 99). Continue on N. 50th to I-5. Take the southbound on-ramp toward Seattle. Once on the freeway move over to the far left lane and take exit # 168A onto Hwy. 520 toward Bellevue/Kirkland heading east. Take the Montlake Blvd. exit. At the traffic signal follow signs to the Arboretum straight through the intersection on Lk. Washington Blvd. E. Follow this route through the Arboretum watching for the Japanese Garden parking, on the right. *Driving distance:* 5 miles; *Estimated driving time:* 20 minutes.

※ Seattle's Japanese Garden

Located at the south end of the Arboretum near the intersection of Lk.
Washington Blvd. and E. Madison St. Seattle Parks Dept. (206) 684-7050,
ticket booth at the Garden 684-4725. Open March 1 through November 30, 10
a.m.-6 p.m., summer 10 a.m.-8 p.m. Entry fee charged. Tours can be
arranged by calling (206) 523-2290 or the ticket booth. Free self-guided tour
brochure with map is available at the ticket booth. A traditional tea ceremony
is demonstrated the third Saturday of the month, at 1:30 in the Teahouse.
✳ RR

At the very heart of a Japanese Garden is the symbolism each element
plays in representing the world as a whole in the microcosm of a
garden. With even a little background to guide children through this
culturally rich experience, Westerners can gain an appreciation for
the Japanese respect and reverence for nature and the discovery that
the world without reflects the world within.

Japan is a country of mountains, forests, streams and lakes. Stone
is prevalent and the indigenous plant palette is subtle and restrained,
noteworthy for characteristics of texture, especially foliar, and plant
structure, especially when pruned to reveal trunk and branching
patterns. The design of Seattle's Japanese Garden centers around the
creation of twin "mountains" (for which 9,000 yards of earth were
brought in), "forests", for which hundreds of trees and shrubs were
planted, and a central "lake", around which the garden is organized. A
common device of "hide and reveal"endows this relatively small site
with the feeling of an expansive natural environment/garden, as
pathways wind past small vignettes enclosed with plantings of trees
which then open onto sweeping views through the garden and out to
"borrowed" views of the Arboretum beyond.

The map and guide that is provided free at the front gate will give
you the Japanese names and significance of various elements
throughout your stroll.

DRIVING DIRECTIONS:
Leave the parking area at the Japanese Garden by turning right onto Lk.
Washington Blvd. E. At the Stone Cottage turn left onto Arboretum Dr. E.
and follow it to the Graham Visitor Center.

WALKING DIRECTIONS:
If it is a lovely day and there is still time for a woodland exploration,
carefully cross Lk. Washington Blvd. to the trail opposite, leading to
Azalea Way, the central route through the Arboretum. This walk leads
you to the Graham Visitor Center.

Graham Visitor Center, Washington Park Arboretum

2300 Arboretum Dr. E., Seattle; (206) 543-8800. (Mailing address, Univ. of Wash. Box 358010, Seattle, WA 98195-8010). Open daily, 10a.m.-4 p.m., except Thanksgiving, Christmas and New Year's Day)

❖ ☂ 🕮 ☆ ✻ RR

❧ **Explorer's Packs** are available for families and groups with children K-6. They can be checked out from the Graham Visitor Center for a self-guided tour that utilizes a whole array of cool equipment, field guides and prepared activity ideas. There are two different inventive and stimulating packs—the "Marsh Madness" Pack or the "Tree-Tective" Pack to help in the observation of habitats, plants and insects. A reservation is required and there is a small fee: $15 for groups of 7 or more, $5 for smaller groups.

❧ 1-1 ¾ hour **Guided Tours**, for kids K-12, are available year-round, led by experienced volunteer guides. These walks stress sensory interaction and discovery. Some topics include: Exploring Native Plants and Ethnobotany; Wetland Ecology; and Seasonal Wonders, or the staff will work with you to design a tour suited to your interests. Three weeks advanced registration is required and there is a small fee.

❧ The **Saplings Program** is a hands-on program for children in grades 3-5 (including home schools). It involves a 1-1¾ hour outdoor adventure centered around interactive games, observation and experimentation, with different topics according to the season. It is offered M, W, F in April, May, October and November, 10-11:30 a.m. or noon-1:30 p.m. This free program requires registration. **Arboretum Adventures** require pre-registration but are offered free every third Sunday of each month. They provide an opportunity for children, ages 7-14, to explore the natural world through interactive tours and hands-on art and science activities.

Driving Directions, End of the Tour:

Leaving the Arboretum **for downtown Seattle**, continue east through the Arboretum on Lk. Washington Blvd. E. to the traffic signal at E. Madison. Turn right and follow Madison all the way into downtown Seattle.
Driving distance: 3.5 miles; *Estimated driving time:* 15 minutes
Should your route take you **northbound on I-5**, on leaving the Arboretum take Lk. Washington Blvd. E. back to Montlake Blvd. E. Turn right at the traffic signal onto Montlake Blvd. E. At the next traffic signal make a U-turn from the left lane then a right turn onto the on-ramp for Hwy. 520. Take the Roanoke St./North I-5 exit towards Vancouver, B.C. onto I-5.
Estimated driving time: 10 minutes to I-5.

Further Resources
Food
Zeek's Pizza: 6000 Phinney Ave. N., Seattle, WA 98103; (206) 789-1778. $, L,D daily. A sure kid pleaser with wild pizzas like the Frog Belly Green (basil pesto does the trick), by the slice or whole pie; generous salads, too.

Lodging
See the "Seattle Travel Notes" in the Introduction for suggestions.

More Resources for (Young) Gardeners
Arboretum Foundation: 2300 Arboretum Dr. E., Seattle, WA 98112-2300; (206) 325-4510. Benefits in this non-profit support group include discounts on shop items, classes and events; monthly newsletter and quarterly *Bulletin*.
Japanese Garden Society: (425) 641-7145
Woodland Park Zoological Society: 601 N. 59th St., Seattle, WA 98103-5858; (206) 615-0397. Join this non-profit organization to help support the Zoo. You'll receive lots of nifty benefits including free admission, Zoo Store discount, a subscription to the *ZooNews*, discounts on classes and lectures and an invitation to a members-only party.

98

WENDING THROUGH WALLINGFORD

———————————— Itinerary Highlights ————————————
creative display garden of organically grown edibles
plant connoisseur's garden of discovery
urban gardener's trusty one-stop shop
Gardener on the Go's best bet for travel maps and books
specialist in terra cotta with pots from around the world

What really enlivened this tightly knit urban neighborhood on the western fringes of the University of Washington district was the innovative recycling of an abandoned circa 1906 schoolhouse. A mixed use plan intermingled up-scale shops and restaurants with trendy but simple apartments in the heart of an established collection of ethnic restaurants, friendly pubs, one of the city's best French bakeries (Boulangerie) and surely the wackiest (the Erotic Bakery). Here one encounters the expected influences of a University population, from the smattering of small bookstores to an excellent movie theater and, true to the contrarian nature of the student set, a serious tea house in Latte-Land.

🦌 **THE ITINERARY IN BRIEF** 🦌

❶ Seattle Tilth

This is the hot spot for what's happening in organic urban farming—whether you are restricted to an 11th story balcony or tilling the soil of a good-sized suburban site. You will find the many productive food display gardens here are at once inspiring and educational. Fruits, vegetables, herbs and ornamentals, many of which will send you to your knees in search of the identification label, intermingle in a fanciful explosion of robust good health.

❷ The Grounds of the Good Shepherd Center

Botanical whiz kid Gil Scheiber has tucked a wide variety of top-notch, uncommon plants throughout the borders that flank red brick buildings and island beds set among peripheral lawns.

Lunch Wallingford restaurants abound or plan a picnic at Gasworks Park.

❸ The Garden Spot

For over a decade gardeners have headed with intent or happened happily upon this delightful garden shop and felt they had entered horticultural heaven. Always distinctive, there is innovation and obvious heart in the choice offerings of plants, pots and paraphernalia.

❹ Wide World Books and Maps

If you are a Gardener on the Go you will no doubt have destinations beyond these itineraries on your agenda. This is a terrific place to stock up on maps and travel guides (local, regional, national and international). There are *many*, for instance, of specific interest to the gardener en route to the British Isles, Hawaii, France, Italy, Portugal or other Western European destinations.

❺ Herban Pottery

City gardeners rejoice in finding such an extensive collection of quality terra cotta from classical to contemporary, teeny tiny to monumental, utilitarian to ornamental. This is a cheery little shop which invites an unhurried browse made especially fascinating by the tremendous effort expended hunting down 20 some domestic artists as well as craftsmen representing over 30 countries around the globe.

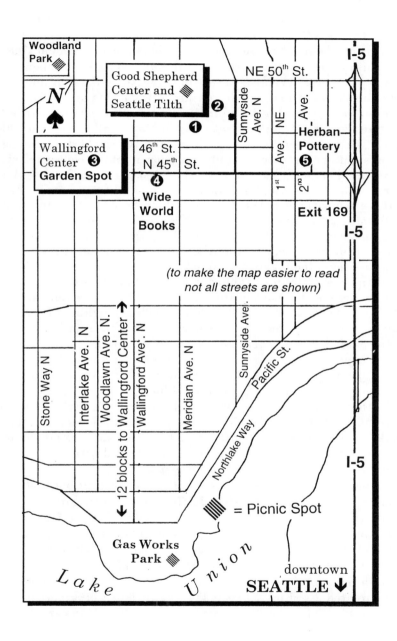

TOUR TIMING ANd TIPS

🍂 All destinations can be visited year round. Herban Pottery is closed Mondays.

🍂 The prime summer growing season would make an excellent time to plan this outing. However, there are a couple of really excellent early and late season events sponsored by **Seattle Tilth** that may well dictate the day you decide to venture forth on this expedition. In the spring, those in the know automatically plan to attend the **Edible Plant Sale** (generally the first Saturday in May – call to confirm 206-633-0451.) A mind-boggling array of herb and vegetable starts, along with some ornamentals, are set out on dozens of tables, well-marked with information and reasonably priced. A separate area is set up for growers selling their own plants along with non-profit organizations and others sympathetic to the Seattle Tilth philosophy of organic and earth-friendly gardening. Events for children, a festive fund-raising auction and food vendors are all part of this popular annual event. In the Fall, as one might expect, there is the **Harvest Festival**, which invites the best of the region's organic farmers to offer the fruits of their labor, ranging from elegant eggplants and luscious lettuces to brilliant bouquets and mouthwatering melons. There are nuts and cheeses and even freshly harvested flower seeds. A highlight for me is the judged tomato tasting contest, where some of this area's most educated palates muster their powers of concentration in a blind tasting in search of the season's most succulent varieties. From the winners' rostrum one can race to the vendor tables to stock up and take notes for *next* spring's visit to the Edible Plant Sale! (If you do attend either or both of these events need I suggest you arrive early to secure a place near the front of the line for the best selection? And I can tell you from personal experience that a little rain does not deter the regulars, who arrive dressed for the weather and with determination and good humor in their hearts.)

🍂 Also consider the valuable classes, walks, demonstrations and workshops offered through **Seattle Tilth** on a wide range of horticultural topics. Call to request their schedule (206) 633-0451. Many are offered on Saturdays and would make a most satisfying start for a weekend *Wending Through Wallingford* adventure.

🍂 In April, 1998 the Wallingford neighborhood kicks off a 10-year urban re-forestation project with a number of gardening and tree planting related activities. On Sunday (the 19th in 1998) there is a free "Walkable Wallingford" tour of private gardens. Maps are available at The Garden Spot.

🍂 **Herban Pottery** throws a couple of dandy sales each year, organized around the theme "Chips Happen." In early April and

September they offer drastic reductions on pots with flaws. There is a festive atmosphere as refreshments are offered and throngs of savvy bargain hunters carefully consider how much they can fit into the family van. Fair warning—come-early-birds catch the best deals! Call for exact dates, (206) 633-1021 (ask to be on their mailing list).

SETTING THE SCENE

The earliest recorded platting of the Wallingford neighborhood was in 1883, but the area remained predominantly a farming community for the next two decades. Annexed to the City of Seattle in 1891, the area took its name from John Wallingford, a resident of the division to the east of Woodland Park. Today's **Wallingford** neighborhood stretches from the shores of Lake Union at Gas Works Park northward to Green Lake and from I-5 where it abuts the University (of Washington) District on the east and the Fremont neighborhood on the west. After annexation the population swelled and the area grew as a bedroom community for blue collar working families, the predominant bungalow style of architecture still characterizing the scale of the neighborhood. In 1907 Seattle Gas Company built a coal-fired gas generating plant which switched later to oil, but not before blanketing the adjacent neighborhood with a filthy grime and filled the air for decades with foul pollution. When natural gas became readily available the plant was rendered obsolete, closed and left to remain a visual blight on an otherwise lovely lakeshore setting. In 1962 the City of Seattle bought the site and turned the project over to landscape architect Richard Haag. Today, Gasworks Park is a gathering place for kite flying enthusiasts, picnickers, dog walkers, joggers and others drawn to the grassy knoll for a respite. The thought-provoking, award- winning design retains the hulk of the gas plant as a symbol of its place in the technological timeline and reminds us of the city's historical context.

The Good Shepherd Center: Under the guiding hand of the Sisters of the Good Shepherd, this substantial institution in the modified neo-classic style was constructed in 1906 on 11.5 acres in Wallingford to house orphaned and "wayward" girls. The project enjoyed an outpouring of support from prominent citizens, and the Order established a nearly self-sufficient community with orchards, vegetable gardens, poultry houses and root cellars. In 1939, a full four-year high school was accredited at the Good Shepherd Home, and over the years more than 8,000 girls were provided shelter, education and the tools to make their way in life. In 1972 financial problems led to the closure and sale of the Home, now in the hands of the Historic Seattle Preservation and Development Authority (the same organization involved in preserving the Pike Place Market). The building houses non-profit organizations, the Wallingford Senior Center, an elementary school and day care program, and several health professionals. Seattle Tilth is housed in the south annex and their gardens are adjacent, as is a community P-Patch garden.

Driving Directions

From I-5 traveling northbound take exit #169, the left fork for 50th St. NW and travel west seven blocks to Sunnyside Ave. Turn left at the traffic signal. Turn right into the grounds of the Good Shepherd Center. You can park in the lot to your left, then follow the path around the south end of the buildings, past the brick smokestack to the office and/or gardens.
Driving distance: 4.5 miles; *Estimated driving time:* 10 minutes

Tour Tip:

One of Seattle's most noteworthy brunch hot spots, **Julia's in Wallingford**, is located in this neighborhood, so if you are in search of a filling breakfast to fuel the day's activity, start here. If your ambitions run to a mouthwatering French pastry and an excellent espresso, head directly to **Boulangerie**, also in the neighborhood (find details at the end of this chapter under "Food").

❋ Seattle Tilth

4649 Sunnyside Ave. N, Seattle, WA 98103; (206) 633-0451. Office open from 9 a.m.-2 p.m. Monday-Friday; garden open daily, dawn to dusk.
Insider's Tip: Seattle Tilth has published a thoroughly updated edition of their "Maritime Northwest Garden Guide" ($10). It serves as a planning calendar for year-round gardening, specifically designed for our region. I highly recommend it as a *must have* for new gardeners and old pros alike!
❖ ✳ RR available in the park

As you wander through this eclectic urban garden, bursting with organically grown vegetables, fruits, berries, herbs and ornamental flowers, it is hard to believe that it sprang forth from a bleak asphalt expanse. In 1978 this garden was the vision of neighbors joining forces to improve their immediate living environment. Their effort has also given life to a city-wide consciousness of the benefits of organic urban agriculture, composting, recycling, and over-all environmental awareness. This is a garden for the whole community: those who visit purely to glean ideas, information and inspiration; those who volunteer their time to help maintain the gardens; those who come to participate in the ambitious and varied educational programs; those children who are given their own garden in which to play and learn; and those who attend the events sponsored for all citizens of this region to enjoy.

What you will find is an earthy, imaginative food garden—one full of texture and humor, intriguing color and dramatic plantings. Be sure to bring a notebook as this is a teaching display garden, whose purpose in life is to present you with new varieties to discover, new techniques to try and new awareness to apply in your own kitchen garden. You'll find, for example, a comprehensive demonstration area of many approaches to composting. Educational signage provides details and hand-outs are available free, too. Be sure to poke into the enclosed Children's Garden beyond the stone wall, where the evidence of the hundreds of young gardeners who spend time here each year will surely bring a smile to your face. If you have come while the office is open, you are invited to ensconce yourself in front of the extensive reference library covering all aspects of gardening. If you have questions, the staff is knowledgeable and anxious to offer advice.

Good Shepherd Center

4649 Sunnyside Ave. N, Seattle, WA. (206) 547-8127. Open year-round, daily, dawn to dusk.

This 11.5-acre site is now owned by the Historic Seattle Preservation and Development Authority. On the grounds you'll also find the Meridian Playground, the gardens of Seattle Tilth and the plots of a Seattle P-Patch community garden project. There has been much contention over the future of this property since the closing of the Home of the Good Shepherd in 1973. Under the current ownership, garden lovers are lucky to find that the grounds are well planted and maintained. There have been no herbicides or pesticides used since 1973 and 100s of cubic yards of compost have fed over 1,000 varieties of plants: trees, shrubs, vines, bulbs and perennials. The mixed borders are packed with a surprising array of unusual gems, the special finds of the head gardener. Here you'll find *Cornus capitata* (Evergreen Dogwood), *Prunus illicifolia* x *Lyonii* (Hollyleaf Cherry), many *Eucalypti, Rosa brunonii* 'La Mortola', specimen Western White Pine, *Populus* x *canenscens* 'Pendula' (Weeping Italian Poplars), Monkey Puzzle Tree, many old roses, collections of *Hellebores* (Lenton roses), *Bergenia, Epimediums* and oaks. Although plants are not identified with markers, tours are available by appointment (fee by donation, call Gil Scheiber, 206-524-9492) and are sometimes offered through the Seattle Tilth education program, as well. Located only a few minutes off I-5, perhaps once discovered this will be one of those quick diversions gardeners favor in any weather just to see what's the "best of the season."

Driving Directions

Leaving the Good Shepherd Center turn right onto Sunnyside Ave. and go two blocks to N. 45th. Turn right. Watch for the Wallingford Center on the left. While you are in the Center you can park in their free lot. Be sure to move your car to a parking spot on the street as you move along on this itinerary, however.

Lunch: Within the Wallingford Center you will find several choices of restaurant fare. The buffet at Chutneys Indian restaurant offers a delicious lunch at a reasonable price in a comfortable environment. If you are looking for a very relaxing light lunch head for Teahouse Kuan Yin, ostensibly a tea house where you can find their version of the trendy wraps (served with a delicious spicy peanut sauce), quiche, pot stickers, scones and the like along with a mammoth menu of teas.

❊ The Garden Spot

Wallingford Center, 1815 N. 45th, Seattle, WA 98103; (206) 547-5137. Open Monday-Friday 10 a.m.-8 p.m., Saturday until 6 p.m., Sunday until 5 p.m.

❖ ☂ ▥ ☆ ✳ RR (available in the building)

One of the charming characteristics of The Garden Spot is the way it spills beyond the boundaries of the interior space, like a container planting bursting with new growth. Out the back door it flows onto a terrace with a top-notch selection of plants and out the front door it rambles onto an interior "courtyard" with an appealing display of comfy outdoor furniture and other alluring gardening-related goods. This place is ideally suited to the urban gardener whose needs are often somewhat less ambitious than their country cousins who garden on acres instead of restricted citified sites. For years I have looked here first for distinctive pots and now they focus also on small water feature "gardens" with Lilliputian fountains appropriate for a balcony (or even for those not blessed with a single square foot of outdoor space). The full range of garden center fare is offered from bagged soil and amendments to quality tools and uncommon seeds, good books and periodicals to goat skin gloves. Keep in mind, also, their elegant cut flower selection for a spirit-lifting bouquet for yourself or a friend.

Walking Directions:

From the Wallingford Center walk one block east, on the same side of the street as the Center, on N 45th Street.

❊ Wide World Books and Maps

1911 N 45th St., Seattle, WA 98103; (206) 634-3453. Open Monday-Friday 10 a.m.-8 p.m., Saturday 10 a.m.-6 p.m., Sunday noon-5 p.m.

❖ ☂ ▥ ☆

Gardeners on the Go are by definition travelers. And as such they recognize the value of good maps (why waste your precious time sitting frustrated behind the wheel of a car or walking aimlessly in search of your destination?) And they need the best of guides and trip planning books. You'll be hard put to find a better selection than in this specialty bookshop. Specifically for the gardener there are books for those lucky enough to have a British or continental European destination in mind, with several hefty guides to gardens open to the public. (In a serendipitous move, the Teahouse Kuan Yin is located in the adjoining space.)

TOUR TIP
Just to keep astute GOG's on their toes, 45th St. changes from N. 45th to NE 45th at 1st Ave. NE.

DRIVING DIRECTIONS:
From the Wallingford Center go eight blocks east, on 45th to 2nd Ave. NE (a one way street, south). Herban Pottery is on the corner, on the left.

✠ Herban Pottery, The Fabulous Terra Cotta Shop

250 NE 45th, Seattle, WA 98105; (206) 633-1021. Open Tuesday-Saturday, 10 a.m.-6 p.m., Sunday, noon-5 p.m.

The newsletter that patrons of HP can receive declares "Hooray for small business!!!!" This sentiment aptly captures the genuine spirit of enthusiasm that shop owners Alison and Dan exude as they endeavor to make their customer's visit a pleasant and rewarding experience. Make that educational, too. There are a lot of misconceptions and perceived problems regarding terra cotta that can be addressed and redressed with a bit of guidance and forethought. An appealing draw for me to this warm and festive shop (besides the exemplary customer service) is the vast selection, unparalleled anywhere in the region, to my knowledge, of quality, unique terra cotta. Along with the vast array of pots are fountains, decorative and utilitarian pot feet, lanterns, bird baths, urns, masonry sealant, pot dollies and pot casters. Ever on the look-out for a good idea, Alison and Dan saw an antique English horseradish-growing pot in a book and decided to commission a local potter to spin some up for them. This clever device comes in two parts, allowing you to lift the top to harvest the root. It is not only handy, and intriguingly historical, it makes a handsome, eye-catching and unique addition to the potager (kitchen garden). If you have whizzed by the shop then perhaps your eye has been caught by the chimeneas (free-standing, wood burning fireplaces) on display at the entry. Yes, they do work ("guaranteed to add warmth to your evening moments in the garden.")

DRIVING DIRECTIONS, END OF THE TOUR:
I-5 is four blocks east of Herban Pottery. The drive to downtown Seattle from here takes 10 minutes.

FURTHER RESOURCES

Food

Boulangerie, 2200 N 45th St., Seattle, WA 98103; (206) 634-2211. $, B,L daily. Croissants, plain and fancy (including luncheon varieties), are heavenly as are the espresso creations. Maybe a stop here on your way home for a crusty baguette or their classic Tarte Normande?

Bow Wow Meow Treatoria, 1415 N 45th, Seattle, WA 98103; (206) 545-0740. My faithful canine undergardeners, Emma and Byron, and my wildly successful mole catcher, Colette, have asked that I pass along their suggestion for their favorite Wallingford dining stop.

Chutneys, Wallingford Center, 1815 N 45th St., Seattle, WA 98103. (206) 284-6799. $$, L,D Monday-Saturday. There is an a la carte menu, though I find the lunch buffet offers an excellent range of their tasty traditional East Indian fare, freshly prepared.

Julia's in Wallingford, 4401 Wallingford Ave. N, Seattle, WA 98103; (206) 633-1175. $$, B daily, (brunch on week-ends), L,D Monday-Saturday.

Teahouse Kuan Yin, 1911 N 45th St., Seattle, WA 98103; (206) 632-2055. $, L,D, Monday-Saturday. The staff is very helpful if you are undecided on which of their 40 teas to try with your light meal. There is a multi-ethnic atmosphere in this haven of relaxation.

Wallingford QFC, 1801 N 45th, Seattle, WA 98103; picnic fare.

❧ PICNIC PlACE

Gas Works Park—if it is a glorious day the views of the cityscape and the Lake Union activity are worth the little effort it takes to get there. From 45th take Wallingford Ave. south 12 blocks to the park.

LodGING

See "Seattle Travel Notes" for suggestions.

FOR MORE INFORMATION

Good Shepherd Center, 4649 Sunnyside Ave. N, Seattle, WA 98103; (206) 547-8127.

Wallingford Chamber of Commerce, P.O. Box 31071, Seattle, WA 98103; (206) 632-0645 – voice mail for this volunteer organization.

MORE RESOURCES FOR GARdENERS

Tweedy and Popps/ Ace Hardware, 1916 N 45th St., Seattle, WA 98103; (206) 632-2290. I will surely date myself, but this is the hardware store of my youth, so unlike the modern mega-stores, though the range of merchandise is vast and varied, and quite naturally caters to the everyday needs of the practical gardener. Pop(p) in for a nostalgic spin down the aisles.

TREE & SHRUB ENTHUSIAST'S TOUR

—————————— Itinerary Highlights ——————————
distinguished private arboretum now a quiet County Park
stately trees, curving shrub borders and expanses of lawn
200-acre arboretum of 4,768 woody plant species, cultivars
highly respected nursery famed for its woody plants

——————————— ❧ ———————————

Woody plants create the primary structure of a garden—providing enclosure or framing views, focal interest or background texture, a sense of permanence or an important link to the neighborhood context. Most of us garden on sites that restrict us to a relatively few tree and shrub selections. A wise decision will reward you daily, through the seasons and years, as you, yourself, grow and mature with your garden. Each destination on this arboreal tour presents an extraordinary collection of mature woody plants— golden opportunities to introduce yourself to distinctive trees and shrubs growing successfully under local conditions. You'll be able to assess plants that represent some of the most consequential decisions you'll face in making a garden.

❶ Rhody Ridge Arboretum Park

One of the loveliest surprise discoveries in the Northwest for those who hold a walk among breathtaking trees one of life's most exalting experiences. Hidden in a quiet neighborhood is a secret arboretum, the horticultural legacy of one couple's love affair with woody plants.

❷ Carl S. English, Jr. Botanical Garden

Over a period of 43 years this magnificent collection of more than 500 plant species of trees, shrubs and herbaceous plants, many rare, was built by Carl S. English, Jr. He was an avid plantsman who exchanged seeds with botanical gardens all over the world and collected seeds of native plants on travels through the western United States. The seven-acre garden/arboretum is set alongside the Hiram M. Chittenden Locks of the Lake Washington Ship Canal.

Lunch There are good opportunities here for a picnic by the Locks, a seafood lunch overlooking the busy marine activity on Shilshole Bay or something ethnic in downtown Ballard where there is an excellent trio of choices: Creole/Cajun, Thai or Italian.

❸ Washington Park Arboretum

Located within the boundaries of Seattle's metropolitan area, this 200-acre urban green space is home to 40,000 trees, shrubs and vines. There are over 4,768 different species and cultivated varieties of plants from around the world—considered one of the finest collections in the country.

❹ Wells Medina Nursery

This stunning nursery offers Seattle area plant aficionados a superior selection, especially for it's carefully considered melange of specimen-sized trees and shrubs.

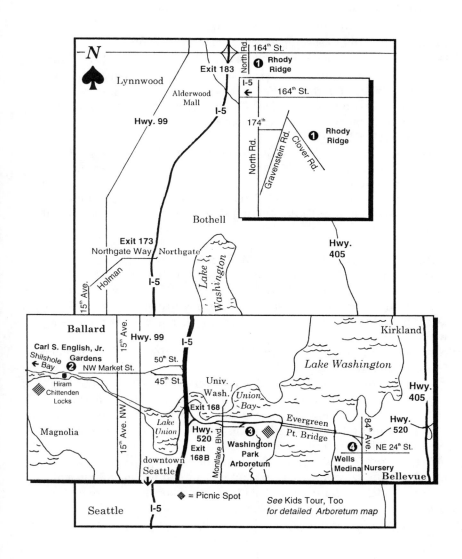

Tour Timing and Tips

🍂 All the destinations are open year-round, daily.

🍂 These are definitely outdoor, woodsy experiences so choose a pleasant day and dress appropriately for the season.

🍂 Visit arboreta in all seasons, at various times of the day. Plan this special trip with a like-minded friend, once in each season and with a mix of early and late light. For an investment of four pleasant day excursions over a year, decades of satisfaction, watching well-chosen woody plants mature, will have been well-earned.

SEASONAL BEST BETS:

Spring and Fall are the two most colorful and dramatic seasons to visit the three arboreta. The spectacle in Spring of outlandish color bursting forth from the somber landscape after months of a million shades of gray and green and Fall's last hurrah of fiery foliage, colorful bark and jewel-like berries should be taken into account in setting a date to visit.

RHODY RIDGE ARBORETUM PARK

Spring: species Rhododendrons; Crabapples (for spring bloom, a marvelous collection here); *Halesia* (Silverbell Tree, low maintenance, high quality tree, rare in Seattle, profuse white bell-shaped flowers in late April-May); *Styrax obassia* (Fragrant Snowbell, also elegant in winter for architectural form)

Summer: *Robinia pseudoacia 'Frisea'*; *Franklinia*; Viburnums for their attractive bloom;

Fall: Viburnums for their spectacular red fruits; Crabapples (for spectacular fall fruit display); *Aronia arbutifolia* (Red Chokeberry, rich scarlet and wine-red foliage followed by bright crimson berries); *Sorbus prattii* (Mountain Ash, white berries form); *Stewartia monadelpha* (deep bronzy-red foliage)

Winter: *Acer griseum* (Paperbark Maple); *Acer palmatum* (Japanese Maple, lovely winter structure, and glorious in fall for foliage color) *Rhododendron caliophytum* (for its spectacular large leaves); *Tsuga canadensis* 'Bennett' (a dwarf Canadian Hemlock); *Stewartia monadelpha* (exceptional mosaic of bark)

CARL S. ENGLISH, JR. BOTANICAL GARDENS

Spring: Rhododendrons (more than 90 difference species); *Lirodendron tulipifera* (tulip tree, for its lovely spring bloom); Japanese flowering cherries; Red (extremely rare in Seattle and a registered "Champion Tree") and Yellow Buckeyes (Horse Chestnuts); *Summer:* *Metasequoia glyptostroboides* (deciduous Dawn Redwood, this specimen is one of the oldest in America from the first seed brought from China in 1947)

Fall: *Liquidambar styraciflua* (sweet gum, perhaps the most photographed heart-stopper with extraordinary fall foliage in orange, red, yellow, and purple); *Stewartia*

Winter: *Trachycarpus fortunei* (fan palm); Pinus patula (Jelecote or Mexican pines, rarely seen in Seattle, do well here in an urban southwest exposure; the silkiest of pines—touch the needles); *Quercus hypoleucoides* and *Q. rugosa* (Silverleaf and Net Leaf evergreen oaks; most grown here by Mr. English from acorns); *Garrya elliptica* (silk tassel-bush, with very long and elegant winter catkins); *Quercus Suber* (Cork tree – the furrowed bark is spectacular; can be stripped for the making of commercial cork); *Rhododendron* x 'Nobleanum' (winter bloomer, sometimes as early as December).

WASHINGTON PARK ARBORETUM

Spring: **Azalea Way** (for azaleas, flowering cherries); the **Japanese Garden** for the flowering cherries; **Loderi Valley trail** (outstanding collections of large leafed and Loderi hybrid rhododendrons); *Magnolias* and *Camellias* (large and noteworthy collections); *Malas* (the Arboretum has a crabapple cultivar evaluation program to help determine the best performers for this region)

Summer: outstanding collections of *Cornus* (dogwoods) and *Hydrangeas*, the Mediterranean collection and particularly divine specimens of *Albizia julibrissen* (silk tree, with a tropical appearance and fluffy pale pink feather-duster-like flowers); *Magnolia grandiflora* (with out-sized white, waxy flowers and enormous leaves); and *Franklinia alatamaha* (Franklin tree)

Fall: outstanding collections of *Acers* (the Japanese maple cultivars comprise the largest public collection in North America); **The Brian O. Mulligan Sorbus Collection** (this is one of the country's most complete collections of mountain ash); Larches; *Quercus* (oaks). Also visit the **Japanese Garden** for the lovely color display of maples.

Winter: **J.A. Witt Winter Garden** with a focus on plants that put on their best performances during the winter months. Also, outstanding collections of *Hamamelis* (Witch Hazel); *Helleborus, Ilex* (hollies, look at the rarer varieties); *Ericas* (Heathers), *Camelias, Mahonia* (Oregon Grape), *Forsythia*, Garrya (Silk Tassel), *Chimonanthus* (Winter Sweet), *Daphnes,* Korean azaleas and *Sarcococca* (Sweet Box)

DRIVING DIRECTIONS

Head north from downtown Seattle on I-5 to exit #183 (164th St.). From the off-ramp turn east (right) onto 164th and drive to North Rd (2nd Ave. W.) At the traffic signal turn right onto North Rd. At 174th Pl. SW (with a directional arrow to Gravenstein Rd.) turn left, ignoring the dead end sign. At the end of the block you'll intersect Gravenstein Rd. Turn left one block to Clover Rd. Turn hard right. Watch for the address on the mailbox on the right and directly across the street is the Park. There is a split rail fence, very unobtrusive signage and modest parking along the street. The gate will likely be closed but not locked—walk in along the drive, continuing past the caretaker's house, to the Arboretum. *Driving distance:* 20 miles; *Estimated driving time:* 30 minutes.

❊ Rhody Ridge Arboretum Park

17427 Clover Rd., Bothell, WA 98102; (425) 743-3945. Open daily, year-round *except* on the occasional day it is necessary to spray in April or May). A call in advance is wise, especially if you are to be accompanied by small children, persons with walking difficulties or are afraid of dogs (to assure that the resident canine will be restricted to the house).

Insider tip: Call in advance to make an appointment with the delightful caretaker, Fir Butler, for an informative guided tour.

❖ ✻

SETTING THE SCENE

Rhody Ridge, the private garden and arboretum of Fir and Merlin Butler since 1960, is now a living trust owned by the Snohomish County Parks system. The Butlers reside on the property as caretakers and continue to lovingly maintain the property and their impressive assemblage of species rhododendrons and vast collection of trees, shrubs and groundcovers. For artful plantsmanship, superb pruning techniques and suggestions about their meticulous maintenance program to battle the inevitable pest and disease problems, this arboretum/park provides an exceptional opportunity for observation and inquiry.

THE PLANTS

Over the years the Butlers have purchased plants at the Arboretum Plant Sale (in their era, one of the few local sources of the unusual plants they dreamed of trying). They also sought out sources for rare and uncommon plants they had read about or admired at the Washington Park Arboretum from specialty nurseries across the country. A wide, well-maintained bark path meanders down a gentle slope through the 11-acre garden with diversions off-trail into the surrounding woodland. Many of the plants are identified with their botanical name. Fir Butler's anecdotes are much like the ones we ourselves would relate: the *Franklinia* that didn't do well in its original site at the front of the property (too cold) – so it was moved to a more protected microclimate and now thrives. The *Robinia Pseudoacacia* 'Frisia' that has matured but not without the painful lessons of wind damage to its brittle branches. The many years spent building this impressive collection are reflected in the sensitive selection and placement of the best of every season with a particular concern for the provision of habitat for birds and woodland creatures.

If you come in late fall, winter or early spring you will see their many sheltering shade cloth structures that protect foliage and bark from the ravages of sun scorching and desiccating winds.

DRIVING DIRECTIONS

Return along Clover Rd. to Gravenstein Rd. Turn hard left. In one block, turn right onto 174th Pl. SW. At North Rd. turn right. At the traffic signal at 164th St. SW turn left. At I-5 take the southbound on-ramp towards Seattle. Take the Northgate Way exit #173, towards 1st Ave. NE (this is 10.7 miles south of Rhody Ridge). Keep right at the fork in the off-ramp and turn right onto N Northgate Way. Follow this road to 15th Ave. NW (the roadway changes names along the way to 105th St, back to Northgate Way then to Holman Rd. N. which becomes 15th Ave. NW (4.5 miles from I-5). Follow 15th Ave. NW about 1 mile to NW Market St., through downtown Ballard and on to NW 54th St. Watch for the Hiram Chittenden Locks parking lot on the left.

Driving distance: 19 miles; *Estimated driving time:* 40 minutes.

❄ Carl S. English, Jr. Botanical Garden

3015 NW 54th St., Seattle, WA 98107; Visitor Center (206) 783-7059. Garden open daily, year-round 7 a.m.-9 p.m. Visitor Center open June 15-September 14, daily, 11 a.m.-8 p.m.; September 15-June 14, Thursday–Monday 11 a.m.-5 p.m. The Garden is managed by the Seattle District of the U.S. Army Corps of Engineers, P.O. Box C-3755, Seattle, WA 98124-2255.

Insider Tip: While the Garden covers 7 acres, there is a quarter-mile long self-guided tour which leads you through a respectable sampling of the collection. Pick up a copy of the color brochure at the Visitor Center and consider taking the time to walk through the displays on the second floor that pertain to the garden's history.

❖ ☂ 📖 ☆ ✳ RR

SETTING THE SCENE

A popular destination for visitors and residents of Seattle is the system of "marine elevators" that allows for the movement of boat traffic from the saltwater of Puget Sound to the fresh water of Lakes Union and Washington (Puget Sound is anywhere from 6 to 26 feet lower than the ship canal level of Lake Union). This feat was accomplished by the U.S. Army Corps of Engineers, under the direction of General Hiram M. Chittenden, from 1911-1917. Later, to facilitate the migration of spawning salmon and steelhead, a $2.3 million 21-level fish ladder was installed as well as an underwater viewing room from which the public can view this spectacle.

It was fortunate that land alongside the locks was, from the outset, designated for expanses of lawn and a few ornamental trees and shrubs that surrounded Cavanaugh House, built in 1913. The house remains on the grounds today, the private residence of the Seattle District Engineer. In 1927 a more formal layout of the garden (in particular the area to the east of the Administration building) was created by a landscape architect and those beds now feature spring bulbs, perennials and annuals.

CARL S. ENGLISH, JR. AND "HIS" GARDENS

But even more to our great fortune, in 1931, Carl S. English, Jr. (1904-1976) joined the Corps staff and began a 43-year career as the horticulturist in charge of the gardens. It is to him that we owe a debt of gratitude for his vision and dedication in creating this noteworthy botanical sanctuary. His skill in acquiring seed (primarily) and cuttings of uncommon woody plants through his connections with botanical gardens, arboreta and individuals from around the world (including Chile and elsewhere in South America, New Zealand, Thailand, China and especially Japan) brought choice, rare and beautiful ornamental plants to the garden he tended. Then through his extensive network he generously shared his progeny with others interested in bringing the best-suited rarities into cultivation. This keen gardener, botanist, horticulturist, taxonomist and nurseryman was likewise devoted to the study and preservation of native plants. He traveled to collect seed throughout the Pacific Northwest (especially the alpine areas), West and Southwest. His work resulted in a highly regarded collection of over 500 different plant species, many of them quite rare. His skill as a propagator is evidenced by the fact that most of the trees and shrubs from his day that you see at the Garden were grown from seed. A favorable microclimate, with a sunny southwestern exposure adjacent to Puget Sound largely free from wind, made it possible to grow plants that would not fare so well elsewhere in Seattle. While the predominance of a mature tropical looking *Trachycarpus fortunei* (Windmill Palm) may seem to fit this category, it is actually quite easy to grow in this region, hardy down to a few degrees below zero. A few of the tender specimen trees you'll find at the Garden are: *Eucryphia glutinosa*, a showy Chilean shrub with large gardenia-like flowers and *Eucalyptus gunii*.

Lunch: If you have decided on a picnic at the Locks, you could stop in Ballard to pick up the fixings at the **QFC** or near-by is the scrumptious **Ballard Baking Company**, where you will find a small but divine selection fresh from the ovens only a few steps away. If this is designated as the kind of day you'll treat yourself to a romantic lunch with a superior view of the Shilshole Bay marine activity, then head directly west to **Ray's Café,** above **Ray's Boat House** (which is not open for lunch). The largely seafood menu will provide a memorable meal. In Ballard proper are three wonderful restaurants I recommend: **Burk's Café** for authentic Creole/Cajun cuisine, **Thai Café** for enticing Thai or **Lombardi's Cucina** for richly sauced, garlicky pastas and lusciously light little pizzas.

DRIVING DIRECTIONS

Go east on NW Market St., through downtown Ballard, continue past 15th Ave. NW. NW Market St. becomes N 46th St. Follow signs for N 45th. The street jogs to the right and merges with N 45th. Continue east about 1 mile. At I-5, take the on-ramp southbound and carefully move across to the far left lane in order to take the Hwy. 520 exit #168A towards Bellevue/Kirkland. After the tunnel you'll merge onto 520 East. Take the Montlake Blvd. exit. At the traffic signal cross Montlake Blvd., go straight, following the signs for the Arboretum, to LK. Washington Blvd. E. Turn left and left again at the stop sign, following the road to the Graham Visitor Center.

❋ Washington Park Arboretum

2300 Arboretum Dr. E, Seattle, WA 98112-2300; (206) 325-4510. Open daily, dawn to dusk; **Graham Visitor Center**, Information Desk and **Gift Shop** open Monday-Friday, 10 a.m.-4 p.m., Saturday, Sunday and holidays (except Christmas and New Year's Day), noon-4 p.m. Free **guided tours** offered Saturday and Sunday at 1 p.m. from the GVC. The **Arboretum Plant Study Program**, through the Center for Urban Horticulture (685-8033) offers a year-round study program Saturday mornings focusing on trees, shrubs, vines and ground covers and includes field study.

Insider Tip: the **Pat Calvert Greenhouse** propagation team (largely composed of volunteers) sells plants through the Graham Visitor Center, with a larger selection offered Tuesdays from 10 a.m.-noon (also April-September the first Saturday of the month 10 a.m.-2 p.m.) The Greenhouse staff will propagate almost any plant in the Arboretum collection for you for a small fee. **NOTE:** there is a small site map of the Arboretum in "Kids Tour, Too!".

❖ 🍴 📖 ☆ ❊ RR

SETTING THE SCENE

Washington Park Arboretum (WPA)

This Seattle treasure provides 200 acres of urban green space within the city boundary, with over 4,768 different species and cultivated varieties of woody plants; 124 kinds of trees; 205 varieties of shrubs; and 23 types of vines. This is, after all, an arboretum, a place you would expect to come to see and learn about specimens collected from all corners of the earth—from over 75 countries (771 wild-collected accessions and 139 plants on the endangered species list). Our mild maritime climate is ideally suited to the strong *Rhododendron* collection (which is world famous) and the stunning *Magnolia* collection. Trees from every continent are represented along with the native flora and 20 species of trees native to Seattle.

THE PLANTS

A good place to prepare for a trip through the Arboretum is an initial stop at the Graham Visitor Center. At the Center pick up a map which will help orient your route and check out examples of what is currently of seasonal interest.

An Arboretum offers the opportunity to view collections of plants, soaking in the beauty of their similarities while noting their unique and distinctive qualities. The Japanese maples (*Acer palmatum* cultivars) here represent the most extensive public collection in North America. Other world-class collections include *Ilex* (Holly, the country's second largest collection), *Quercus* (Oak), *Sorbus* (Mountain Ash), *Abies* (Fir), *Acer* (Maple) and *Magnolia* species. Other important plant collections include *Camellia*, *Hamamelis* (Witch Hazel), *Viburnum*, *Prunus* (Cherry), and *Rhododendron* (including *Azaleas*).

A curious student of the arboreal offerings would be wise to purchase a copy of *The Woody Collection in the Washington Park Arboretum* (1994), the catalog of trees and shrubs in the Arboretum. It is arranged in alphabetical order by botanical name, followed by the common name, country of origin and map co-ordinates that locate the plant in the grounds. Staff at the Center can help identify a plant if you supply the label number from the plant tag. Arthur Lee Jacobson's *Trees of Seattle*, also includes a fold-out map of the Arboretum and provides more text identifying and describing many of the trees you will find as you wander through the WPA collection.

DRIVING DIRECTIONS

From the Graham Visitor Center follow the road north to Lk. Washington Blvd. Turn right then take the on-ramp for Hwy. 520 east and merge onto the Evergreen Point Floating Bridge. Take the 84th Ave. NE exit. Turn right at the stop sign and proceed two blocks to the traffic signal at NE 24th St. Turn right and watch on the right for the entrance to the nursery. *Driving distance:* 4.5 miles; *Estimated driving time:* 10 minutes

🌸 Wells Medina Nursery

8300 NE 24th St., Medina, WA 98039; (425) 454-1853. Open Monday-Saturday 9 a.m.-6 p.m., Sunday 10 a.m.-5 p.m.; winter hours Monday-Saturday 9 a.m.-5 p.m., Sunday 10 a.m.-5 p.m.

❖ 🌱 ✳ RR

When horticultural luminaries are in town, *this* is where they are taken for a look-see.

In 1971, Wells Medina began as the inspiration of Ned Wells. It has grown over the years as a family business, anxious to enthuse its patrons about the marvelous plant choices there are for every gardener, from quality, well-grown common varieties to great rarities. There is a woody plant specialty here, in deference to the heart and soul of the Northwest garden. You'll find an outstanding selection of conifers, Japanese maples, flowering trees and shrubs, species and hybrid *Rhododendrons*, shade trees and, of course, the full complement of other plants are well represented also. In 1997 Wells Medina Nursery introduced a Collection of **Rare Chinese Trees**, never available before in the Pacific Northwest. The plants were rescued from China where they were threatened with imminent extinction. While there is little botanical literature on them, this is a remarkable opportunity for adventurous gardeners to try something truly new in the hopes their effort will be rewarding on a personal level and in the broader context of helping save endangered species.

Ned Wells is still very actively involved in the running of the nursery, along with four Wells (adult) children. Ned spends a great deal of time traveling in search of the uncommon, hand-picking the best he can find. Some examples are *Magnolia* x 'Caerhay's Belle', 'Sayonara' and 'Vulcan' – all big flowering varieties. There are 136 varieties of Japanese Maples to choose from, including *Acer palmatum* 'Aka shigitatsu' and *A. p.* 'Ukigumo'. If you are on the hunt for an uncommon Sorbus they have 'Vilmorinii', *Sorbus aria* 'Lutescens' and *S. cashiriana*. There are 12 varieties of lilacs on offer, including the elusive pale yellow one called 'Primrose'. For conifer fanciers there is *Taxus baccata* 'Amerisforte' and *Cephalotaxus harringtonia* 'Fastigiata' and *Juniperus communis* 'Gold Cone.'

The five-acre nursery is blessed with a dazzling display garden, designed and maintained by the Seattle professional design duo, Glenn Withey and Charles Price. Because this border has become an institution among aficionados (from far and wide) who make it a point to stop by often to watch seasonal progress, there are periodic make-overs, introducing fresh ideas, new plants, and the satisfaction of watching a young garden mature. Don't miss the lush Wells-Medina streetside display bed as well!

Driving Directions, End of the Tour

Go east on NE 24th St. one block and turn left onto 84th Ave. NE which takes you to Hwy. 520. Take the westbound on-ramp, cross the Evergreen Floating Bridge, follow signs onto I-5 for Seattle's City Center. *Driving distance:*7 miles; *Estimated driving time:* 15 minutes.

FURTHER RESOURCES

Food

QFC: turn right onto 24th from NW Market St.

Ballard Baking Company: 5909 24th Ave. NW, Seattle, WA 98117; (206) 781-0091. $-$$, B,L,D. Open daily. One of the joys of a visit are the aromas wafting from the bakery as natural breads and fine pastries emerge and make their way to the old fashioned case up front. Expert espresso, sandwiches, soup, dynamite treats.

Ray's Café upstairs at **Ray's Boathouse**: 6049 Seaview Ave. NW, Seattle, WA 98107; (206) 789-3770. $$ L. Open for lunch daily. Outdoor seating or take in the captivating view from within. Imaginative seafood, a bit less upscale (and less expensive) than the parent restaurant.

Burk's Café: 5411 Ballard Ave. NW, Seattle, WA 98107; (206) 782-0091. $$, L,D. Open Tuesday-Saturday. From the traditional spicy pickled okra in crocks on each table, through a smokey shrimp gumbo and on to the perfect pecan pie, this is authentic Creole/Cajun cuisine.

Thai Café: 5401 20th Ave. NW, Seattle, WA 98107; (206) 784-4599. $$, L,D. Open Monday-Friday 11 a.m.-10 p.m., Saturday 5-10 p.m. One of my favorite Thai restaurants anywhere. I especially return for the satays.

Lombardi's Cucina: 2200 NW Market St., Seattle, WA 98107; (206) 391-9097. $$, L, Monday-Friday D daily, Sunday Brunch. Generous servings, richly flavored sauces, and a tradition of serving savory baked garlic with their complimentary basket of fresh French bread.

Lodging

See "Seattle Travel Notes" in the Introduction for accommodation suggestions

More Resources for Gardeners

Arboretum Foundation: 2300 Arboretum Dr. East, Seattle, WA 98112. (206) 325-4510. This non-profit organization provides financial and volunteer support to the Arboretum. Members' benefits include a full-color quarterly, a monthly newsletter and educational program discounts.

E.B. Dunn Historic Gardens: P.O. Box 77126, Seattle, WA 98177; (206) 362-0933. The private garden of the late E.B. Dunn, now in the hands of a trust. An Olmsted design from 1915, on a woodland bluff overlooking Puget Sound. By appointment, Fridays and Saturdays, April-September, 10 a.m. and 2 p.m., limited to 12 / 7 cars. A guided tour is provided, a fee is charged.

Elisabeth C. Miller Botanical Garden: P.O. Box 77377, Seattle, WA 98177. The garden of the late Elisabeth Miller, now in a trust, known for its exceptional collection of fine trees, shrubs and woodland herbaceous plants. The garden is open on a limited basis for tours by *appointment only*. Tour times are 10 a.m. and 1 p.m. Wednesdays and Thursdays (without exception), March-October. Tours are limited to 15 people; free.

Trees of Seattle, Arthur Lee Jacobson (1989, Sasquatch Books, 432 pages., color photos) and ***North American Landscape Trees*** (1997, Ten Speed Press, 722 pages). Both are extraordinary reference resources

NURSERY HOPPING LOOP/North

———— Itinerary Highlights ————
nursery turns to China, Europe for new plant introductions
displays of rare specimen trees, endangered-bird aviary
glorious peonies, daylilies flaunt beauty in wooded setting
stone garden ornaments of exquisite craftsmanship
colossal country nursery offers acres of great plants

Some of my most cherished memories of "gardening with friends" come from the days we have piled into the van for an adventurous day of nursery hopping. Bringing together our collective aspirations and diverse backgrounds always makes for stimulating botanical chatter along the way and especially while prowling the nursery aisles. There is a genuine sense of camaraderie in seeking one another's valued opinion on the merits of this chartreuse hosta or the shade tolerance of that lacecap hydrangea. There is a marvelous air of excitement and self-satisfaction as flat after flat of plants, large (too large?!) and small, are carted off to a vehicle already crammed with personal prizes and hard-earned plunder!

🌱 **THE ITINERARY IN BRIEF** 🌱

❶ Sky Nursery

This superb garden center continues to be a much loved and respected destination for gardeners of every sort, from the novice to the seasoned veteran to the professional in search of quality plants for a customer. The reason for this loyalty is obvious—great plants, knowledgeable staff, pleasant ambiance and a full range of non-plant supplies and equipment.

❷ Emery's Garden Nursery

This is one of those, "Have YOU heard about ..." kind of nurseries. The kind that people can hardly wait to tell their gardening friends about. This place literally pulsates with staff competence and enthusiasm, as they are encouraged to express their innovative ideas to keep abreast of the fast-paced Northwest gardening world.

❸ A & D Nursery

A & D is the designated display Garden of the American Hemerocallis Society and is the first and only such daylily garden in Puget Sound. Their selection and display collection of daylilies and their extensive collection of peonies is probably the most comprehensive in the region. The Hosta Walk provides the opportunity to see hundreds of mature plants in a woodland setting among favored companions.

Lunch A famous "destination restaurant" in this rural outpost! The **Maltby Café** is a great place to eat (a good thing, with virtually no other contenders in the immediate vicinity!)

❹ Nichols Brothers Stoneworks

The Nichols Brothers' European-styled pieces (classical urns, elegant pots, pineapple and artichoke finials) of reconstituted sandstone are marketed throughout the country to discerning landscape design professionals. The public is invited to shop the sales yard at this quality garden ornament manufacturer (save on flawed pieces).

❺ Flower World

The Toys-R-Us of the plant world, with 10 acres of indoor plants, bedding plants, flowering baskets, trees and shrubs, vines, pond plants, perennials, fruit trees and berry bushes, cacti and succulents, ornamental grasses...

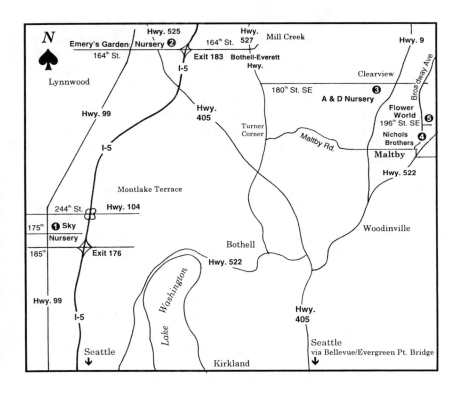

TOUR TIMING AND TIPS

This makes an excellent OUT OF TOWN VISITOR TOUR:
Out-of-town company with an interest in gardening would enjoy the
little "extras" to be found along this tour. **Sky Nursery** has installed
a number of tiny but very interesting displays within the nursery of
which the lushly planted koi pond is my favorite. At **Emery's
Garden Nursery** an innovative Northwest/Japanese display garden
is built around a number of dramatic specimen trees; a handsome and
informative aviary reflects the owner's special interest in preserving
endangered birds (particularly the exquisite pheasants of China); and
there are a number of resident farm animals retaining and enhancing
the rural character of this location. **A & D Nursery** is the epitome of
the small, specialty nursery for which the Northwest is gaining
national acclaim. The country setting paired with the peak bloom of
peonies or daylilies is sure to wow your company. The **Maltby Café** is
an obvious people-pleaser judging from the long lines of patient
patrons who willingly wait for a table when they arrive on a
particularly busy day (Sunday Brunch, certainly, and noon hour
almost always). **Flower World** is one of my favorite places to take
plant loving friends and relatives because of the sheer vastness of the
place. Just wandering through the cavernous greenhouses,
overflowing with flourishing foliage and towering indoor plants, is a
little like getting lost in a leafy green maze.

🐛 All the destinations on this itinerary are open year round with the
exception of **A & D Nursery**. They are open daily March-June and
Wednesday-Sunday July-November. See the destination profile for
exact details. **Nichols Brothers** is open Monday-Friday year round.

🐛 Plan to be at **Sky Nursery** as the doors open at 9 a.m. (Sunday at
10 a.m. November-March)—this itinerary will keep you hopping!

🐛 As there are potentially three nursery stops before my suggested
lunch destination, consider fueling up with a hearty breakfast to keep
up your stamina or pack along a mid-morning snack. As an
alternative, if you decide to be creative and do this tour backwards,
the **Maltby Café** turns out to be one of the Seattle area's most
renowned breakfast destinations!

🐛 From mid-May through June the fields of beautiful blooming
bearded irises at **Walsterway Iris Gardens** are worth a stop!

🐛 **Sky Nursery** holds its annual "Garden Party" the second weekend in September. There are speakers, special prices and prizes, and the Nursery donates space for one of my favorite plant events of the year: the "Odd Plant Show and Sale" sponsored by a number of non-profit organizations (Carnivorous Plant Society, Cactus and Succulent Society, Bamboo Society, etc.)

❧ Both **Sky Nursery** and **Emery's Garden Nursery** offer free newsletters. Just ask to be added to the mailing list and plan your tour to coincide with fat savings or a fact-filled workshop.

❧ **A & D Nursery Bloom Time Best Bets:**
Single Type Peonies – all through May
Tree Peonies – early-May through mid-May
Double and Japanese Peonies – late May through mid-June
Daylilies – July through August
Hostas – May and June for foliage; late summer for flowers

SETTING THE SCENE

This "Loop to the North" starts out by heading up to the boundary between King and Snohomish Counties. **Sky Nursery** is located along a busy business-lined thoroughfare, Aurora Avenue (also called State Highway 99). When the nursery was established here in 1953 by Eileen Landry, it was way out in the country. Today her memory is commemorated in the form of a scholarship to a student of horticulture at Edmonds Community College, funded through the September "Garden Party" festivities at the nursery.

Lynnwood is famous with aspiring landscape designers and horticulturists for the very good program offered at Edmonds Community College. It is also home to the Alderwood Shopping Mall. Traveling east you will find an area that has been home to horse farms and rural folk for decades, but is quickly being discovered and developed as a countrified suburban bedroom community for the wider King/Snohomish County work force.

DRIVING DIRECTIONS:

From mid-town Seattle drive north on I-5 to the N. 175th St. exit #176. Go west on 175th about 1 mile. Turn right on Aurora Ave. N. .5 mile
Driving distance: 12 miles; *Estimated driving time:* 20 minutes.

❇ Sky Nursery

8528 Aurora Ave. N, Seattle, WA 98133; (206) 546-4851. Open year-round, daily 9 a.m.-6 p.m. (Sundays November-March 10 a.m.-5 p.m.)
Web site in process at press time, call for URL
❖ 🎄 📖 ☆ ✳ RR

I once asked Art and Mareen Kruckeberg (he of native plant fame, she of MsK Rare Plant Nursery fame) where it was that *they* shopped when looking beyond the rarities and native plants in their own highly regarded nursery. Of a voice, and with enthusiasm, they answered

"Sky Nursery, of course!" My investigation bore out their recommendation as this is a very appealing place to prowl in search of just about everything for the garden. I have been impressed with the effort they put into obtaining the less common and best performing plants (from specimen-sized trees to vegetable starts) and look to them now for imports from China (rare Tree Peonies, trees and shrubs), New Zealand (they work with the plant through it's year of seasonal jet lag) and Europe. Look to them also for more uncommon plants, propagated in-house.

It isn't sheer coincidence that there is an Information Booth smack in the center of the sales yard, because Sky Nursery is committed to offering their expertise to gardeners. A terrific set of fact sheets is available; they offer seminars (not only in the nursery but in the public schools and through the Shoreline Parks Department); they donate soil and plants to local charities; and they sponsor a scholarship for a student in horticulture at Edmonds Community College. They were one of the first nurseries in the area to make their premises more accessible to customers with mobility limitations.

As a full-service garden center they offer everything from bulk soil and amendments (delivery available) to an excellent batch of seed companies, a broad range of gardening books and quality tools large and small.

DRIVING DIRECTIONS:
From Sky Nursery turn right onto Aurora Ave. N. Turn right on 244th St. (Hwy 104). At I-5 take the northbound on-ramp. Take the 164th St. SW exit #183 and turn left, traveling west about 1 mile.
Driving distance: 7.5 miles; *Estimated driving time:* 20 minutes.

Emery's Garden Nursery

2829 164th St. SW, Lynnwood, WA 98037; (425) 743-4555. Open year round daily during daylight savings time 9 a.m.-6 p.m. (earlier on Saturday and later on Friday in the busy gardening season) and otherwise 10 a.m.-6 p.m.
❖ ⌂ 📖 ☆ ✳ RR

For forty years nursery patrons loyally came to this location to buy plants at the Uyeda Nursery. After Mr. Uyeda's death the nursery languished until, in 1996 it was resurrected to become a plant haven filled with healthy plants and a dedicated staff. The "Emery" of Emery's Gardens is Emery Rhodes, a man bursting with enthusiasm to make this, once again, one of Seattle's best nursery destinations. To that end he has successfully drawn a cadre of top talent from around the region to make up a staff imbued with high standards of quality, filled with innovative ideas, experienced in the nursery industry here and as anxious as he is to build a loyal customer base.

What especially catches my eye are the well-organized tables, neatly packed with healthy, happy plants, attractively displayed. Even in the most challenging of "between" seasons, a stop here will yield fresh temptation. There is excellent choice in everything from dwarf conifers to traditional bonsai (starter plants as well as finished.) Look here for larger trees when you are seeking the benefits of maturity. The staff has been careful to assess which varieties are best suited for Northwest gardens and can provide experienced advice on care requirements for transplanting large specimens.

Creative display beds throughout the nursery reflect an attitude of customer service—the importance of providing inspiration and the opportunity to see mature and massed plantings. While Mr. Uyeda was alive the nursery was most famous for its spectacular collection of conifers not typically found in Seattle at the time, such as Atlas Weeping Cedar, Australian Black Pines and Golden Threadbranch Cypress. Today, an area of about three acres has been dedicated to the development of a botanical garden, reclaiming land where historically and horticulturally important trees have survived untended for many years. A dedicated nursery owner and a talented staff are working to properly prune and rejuvenate these distinctive specimens and integrate native woodland features that occur on the site as well. Respectful of the heritage of this nursery, Emery has retained and revitalized the Uyeda's traditional Japanese display garden and has integrated several of his own choice species rhododendrons from China. An aviary displaying rare and endangered birds (in particular pheasants from China) makes an intriguing diversion for visitors of all ages. (This commitment to animal preservation is further evidenced by his position on the Board of Directors of the Woodland Park Zoo).

DRIVING DIRECTIONS:
Leave Emery's Nursery turning east on 164th St. SW, cross over I-5 and continue on 164th 2.5 miles to the Bothell-Everett Highway (at Mill Creek Plaza) turn right approximately 1.5 miles to the North Creek Shopping Center. At the traffic signal turn left onto 180th SE and proceed east about 3.5 miles. Watch for the "A & D Nursery" sign on the right. *Driving distance:* 8 miles; *Estimated driving time:* 20 minutes.

TOUR TIP:
If you are famished now you may want to stop at one of the two shopping centers en route to A & D Nursery for lunch or refreshment.

❀ A & D Nursery

6808 180th SE, Snohomish, WA 98290-8340; (360) 668-9690. Open March-June weekdays 9:30 a.m.-4:30 p.m.; July-mid-November, Wednesday-Friday 9:30 a.m.-4:30 p.m.; Saturday-Sunday 9 a.m.-5 p.m. Catalog $2. bbbloom@mcione.com

❖ ☂ 📖 ✳ RR

A & D first opened for business in the early seventies on the basis of the famed Goldsmith collection of peonies, brought to the west from Clinton. N.Y. by Roy Leighton. Many peonies of America's first major peony hybridizer, Professor Saunders, are still grown at the nursery, though they are difficult to locate elsewhere. Through A & D's commitment to quality you'll find here the best of America's major hybridizers' work.

Over the years that I have been returning annually to A & D one thing has remained consistent. Each visit dazzles and delights me with the dedication Don and Keith muster to offer their patrons the best of the best -- cultivars of the special, the rare and the proven performers they work hard to seek out, cultivate and display for their plant-loving friends and valued customers.

As someone who gardens in a largely shady location, it is a joy and rare treat to find such an extravagance of choice in one fell swoop. Consider (and relish) the extensive woodland Hosta Walk. Covering a wide range of micro-conditions (dry shade, dappled sun, boggy), there is much to learn from their example.

In the delightfully rustic Potting Shed there are thousands of color slides of peonies and daylilies for customers to peruse.

DRIVING DIRECTIONS:
Leaving A & D Nursery turn right onto 180th SE. Follow it through Clearview and on to Broadway, about 1.5 miles. Turn right onto Broadway Ave., which becomes Maltby Rd. Watch for the Maltby Café on the right – it's in the basement of the old Maltby School Gymnasium building, circa 1937, a WPA project.
Driving distance: 3.5 miles; *Estimated driving time:* 10 minutes

Lunch: At the ever popular **Maltby Café** it is wise to arrive with a ravenous appetite for generous portions of hearty fare are the name of the game here. Sandwiches are served on thick slices of freshly baked bread (the delicious Reuben is made with freshly baked corned beef), salads are huge (my favorite is the Spinach), imaginative concoctions, desserts are divine.

DRIVING DIRECTIONS:
Leaving the Maltby Café, retrace your route to Broadway Ave. about 1 mile to Nichols Brothers Stoneworks (on the right).

❋ Nichols Brothers Stoneworks

20209 Broadway Ave., Snohomish, WA 98290; (360) 668-5434, (800) 483-5720. Call or write for a catalog. Open year- round Monday-Friday 8 a.m.-5 p.m. (Located in Maltby, just off Hwy. 522).

If you have been in the market for an English style sandstone urn, planter, pot, pedestal or stone garden bench, you will have seen the Nichols Brothers work in garden shops. What makes a trip to their business rewarding is the potential of a great bargain, as there is a corner of the sales yard set aside for pieces with flaws. The price break (sorry, bad pun) may be just what you needed to get what you've wanted. NEW! This company has negotiated the rights to exclusively reproduce the stone garden work designed by Frank Lloyd Wright, the first firm allowed to do so.

DRIVING DIRECTIONS:
From Nichols Brothers turn right onto Broadway Ave. and follow it to 196th St. SE. Turn right. *Estimated driving time:* 5 minutes

❋ Flower World

9322 196th St. SE, Maltby, WA 98290; (360) 668-9575 (mailing address: 19127 99th Ave. SE, Snohomish, WA 98290). Open year-round, daily 9 a.m.-5 p.m. (Spring 9 a.m.-5 p.m. except Friday 9 a.m.-8 p.m., Sunday 9 a.m.-5 p.m.)

❖ ⍏ ✳ RR

On my first visit to Flower World, some years ago, I actually lost my husband Larry who had "gone missing" among the 5-acre botanical bounty (and the nursery has since doubled in size!) You can pick up a convenient map at the front counter to help organize your shopping strategy and provide a means of finding your way back to the sales counter! Should you arrive on a nasty wet day, fear not. There are several acres of plants under cover in large plant houses, well lit and invitingly displayed (in addition to the extensive sales yard). As the grower of something like 90% of the stock they sell, prices are kept competitively low and plants are fresh from the field or greenhouse.

DRIVING DIRECTIONS, END OF THE TOUR:
From Flower World return on 196th St. SE to Broadway Ave. Turn left. At the intersection at the R/R tracks, turn left crossing the tracks, turn right on Yew Way, then left on Paradise Lake Rd. to the traffic signal at the intersection with Hwy. 522. Turn right (south). Take the I-405 South exit towards Bellevue/Renton. After 8 miles take the Hwy. 520 East/520 West exit #14 towards Redmond/Seattle keeping to the right at the fork in the ramp. Merge onto Hwy. 520 traveling west which takes you across the Evergreen Floating Bridge. Take the I-5 South exit towards the City Center. *Driving distance:* 25 miles; *Estimated driving time:* 35 minutes.

FURTHER RESOURCES

Food

Maltby Café: 8809 Maltby Rd., Maltby, WA 98290; (425) 483-3123. $$,B,L. Open daily 7 a.m.-3 p.m. (breakfast until 11:20 a.m. week-days and all day Saturday and Sunday). Limited reservations for large groups only. The Maltby Café is 6 miles north of Woodinville.

Lodging

A Cottage Creek Inn: 12525 Avondale Rd., Redmond, WA 98052; (425) 881-5606. This is a secluded Tudor-style Bed and Breakfast Inn set in park-like grounds surrounded by gardens, a romantic gazebo, woodland walk, koi and goldfish pond and a creek running alongside the front of the property. Reasonable rates. See photos on their site www.brigadoon.com/~cotcreek/

More Resources for Gardeners

Basetti's Crooked Arbor Gardens: 18512 NE 165th, Woodinville, WA 98072; (425) 788-6767. Open April 15-October 31, Saturdays 10 a.m.-3 p.m. and by appointment. Come for dwarf conifers, alpine plants, garden sculpture and accessories and to see Leonette and Bill's highly respected display gardens. Garden Art events are very special, request current dates!

Specialty Nursery Guide: 1220 NE 90th, Seattle, WA 98115. This guide gives excellent profiles and directions to around four dozen small specialty nurseries in the greater Seattle area. Send SASE with two stamps.

Walsterway Iris Gardens: 19923 Broadway Ave., Snohomish (Maltby), WA 98290; (360) 668-4429 or 485-6470. Open late May to September 15, daily 9 a.m.-5 p.m. Located directly along Broadway Ave. in Maltby, the two acres of irises in bloom mid-May to mid-June draw many a passer-by in for a closer look. Tall bearded iris are the specialty (Japanese and Siberians, too.)

GARDEN
& NURSERY
LOOP/South

—————————— Itinerary Highlights ——————————
world's finest collection of species rhododendrons
spellbinding outdoor gallery with ancient bonsai
Northwest nursery with sublime English country flare
blue poppies amid formal elegance in lakeside estate garden
terrific shop and its teeny tiny nursery of collector plants

*How often does one emit a heavy sigh when garden loving visitors from afar recount their ambitious itineraries and we feel the pangs of guilt and envy that they can pack **so much** into a few days and we have trouble managing to put a dent in even a fraction of our local "must see" gardens and nursery list! Sigh.*

A bevy of outstanding destinations that draw enthusiasts from across the country cluster to the south of Seattle in the Tacoma/Federal Way area. Yet when greatness is in one's midst, it is often too close to see -- and sometimes a little too far away to inspire a spontaneous visit. Winter-worn Northwest Gardeners on the Go, put this heavenly springtime "day of exploration" on your calendar!

❦ THE ITINERARY IN BRIEF ❦

❶ Rhododendron Species Botanical Garden

One is easily charmed by the intriguing bloom of Washington's state flower, the *Rhododendron macrophyllum* (one of two species native to Washington). This Botanical Garden displays over 10,000 individual Rhododendrons—2,100 varieties of 435 species, one of the finest collections in the world.

❷ Pacific Rim Bonsai Collection

This magnificent outdoor gallery presents 50 displays of more than 100 prized bonsai, some several hundreds of years old, amidst towering Douglas firs. The juxtaposition is brilliantly and sensitively conceived. A Tropical Bonsai Conservatory makes a particularly inviting destination on rainy days and in cooler months.

❸ Edgewood Flower Farm

Leave the bustle and clutter of suburban sprawl behind. This charming country nursery welcomes visitors with colorful flowers spilling from extraordinary hanging baskets and European style window boxes. It is easy to be diverted en route to the plant display and sales area by the appealing shop, tastefully reflecting an English gardening influence.

❹ Lakewold Gardens

This inviting 10-acre estate garden nestles along the shores of Gravelly Lake, blessed by a favorable micro-climate and the adventurous and sophisticated gardening ambitions of Corydon and Eulalie Wagner. Their personal involvement was happily married with professional guidance from renowned landscape architect Thomas Church, who practiced what he preached, that "gardens are for people."

❺ The Garden Shop at Lakewold Gardens

With a keen appreciation for outstanding plants and a passion for garden books and an enviable selection of gardening periodicals, many from abroad, Vickie Haushild has assembled an outstanding garden shop – with one eye firmly on the practical and the other giving a playful wink to fanciful necessities. Set on the grounds of Lakewold Gardens, a browse through this shop makes a fitting finale to a delightful day of exploration and discovery.

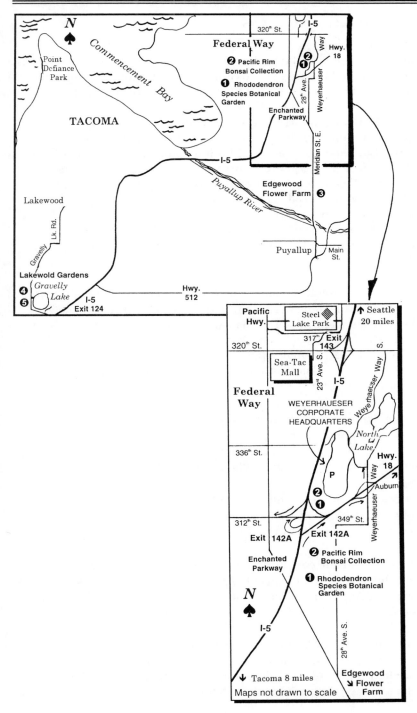

TOUR TIMING AND TIPS

🌿 Timing is a bit tricky for this itinerary because of the uncoordinated opening days and seasons for the two major gardens. If your exploration day turns out to coincide with one of the closing days, however, fear not. At the end of this chapter you'll find additional options for Gardeners on the Go.
The **Pacific Rim Bonsai Collection** is **open** March-May, Friday-Wednesday 10 a.m.-4 p.m. (*closed* Thursdays); and **open** June-February, Saturday-Wednesday 11 a.m.-4 p.m.(*closed* Thurs. - Fri.).
The **Rhododendron Species Botanical Garden** is **open** March-May, Friday-Wednesday 10 a.m.-4 p.m.(*closed* Thursday); and **open** June-February, Sat.-Wed. 11 a.m.-4 p.m. (*closed* Thursday -Friday).
Lakewold Gardens is **open** April-September, Thursday-Monday 10 a.m.-4 p.m except Friday, noon-8 p.m. (*closed* Tuesday and Wednesday); October-March, Friday-Sunday 10 a.m.-3 p.m. (*closed* Monday-Thursday).

🌿 Species rhododendron bloom runs from January through July. The most ravishing bloom is March through May, when the largest number of rhododendrons and seasonal companions strut their stuff. The next greatest show of color is in fall when the landscape is ablaze with the vivid reds, oranges and yellows of the extensive Japanese maple collection, azaleas, fothergillas, sweet gums and many other ornamental trees and shrubs.

🌿 A signature plant at **Lakewold Gardens**, the Himalayan Blue Poppies (*Mecanopsis betonicifolia*), are at their best in late spring (June) before the heat of the summer sets in. Their waves of blue pool beneath the sunny golden Honeylocust, *Gledista triacanthos*.

🌿 **Lakewold Gardens** celebrates it's peak season "Festival of Flowers" April-May and in early August sponsors a "Picnic and Pops" concert in the garden with the Tacoma Concert Band.

🌿 The **Rhododendron Species Foundation** holds two extensive **plant sales** each year: in spring (a Friday and Saturday, usually the first week of April) and in fall (usually mid-September). The Garden is open for free on these days.

🌿 The **Pacific Rim Bonsai Collection** offers free Introductory Bonsai lectures on alternative Sundays, mid-April through early October at 1 p.m. and Saturdays once a month, mid-June through mid-September. Call (253) 924-3153 for more information. There are usually two or three Special Exhibits each year as well.

🍂 There are major bulb growers in the country surrounding Puyallup and a drive through the area in spring yields spectacular vistas of the commercial fields in bloom. Farm stands and u-pick fields are common along the picturesque country roads during the season's harvest, fresh produce and cut flowers can be had at the Farmer's Market at Pioneer Park Saturdays, May-September.

SETTING THE SCENE

Rhododendron Species Botanical Garden: The origins of the Garden go back to 1964 and to Eugene, Oregon, when botanist Dr. Milton V. Walker, along with a dedicated group of American Rhododendron Society members, began the daunting task of assembling a comprehensive collection of species rhododendrons. Their mission was the preservation, distribution and display of authenticated species rhododendrons. The first acquisitions were planted in the personal gardens of Dr. Walker and P.H. Brydon (retired director of San Francisco's Strybing Arboretum). Many of the species were then introduced into cultivation through distribution to individuals, nurseries and other gardens.

A decade later the Weyerhaeuser Company generously offered a 24-acre site in Federal Way, WA., at their Corporate Headquarters campus, along with site preparation, construction of offices, a greenhouse and lathhouse, access roads and an irrigation system. The entire collection was moved from Oregon to Washington in 1975. Since that time an active plant propagation program has been developed and research relationships have been established with other institutions. A public display garden has opened with companion plants being added, a Volunteer Program has been developed and a Garden Master Plan has been written.

The Rhododendron Species Foundation (RSF): This private non-profit organization is an internationally recognized leader in rhododendron conservation. Their staff and a cadre of loyal volunteers (some driving as much as 140 miles weekly to work in the gardens) support programs in plant collection; plant, seed and pollen distribution; public education; and research. This genus, one of the largest in the plant kingdom, is represented by nearly 815 known species. As natural habitat for these plants is under threat worldwide, they have endeavored to provide a place to preserve, protect and propagate the species rhododendron. To that end, they make reciprocal arrangements with other botanical gardens to share plant material in hopes of establishing auxiliary collections.

Weyerhaeuser Company: This forest products company is the largest private owner of softwood timber in the world. Founder, Frederick Weyerhaeuser was born in Germany in 1834. After immigrating to Illinois in 1852, he worked in a sawmill and married a German compatriot, Elizabeth Bloedel. Five years later Frederick and his brother-in-law purchased the bankrupt mill and expanded west through timber purchases and harvesting from Illinois to the Pacific Northwest. A group of investors led by Frederick Weyerhaeuser incorporated as the Weyerhaeuser Company in 1900. They opened offices in Tacoma following the purchase of 900,000 acres of forest land for $6 per acre. In 1902 they acquired the Pacific Coast Lumber Mill in Everett and in 1931 built their first pulp mill, in Longview, WA. They established the nation's first tree farm, the Clemons Tree Farm, in Montesano, WA., initiating private forest stewardship that today includes more than 70,000 landowners nationally and 95 million acres. In 1990 their reforestation program produced the 500 millionth seedling grown at Mima Tree Nursery.

Puyallup: (pronounced pew al' up) Dr. William Fraser Tolmie, who was attached to the Hudson's Bay Company trading post at Fort Nisqually, was the first recorded white settler in this rich agricultural valley in 1833. After resolution of the American/Canadian boundary in 1853 more American settlers began to arrive and among them was the Jacob Meeker family. They are noteworthy as the first to grow hops, a wildly successful crop that would make son Ezra "Hop King of the World" with a claim to be the wealthiest man in the Pacific Northwest having earned more than $500,000 in a single year. In the mid-1890s, however, an infestation of hop lice decimated the crop, after which farmers moved into berries, small fruits, flowers and bulbs. Today the farming sector relies on bulbs (tulips, daffodils and irises), hot house rhubarb and berries. The bulb industry dates back to the early 1900s when bulbs were imported from England and continental Europe. In the early 1920s Simon VanLierop came from Holland to sell bulbs and ended up settling in the Puyallup Valley in 1934 to grow bulbs himself. The Puyallup Daffodil Festival claims to be "the fourth largest floral festival" in the nation.

Lakes District of Tacoma: From about 1839 to 1870 the area west of Nisqually and south of Tacoma was claimed by the Puget Sound Agricultural Company (a subsidiary of the British Hudson's Bay Company) to grow produce for trade with Russian posts further north in exchange for furs. Prairie grasslands predominated here because local Indians burned the land frequently to discourage fir trees and to encourage the growth of the native camas, the root of which was a staple of their food stores, and blackberries which in turn drew deer and bears—resulting in an ample supply of fruit and game. With pioneer settlement, Douglas fir forests began to establish themselves and by the turn of the century the region was heavily forested. The area also boasted a number of lovely lakes. Gravelly Lake was so named for the coarse pebbly soil that epitomizes the outwash of gravel-laden melt water from retreating glaciers (in this case, Vashon Glacier which extended from Oregon to the San Juan Islands and was responsible for the formation of these lakes). The area, now Lakewood, was known in the early 1900s as Interlaaken. In the early days it was fashionable to take the trolley out to American Lake, where a grand dance pavilion had been built and the big bands of the day played into the night. This lakeland paradise was fertile ground for the region's elite to establish their summer retreats and then grander estates, many of which had enormous gardens. Lakewold is one of only a couple of the great gardens to survive, and is open to the public under the auspices of the Friends of Lakewold, non-profit organization.

DRIVING DIRECTIONS:
From **mid-town Seattle** drive southbound on I-5. Follow signs for Tacoma/Portland for approximately 20 miles. Take the Federal Way/S. 320th St. exit #143. At the stop light turn left onto 320th traveling east (back over I-5). At Weyerhaeuser Way S. turn right. Follow the signs for the Rhododendron Species Botanical Garden, turning right at the East Entrance. You will circle behind and around the Weyerhaeuser Headquarters main building to the Visitor Parking Lot. (Turn left at the Garden entrance to let off passengers with walking difficulties.) From the Visitor Parking lot there is a short walk back to the Garden entrance. *Driving distance:* 25 miles; *Estimated driving time:* 40 minutes.
From **Tacoma and south**, drive north on I-5 to the Hwy. 18/Auburn exit #142A. Exit right from I-5 onto Hwy. 18 then take the first exit right, to Weyerhaeuser Way. S. Turn left onto Weyerhaeuser Way S. going north. Follow signs for the Rhododendron Species Botanical Garden turning left at the East Entrance. Follow directions to the Visitor Parking Lot.

NOTE: The Rhododendron Species Display Garden and the Pacific Rim Bonsai Collection are located adjacent to one another.

❇ Rhododendron Species Botanical Garden

2525 S. 336th St., Federal Way (mailing address: P.O. Box 3798, Federal Way, WA 98063-3798); (253) 838-4646; gift shop 661-9377; tour groups require a reservation 661-9377. Open March-May, Friday-Wednesday 10 a.m.-4 p.m.(*closed* Thursday); and June-February, Sat.-Wed. 11 a.m.-4 p.m. (*closed* Thursday -Friday). There is an entry fee. Free entry days are: all of January and February, Mother's and Father's Day and plant sale days (see "Tour Timing"). Web site: www.trine.com/GardenNet/RSFG/
Insider Tip: Knowledgeable docents provide free guided tours to groups of 15 or more participants. During the peak season March-May they need two weeks advance notice.
❖ ♈ 📖 ☆ ✳ RR

For some years I visited the botanical garden here with the eyes of a novice gardener, most interested in soaking up the beauty of spring rhododendron bloom. As I began to develop my skills as a gardener and my background broadened, my eyes also focused on a large and varied collection of fascinating trees, like the Dove Tree (*Davidia involucrata*), with its breathtaking white bracts that resemble delicate butterflies, and Japanese Stewartia (*Stewartia pseudocamellia*) with attractive peeling bark, lovely white flowers in early summer and brilliant fall foliage. I began to discover the many diverse micro-habitat gardens here, like the Alpine Garden and the Pond Garden, and to appreciate the mission of the garden in conserving a major plant family and providing a glorious display of rare, uncommon and valuable plants one would not have an opportunity to see elsewhere.

If you would like to expand your knowledge of rhododendrons, I suggest you pick up the printed self-guided seasonal tours that point out significant plants and provide subsidiary cultural information. This is an opportunity to note the striking differences among rhododendrons commonly stereotyped as rather boring green-leafed bushes with a burst of (sometimes outlandishly bright) color in spring. In fact, the rhododendron collection here represents 2,100 forms of the species and can boast a bloom season from January through October.

While much of the garden meanders through a woodland setting, which provides the quintessential growing environment for most wild species, the inclusion of a sunny **Alpine Garden** of gravely soil and boulders simulating Himalayan mountain scree provides a representative habitat favored by high elevation rhododendrons whose growth habit is compact, ground hugging and drought tolerant. Hundreds of species come from the mountainous regions of the world, from the Himalayas of Nepal, to the Swiss Alps, to the Northwest Province of Sichuan in China. More than 200 tons of granite were brought in from the Cascades to create the growing conditions favorable to these plants. Overlooking this garden and providing a marvelous panoramic view is a **Gazebo** built entirely from one cedar log. The **Pond Garden** attracts frogs, salamanders, many species of birds and a variety of woodland creatures and displays a fascinating array of water-loving plants, including hardy carnivorous plants.

Each of the gardens has been richly planted with seasonal showpieces, so that even in winter there are exquisite berries, heathers in bloom, startling silhouettes of deciduous trees and winter blooming species rhododendrons, *Cornus mas*, flowering plums, quince, trilliums, hellebores, cyclamen and species crocus. There is an impressive collection of Japanese maples and species primula. Several horticultural groups have contributed collections to enhance the overall botanical interest of the garden-- Hardy Fern Foundation, NW

Chapter of the American Bamboo Society, Cascade Chapter of the Carnivorous Plant Society and Cascade Heather Society.

❊ Pacific Rim Bonsai Collection

33663 Weyerhaeuser Way. S., Federal Way, WA 98003; (253) 924-5206; Group tour reservations 924-3153. Open March-May, Friday-Wednesday 10 a.m.-4 p.m. (*closed* Thursdays); and June-February, Saturday-Wednesday 11 a.m.-4 p.m. (*closed* Thurs.- Fri.). The exhibit is free. Group Tours are available for groups of 10 or more, free, by appointment, (253) 924-3153.

Insider Tip: Free guided tours are offered Sunday at noon, when reservations are not required. You may request a tour at the Rhododendron Garden Shop adjacent to the Bonsai Collection. Also, there is a complimentary guidebook that will add enormously to your enjoyment of the bonsai gallery.

❖ 🌱 ✳ RR

I love this quip from Weyerhaeuser Company greenhouse/nursery director, Bob Seldon: "It's got to be the first time in history that Weyerhaeuser has bought a runty bunch of trees and hoped they *wouldn't* grow!"

Dare I admit that I was not particularly drawn to bonsai until I spent a most engaging morning viewing this exhibit a few years ago with my husband and his parents? We took advantage of the free guidebook that provides fascinating information on each of the displays and read each and every one as we made our way through the exhibit. I not only began to learn about the art of bonsai, I began to truly appreciate the artist's skill in eliciting an emotional response from the viewer. It became easier to transport myself into the miniaturized world evoking a windswept ocean bluff or a serene forest grove carpeted in velvety green moss. As with the best of Japanese Gardens, the cultural implications of this collection inspire serenity, contemplation and reflection.

From a horticultural perspective, the plants in the **Pacific Rim Bonsai Collection** provide year-round interest, with unlikely subjects bearing tiny, colorful fruit (Golden Bean Kumquat, *Fortunella hindsii*) and Crab Apple, (*Malas sp.*) and striking autumn foliage (*Ginko biloba* and Japanese maples). In winter come to see the bark of Cork Oak (*Quercus suber)* and Paperbark Maple (*Acer griseum*); in spring the delicate bloom of Wisterias, Pear and Flowering Plums; and in summer the flowers of Bougainvilleas and Pomegranate.

LUNCH/alternative 1

I have a couple of suggestions for lunch. There is no sanctioned picnic spot on the Weyerhaeuser Headquarters grounds, so if you are up for a quiet place to sit and enjoy lunch, retrace your route to S. 320th at I-5. Continue west on 320th over I-5 to 23rd Ave. (this is fast food country, for those so inclined). Turn right onto 23rd Ave. S. which jogs to the right and becomes 28th Ave. S. Turn left on S. 312th St. and enter Steel Lake Park. This is a 5 minute drive from the RSBG.

Another idea is to continue on to Edgewood Flower Farm, then follow the driving directions into Puyallup to an excellent little brew pub restaurant – an historically interesting building and good food. See "LUNCH/alternative 2" below

DRIVING DIRECTIONS:

From the RSBG parking lot, turn left and proceed to Weyerhaeuser Way S. Turn right to Weyerhaeuser Way S. Cross over Hwy. 18 and continue south on Weyerhaeuser Way S. The road jogs to the right on S. 349th then left onto 28th Ave. S. After 2 miles it terminates at Hwy. 161/ Enchanted Parkway S. Turn left, heading south. This road becomes Meridian St. E. Watch for Edgewood Flower Farm on the left after about 1.5 miles.

Driving distance: 5 miles; *Estimated driving time:* 15 minutes.

▧ Edgewood Flower Farm

2017 E. Meridian, Edgewood (Puyallup), WA 98371; (253) 927-0817. Open year round, Monday -Saturday 9 a.m.-5:30 p.m., Sunday 10 a.m.-4:30 p.m. (closed Sunday January-Valentine's Day), and apt to vary opening and closing hours seasonally.

❖ ☂ 📖 ☆ ✳ RR

It is not difficult in looking around Edgewood Flower Farm to imagine that it originated as a farm and at a time when farmland surrounded it in all directions. When the O'Ravez family moved to the property in the 1950s there were peach orchards here, which they replaced with a berry farm featuring strawberries and raspberries. Son Bill would join his mother at the stand out front—she sold berries and he sold fuchsia baskets he'd bought from a local grower. As a college student in 1974 he built his first greenhouse and began to grow his own fuchsias. He married Donna and their business expanded to include the holiday poinsettias. In order to keep their valued staff they made the decision to open year-round with a more full-service nursery.

While they still specialize in quality planted hanging baskets, they have made an effort to stay on top of what is happening in the nursery trade. So, for instance, you can expect to find perennials imported from England's Blooms of Bressingham and from this area's best growers. They also pride themselves on their selection of specimen trees and shrubs.

The gift shop has an excellent section dedicated to garden books and offers a particularly tasteful and elegant array of home and garden accessories. Expect to dawdle here as the attention to detail will capture your imagination as it did mine.

DRIVING DIRECTIONS:
Leave Edgewood Flower Farm turning left and traveling south on E. Meridian toward Puyallup. Turn left on Stewart Ave., which becomes Main St. The Powerhouse Restaurant is on the right.
Driving distance: 4 miles; *Estimated driving time:* 10 minutes.

LUNCH / alternative 2
The **Powerhouse Restaurant and Brewery** is located in the Puyallup Substation, constructed for Puget Sound Electric Railway in 1907, to supply current for the southern leg of the Interurban Electric Trolley that ran from Seattle to Olympia. As demand outgrew its capabilities the building was relegated to storage and was vacated by Puget Power in 1969. From a derelict shell it has been restored by Tacoma architect Dusty Trail into the elegant red brick building it had been. They offer generous portions of creative pastas and pizzas, innovative salads and sandwiches and attention-grabbing appetizers such as "Breasts of Fire" (tender pieces of chicken sautéed in a delicious red chili cream sauce).

DRIVING DIRECTIONS:
Turn left, go west on E. Main Ave. which becomes E. Stewart Ave. Turn left onto Meridian St. N. Take the Hwy. 512 West on-ramp traveling west. After 10 miles take the I-5 exit South toward Portland. From I-5 take the Gravelly Lk. Dr. Exit #124. Turn right. Follow signs for Lakewold Gardens, keeping left at the fork in the road. The Gardens entrance is on the right after about 1 mile.
Driving distance: 15.5 miles; *Estimated driving time:* 25 minutes

❀ Lakewold Gardens

12317 Gravelly Lk. Dr. SW, Lakewood, WA 98499; (253) 584-3360 or toll free (888) 858-4106. Friends of Lakewold, P.O. Box 98092, Tacoma, WA 98498. Open April-September, Thursday-Monday 10 a.m.-4 p.m. except Friday, noon-8 p.m. (*closed* Tuesday and Wednesday); October-March, Friday-Sunday 10 a.m.-3 p.m. (*closed* Monday-Thursday). There is an entry fee. www.lakewold.com

Insider Tips: There is an extremely well done video about Lakewold that I urge both first-time visitors and those who have walked the gardens before to see. You will gain a much deeper appreciation not only for the significance of the garden itself, but of the historical context of Northwest estate gardens, the eminent professionals of this area and others who worked over the years with the Wagners and the role being played here today in conserving endangered species from around the world. "Lakewold, Where the Blue Poppy Grows" is available through the Garden Shop at Lakewold, $29.95.

🍂 Saturday is Family Day at Lakewold Gardens—one car, one family, one reduced entry fee. Also, as I went to press, the staff at Lakewold was conjuring some special event(s) for their Friday night late opening. Whether a buffet dinner or a concert in the Garden, they had not quite decided. If your visit is for the end of the week, give them a call in advance to see what has been devised for your entertainment.

❖ ☂ 📖 ☆ ✳ RR

What is known as Lakewold Gardens was originally the summer retreat of Tacoma resident Emma Alexander, who bought this desirable lot on the western shore of Gravelly Lake soon after it was platted in 1912 and built a small cabin. The landscape of towering Douglas firs and Garry oaks, shrubs and ground covers was largely left intact. The adjacent property was purchased and in 1918 the property was transferred to Emma's son H.F. Alexander and his wife Ruth, who built a larger home and began to develop a garden. In 1925 the property was sold to Major Everett Griggs and his wife Grace. They changed the name from "Inglewood" to "Lakewold" (Middle English for "lake woods"). In 1940 the property changed hands again, purchased by Grigg's nephew, Corydon and his wife, Eulalie, Wagner both of whom were dedicated to their new home, the family they raised there and the gardens they worked tirelessly to develop. Over the years the tree canopy gave way to the formal gardens and rolling lawns which provided the palette on which the Wagners devoted their life's love affair with Lakewold. They began to build collections of rhododendrons, Japanese maples, shade plants, roses and rare rock garden and alpine plants. In 1958, the noted landscape architect Thomas Church was engaged to work with the Wagners, a relationship that endured for over 25 years. Many of the formal details of the garden are fine examples of Church's sensitivity to the property, the plant palette and the sensibilities of his clients. The quatrefoil (formal four-lobed) pool was a design solution for a husband who wanted a practical pool in which to swim and a wife who was fearful a traditional approach would spoil the formal garden effects they had worked hard to achieve. This pool was a brilliant compromise that suited them both. Today work is proceeding to develop this area into a formal water garden.

The Georgian-style house is open to the public. The Friends of Lakewold have turned their attention to re-building the library for the use of visitors. The sunroom has become another focus of restoration, with the planting of bird habitat in front of the windows. This lovely space is at its best in winter, when visitors can bask in the warmth of the sun and watch the birds at the window and in the garden beyond.

❋ The Garden Shop at Lakewold Gardens

P.O. Box 98092, Lakewood, WA 98499; (253) 584-3360. Open the same hours as the Gardens.
Insider Tip: This shop is only five minutes off I-5. Even if you don't have time for a walk through the Gardens, you can pop off the freeway and over to the shop for a quick browse.

❖ 🍄 📖 ☆

A most appealing garden shop is located in the Lakewold Gardens' old carriage house (circa 1920). What immediately won my heart was manager Vickie Haushild's talent at tracking down a top notch selection of gardening periodicals. If you are addicted to magazines as I am, you'll be pleased. Her interest in gardening literature certainly doesn't end there, for she has built a meritorious collection of books as well. Beyond this passionate specialty, there is the distinct impression throughout the shop that *a gardener lives here*, with a balance of the best "Tip Bags" (for garden refuse) and Felco pruners side-by-side with Microcrop sea kelp powder (a useful but expensive amendment she re-packages herself into affordable packets). She is well stocked with the Lakewold signature Himalayan Blue Poppy plants (*Mecanopsis sheldonii, M. betonicifolia and M. grandis*) and seeds which she imports from Chilterns in England, and offers uncommon Canadian and local seeds as well. Be sure to peruse the tiny nursery because it is an absolute gold mine of treasures. A couple of local craftsmen supply Vickie with well-built twig and barnwood benches and bird houses and she has a sharp eye for gardening-themed collectibles, good old-fashioned gardening tools and antiques

DRIVING DIRECTIONS, END OF THE TOUR:
From Lakewold return to I-5 by turning left onto Gravelly Lk. Dr. SW. Take the I-5 North ramp and follow to Seattle.
Driving distance: 42 miles; *Estimated driving time:* 60 minutes.

FURTHER RESOURCES

Food

Powerhouse Restaurant and Brewery: 454 East Main St., Puyallup, WA 98371; (253) 845-1370. $$, L,D. Open daily. Eclectic menu, good food, great ambiance. They feature fresh ales and a 20 oz. Imperial pint.

LODGING

Chinaberry Hill: 302 Tacoma Ave. N., Tacoma, WA 98403; $$. (253) 272-1282. This Grand Victorian, circa 1889, on the National Register, is a stunning bed and breakfast offering suites and a two-story carriage house, and a full gourmet breakfast for their Gardener guests to get up and Go. There is the distinction that the grounds are purported to be the earliest example of landscape gardening in the Pacific Northwest, when this concept was scoffed at locally. The location is ideal—near Wright Park, downtown and

Commencement Bay. The gardens at Chinaberry were designed by the same landscape architect, E.O. Schwagerl, who also provided the plan for Wright Park and Point Defiance Park. www.virtualcities.com

Thornewood Castle Bed and Breakfast: (253) 589-9052. $$. This 28,0000 square foot castle located on the shores of American Lake dates from the turn of the century (1908-1911). The cost, in 1911, is said to have been $1,000,000, with much of the exquisite interior woodwork imported from a 15th century mansion in England. While there are 54 rooms all told, four suites have been beautifully decorated for guests. The gardens are undergoing restoration, with a ¼-acre sunken English perennial garden fully returned to its former glory. www.thornewoodcastle.com

Camping: Kopachuck State Park -- a mere 12 miles northwest of Tacoma find a peaceful, wooded, beachfront 103-acre park on Henderson Bay. There are only 4 campsites ($10), open late April-early October, reservations available for a $6 extra fee, (800) 452-5687. (No RV hook-ups).

FOR MORE INFORMATION

Tacoma-Pierce County Visitor and Convention Bureau: 906 Broadway, Tacoma, WA 98401; (253) 627-2836.

Tacoma Bed and Breakfast Association: toll free (888) 593-6098. There are many historic homes that are now bed and breakfast inns.

Western Washington Fair, Puyallup, Spring Fair, mid-April and big Fall event 2nd week in September, (253) 841-5045.

MORE RESOURCES FOR GARDENERS

Daffodil Festival, (253) 627-6176 (a major **Spring Fair** is held concurrently), (253) 841-5045

Jungle Fever Exotics: 5050 N. Pearl St., Tacoma, WA 98407; (253) 759-1669. Profiled in the "Tropicals and Exotics" tour, and worth a detour if you are in the area and even the tiniest bit inclined to hardy plants with bold foliage, exotic flowers, exuberant vines and a nice selection of wonderful, less common Washington natives.

Lakewood Garden and Pet Center: 6306 Mt. Tacoma Dr. SW, Lakewood, WA 98499; (253) 584-7898. Open daily. Tom and Carol Prest specialize in unusual plants along with bamboo, perennials, herbs, vegetables, aquatic plants, and all manner of wild bird and pet supplies. 3 miles from Lakewold.

Metropolitan Park District of Tacoma: 4702 S. 19th St., Tacoma, WA 98405; (253) 305-1000. Request a copy of their brochure profiling the many public parks in Tacoma, including **Wright Park** with its impressive arboretum and Victorian **W.W. Seymour Botanical Conservatory**; delightful **Puget Gardens** tucked just off Ruston Way on Commencement Bay; the **Nature Center at Snake Lake**; and, of course, the extensive 698-acre **Point Defiance Park** with many specialized gardens, five mile drive, and the highly respected Zoo and Aquarium.

VanLierop Bulb Farm: 13407 80th St. East, Puyallup, WA 98372; (253) 848-7272. Open mid-January to mid-June and mid-September to mid-November. This would make a splendid destination if your tour takes you to this area in the spring when their display gardens burst forth with daffodils, tulips, hyacinths, crocus, iris and companion plants. In fall, buy fresh bulbs They have a splendid gift and garden shop.

NURSERY HOPPING LOOP/East

―――――――――――――― Itinerary Highlights ――――――――――――――
country nursery capitalizes on a charming, big gray barn
the romantic whisper of a breeze rustles through bamboo
a botanical garden features a legendary perennial border
plant pilgrims from home and abroad find this nursery Mecca

―――――――――― 🍂 ――――――――――

When I was a child growing up in Montana, my Mother used to plan summer "days of exploration" out into the country. We'd make arrangments to pick up farm-fresh eggs and milk and we'd stop to pick berries for a pie. We'd always pack a delicious picnic lunch and then head for one of the many dusty ghost towns that are tucked back in the sagebrush-covered foothills. I never outgrew the excitement of setting off to explore, the thrill of discovery and the gratification of treasures acquired along the way. Part of the thrill of this nursery hopping journey is leaving behind the hubbub of Seattle, heading east over the Evergreen Floating Bridge, winding along the freeway network past suburban communities and into the country beyond. Arriving at a big gray barn in its rural setting takes me back to those cherished childhood memories.

THE ITINERARY IN BRIEF

❶ Gray Barn Garden Center

An old timer, this nursery had been put out to pasture until new owners took on the task of resurrection, restoration and revitalization. A handsome destination now welcomes Gardeners on the Go. There is a full range of well-selected plants with garden related gifts, gear and supplies on display in the spacious and spiffy Gray Barn.

❷ Bamboo Gardens of Washington

For years bamboosaros-in-the-know have headed to Redmond in search of wondrous and uncommon bamboo and bamboo products. Come also for the inspiration of the bamboo, ornamental grass and water plant display gardens. If you are enamored of the simple elegance of Japanese Garden features you'll find a number of handsome vignettes with granite basins, bamboo water pipes and gracious bamboo fencing.

Lunch A picnic at the park adjacent to Bellevue Botanical Garden (with a stop at near-by Larry's Market for the fixings) or for something special, treat yourself to lunch at an excellent Italian restaurant in Redmond or in the tiny courtyard garden at Bellevue's simply elegant Azaleas Fountain Court.

❸ Bellevue Botanical Garden/NPA Borders

Word about the Northwest Perennial Alliance's extraordinary mixed perennial borders found here has sent botanical shock waves through the national (and even international) horticultural press. It is common to find horticultural luminaries from across the country and abroad marching along in appreciation for the talent and effort that have given birth to this showplace. In all seasons the faithful and the curious troop across to Bellevue to see what is putting on a good show.

❹ Wells Medina Nursery

If Wells Medina were a restaurant you might call it "gourmet". This beloved nursery serves up a distinguished collection of choice trees, shrubs, perennials, vines, ornamental grasses, ground covers, annuals and, in addition, offers a tasty selection of rare Chinese plants they have imported for adventurous gardeners to try here.

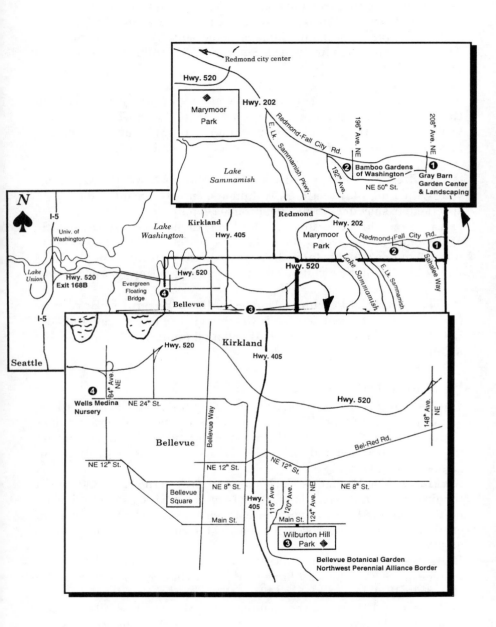

Tour Timing and Tips

◆ All the nursery/garden destinations on this tour are open daily, year round, except **Bamboo Gardens of Washington** which closes on Sunday during Standard Time (as opposed to Daylight Savings Time, when they remain open on Sunday). Also, call first if planning a visit on a holiday.

◆ You will be venturing out through commuter country, especially on the floating bridge crossing to the "Eastside" (of Lake Washington and back to the Seattle side at journey's end.) 770 AM is the radio station I listen to for frequent traffic updates (every 10 minutes).

◆ The **Bellevue Botanical Garden** celebrates Mother's Day each year with a big **plant sale**, refreshments, entertainment and spectacular showing of rhododendrons (1-3 p.m., free). Their extravagant Christmas display, Garden D'Lights, through the month of December, drew over 35,000 admirers in 1997. What makes this a unique and dazzling botanical showcase is the replication of a flowering garden magically done up intricately in tiny colored lights.

◆ The Northwest Perennial Alliance's **Mixed Perennial Border** at the Bellevue Botanical Garden is worth a visit *in any season* and, for the obsessed, *in any weather*. This splendid public garden has many lessons to teach keen gardeners.

Setting the Scene

The **Eastside** is the local lingo for the countryside and communities along the shore of Lake Washington sweeping eastward through the communities of Woodinville, Redmond, Kirkland, and Bellevue and on to Duvall, Carnation and Snoqualmie Falls and to the foothills of the Cascade Mountains.

Kirkland: The Eastside's "early days" go back to the late 1880s when the first community, Kirkland, the site of Peter Kirk's steel mill, was built. Founding father Leigh Smith Jones Hunt lured Kirk away from establishing his enterprise in Tacoma by offering to name the town after him.

Bellevue: The first reported land acquisition was made by Aaron Mercer in 1863 on the west bank of Mercer's Slough. This became the site of the Wilburton Lumber Mill at the turn of the century but the mill closed in 1916 when the opening of the Hiram Chittenden Locks resulted in the lowering of Lake Washington by 9' – rendering the slough unnavigable. There was a strong contingent of Japanese strawberry farmers in this area and the annual three-day Strawberry

Festival drew thousands of visitors from 1925 until 1942, when the farmers of Japanese descent were sent to internment camps. In 1946 Kemper Freeman, Sr. opened Bellevue Square, his innovative idea for the first regional suburban shopping center. That same year a whaling fleet that had made Meydenbauer Bay its winter port moved elsewhere. Until the first of two floating bridges to the Eastside (via Mercer Island) was completed in 1940 there was a fleet of steamers that made daily rounds to residential and community docks to gather commuters and shoppers for the trip across the lake to Seattle.

The Gov. Albert D. Rosellini Evergreen Point Floating Bridge (known to most as the Evergreen Point Bridge) is the world's longest floating bridge at 1.4 miles (floating portion). Dedicated in August of 1963, this bridge was needed to relieve traffic pressure on the **Lacey V. Murrow** (also called the Lake Washington, I-90 or Mercer Island) **Bridge**, completed in July of 1940. The depth and unstable nature of the lake bottom were inappropriate for conventional bridge construction, suggesting the notion of using floating concrete cells. Developed for WWI barges, this technology could bear the demands of heavy vehicles and gale force winds whipping up powerful waves across the lake. Near the center of the Evergreen Point Bridge there is a draw span which allows ship traffic to pass through at a point where the lake is 200' deep.

A thumbnail sketch of the Eastside today: Not long ago this region was largely bucolic, a place one might explore on a Sunday drive. Then the seams burst on Seattle's metropolitan britches and folks spilled out in droves to escape the tight fit of an urban lifestyle in exchange for space to stretch—and, I suspect for many, to garden. Throw into the mix the establishment of Silicon Valley North with Microsoft and friends attracting flocks of bright young techies, and suburban sprawl has begun to make a strong impression on these farmed and forested hills and dales. Yet with lifestyles that value lakeside walks and bicycle paths, equestrian trails and boats with sails, there is much of the original appeal of greenery and open space to commend this side of the pond.

DRIVING DIRECTIONS:
From mid-town Seattle drive north on I-5 to the Hwy. 520 east exit # 168B
for Bellevue/Kirkland. This takes you across Lake Washington on the
Evergreen Floating Bridge. Keep following Hwy. 520 east all the way to
Redmond Way where it terminates. Turn right. The road becomes the
Redmond-Fall City Rd. (Hwy. 202). At Sahalee Way NE there is a traffic
signal. Turn right and into Gray Barn Nursery's parking area.
Driving distance: 15 miles; *Estimated driving time*: 25 minutes.

Gray Barn Garden Center & Landscape Co.

20871 Redmond-Fall City Rd., Redmond, WA 98053; (425) 868-5757. Open
daily spring and summer 8 a.m.- 6 p.m. (open later Thursday and Friday and
as the season dictates), fall 9 a.m.-6 p.m., winter 10 a.m.-6 p.m. (with extended
holiday hours in December).

❖ ♀ 📖 ☆ ✳ RR

The signature gray barn has housed a nursery for several years, but it
was not until 1997 that new owners came along and spiffied up the
facility to its present glory. In a long ago life this barn served the farm
that occupied this site and even today customers tell tales of playing
in the hay loft, now the spic and span and spacious home to a garden
art, home furnishing and gift gallery. You may find botanically-
themed area rugs displayed adjacent to a buttercup yellow Adirondack
chair beneath a fabulous hand-crafted metal arbor. The main floor is
a garden center with tools, seeds, pots, soil amendments, pest controls
and the like.

In the nursery that surrounds the barn you will find the full range of
plants, with a greenhouse up front for annuals and seasonal color
plants. Perennials are displayed under a sheltered roof and there is a
sales yard for trees and shrubs from 1 gallon to landscape-sized
specimens. The staff prides itself on seeking out varieties that are
"hot new picks" – those that have been developed to be disease
resistant or are bred for better or unusual color. If you are looking for
something particularly special there is also a collector's corner of one-
of-a-kind and uncommon plants they have discovered.

Displays are scattered here and there based on such themes as a
Japanese Garden, a waterfall/water garden, a shade garden, a formal
garden and one featuring edibles. Still new in 1997, the plantings will
show greater depth and maturity with time and a continued
commitment to their value as *educational tools*. Stop by to see how
the Wildflower Field is doing. This was planted in March of 1998 by
participants of a workshop on planting wildflower gardens. The
colorful scene will brighten the countryside for passing motorists and
arriving nursery patrons alike. For younger Gardeners on the Go,
bored with nursery hopping, there is a playground.

DRIVING DIRECTIONS:
From Gray Barn Nursery turn left onto Sahalee Way NE, then right on NE 50th and again right on 196th Ave. NE.
Driving distance: 1.75 miles; *Estimated driving time:*: 5 minutes.

▓ Bamboo Gardens of Washington

Location: off 196th Ave. NE, Redmond, WA; (425) 868-5166
Office/Mailing address (adjacent): 5016 192nd Pl. NE, Redmond, WA 98053.
Open during Daylight Savings Time daily 9 a.m.-6 p.m. During Standard Time open Monday through Saturday 9 a.m.-4 p.m. On holidays it is best to call in advance.
Insider's Tip: With a call in advance you can set up a guided walk through the nursery and display gardens. There is a great deal of fascinating information to learn about bamboo from this experience!
❖ ＊ RR

A visit to Bamboo Gardens of Washington will inspire and educate most gardeners. There is a love-hate relationship with bamboo that is only partly deserved. For one thing, there are many different varieties of bamboo, so if you are attracted to using this valuable plant but afraid it will take over your garden, then look for one of the "clumpers" that are much better behaved than the "runners". Containing even the runners is very do-able with forethought of containerization or the installation of bamboo root barrier material, available at the nursery. It is a shame to miss out on the exciting uses to which bamboo can be put in the garden! Not only is it a statuesque and graceful architectural plant, useful in adding structure and verticality, there is the added benefit of its seductive rustling through even a small planting with the slightest breeze. There are many small display gardens here that demonstrate the usefulness of bamboo and the ornamental grasses and wetland plants that are also a specialty. For those in search of ideas for creating an evocative Japanese garden vignette with the use of stone, water and plants, there are a number of elegant examples. You can purchase stone basins, water pipe fountains, bamboo poles and finished bamboo fencing here as well. A number of improvements to the nursery property were made in the winter of 1997-98, so if you have not visited in awhile, you'll find a new entry and many more display gardens.

Lunch: Consider **Il Bacio** on the main street of Redmond or, if it is too early for lunch, then consider holding out for an equally up-scale lunch in Bellevue at **Azaleas Fountain Court** where you'll have the added benefit of a very charming courtyard garden or intimate indoor setting. For Gardeners on the Go intent on spending more time in gardens and nurseries than lingering over a terrine or a cream soup, then I suggest a picnic at the Wilburton Hill Park/Bellevue Botanical

Garden, as **Larry's Market,** an excellent source of gourmet goodies for lunch, is conveniently located en route.

DRIVING DIRECTIONS:
Leave Bamboo Gardens of Washington turning left onto 196th Ave. NE then carefully turning left (west) onto the Redmond-Fall City Rd. (Hwy. 202) which becomes Redmond Way. Turn left at the signs for Hwy. 520 west. Take the 148th Ave. NE exit and turn left onto 148th Ave. NE. Turn right onto the Bel-Red Rd. Turn left onto 124th Ave. NE. Turn right onto Main St. Turn left into Wilburton Hill Park / Bellevue Botanical Garden. *Driving distance*: 10 miles; *Estimated driving time*:: 25 minutes.

Bellevue Botanical Garden and Northwest Perennial Alliance Border

12001 Main St., Bellevue, WA; (425) 868-5166. Open daily, year round, 7:30 until dusk, except for December, when their extravaganza, Garden D' Lights takes advantage of the evening and puts on an enchanting holiday light display. Visitor Center is open 10 a.m.-6 p.m. There is no admission fee. *Insider's Tip: Garden Design* magazine selected BBG as one of the Top 34 Public Gardens in the U.S. You can arrange to have a docent lead your group on a tour, including experiences designed especially for kids. (425) 451-3755.

❖ ⊤ ☐ ☆ ✷ RR

From 1947 until 1984 this site on Bellevue's Wilburton Hill was the home of Harriet and Calhoun Shorts. They not only created a garden, but designed a rhododendron glen within a seven-acre woodland setting, displaying a treasury of native and ornamental trees underplanted with rare shrubs and ground covers. They donated their house, designed by Paul Kirk, a renowned local architect, and seven acres to the community. The Bellevue City Council added 29 acres for the **botanical garden** in 1989 (amid an over-all 103-acre Wilburton Hill Park). The Parks and Community Services Department, along with a dedicated group of volunteers, spent countless hours preparing the garden for its public debut, June 27, 1992.

The **Northwest Perennial Alliance**, a non-profit group of plant enthusiasts, proposed that they design and maintain an ambitious mixed perennial border on the site, which they have accomplished with remarkable skill. A number of beds and borders featuring fuchsias, dahlias and hardy ferns have also been created and are maintained by a number of other non-profit gardening groups.

A monumental undertaking has been the construction of the **Alpine and Rock Garden**, with alpine meadow and alpine bog reserve plants native to the northwest including dwarf forms of conifers and deciduous trees. Growing alongside these natives are their showy relatives, species from around the world and many small and dwarf plants chosen for their form and beauty. 250 tons of rock were imported to the Garden for this project. A **Waterwise Demonstration Garden** features a diverse selection of plants that thrive in the Northwest when water is at a premium (if you happen to be visiting from outside the area I can assure you that it does *not* rain all the time in the Pacific Northwest and drought tolerance can be a real concern here). The **Yao Garden**, representing Phase I of the Eastern Garden, combines traditional and contemporary design concepts using plants native to Asia and the Northwest. Basalt quarried in Oregon and hand-picked by the architect was imported to form the base of the enclosed garden. A major feature is the imposing double gate at the entry, with a stunning copper adornment at the peak. The Shorts were dedicated species and hybrid Rhododendron collectors, so many of the specimens in the woodland are over 40 years old and reach to 20'. Native plants and Groundcovers, their other great loves, are well used and displayed in a special setting.

The Perennial Border (actually more than a single border) is the contribution of the Northwest Perennial Alliance (NPA) and has received a great deal of national and even international acclaim. Integrated beautifully into the BBG as a whole are a number of extraordinary borders created originally by a team of four designers (Glenn Withey, Charles Price, Bob Lilly and Carrie Becker) and a cadre of volunteers under the auspices of the NPA. The scale is enormous, with the central island bed of mixed perennials measuring 300 feet in length and 90' deep. (They also maintain a 6,000 sq. ft. mixed border dedicated to shade conditions and a 4,000 sq. ft. shrub border adjacent.) The praise heaped onto the accomplishments of the NPA reflect deep respect for the brilliant planting combinations that result in a complex orchestration of color, texture, timing and seasonal growth. A strong skeleton of woody plants, roughly the spine of the border, provides year-round structure and the scale of height such a deep border demands (though in actuality it is a bed that spills over a steep hillside). Sophisticated plant combinations marry perennials with thousands of bulbs, ground covers, shrubs and small trees, vines and even some unusual annuals. One of the features of this botanical labyrinth is the variety of perspectives given a visitor to capture essences of these combinations. From the grassy expanse where one first views the main border, it appears to move in a fairly traditional progression from shorter plants in the foreground to taller ones behind. On closer inspection there are paths that beckon the visitor to explore within, at which time it becomes evident that the rather deep bed that greeted our attention so pleasantly was only a small sampling of what lay beyond. At this point the plantings can be examined on an intimate basis, as though the garden had gulped you up and you are moving within, seeing from the inside out. Emerging at the bottom of the slope, you view the garden from below. Plants gracefully arch up and out, raucously scramble down the hillside or form rivulets of massed plantings that form floral and foliar streams of color and texture.

In keeping with the nature of a botanical garden there are many, many plants that have been donated to this border that even the most experienced of horticultural minds will find puzzling. Species not yet in cultivation are likely to coexist alongside time-honored favorites your grandmother grew. But much of what is planted here *is available* from a nursery or seed house, and for some that is the most exciting game of all—to track down the name and source of an uncommon plant that has captured your heart, making the winning of that "prize" all the more valuable. You can begin by checking with the Visitor Center for a list of plants in the NPA border. An on-going program of adding new plants, taking out deceased or unsuccessful plants, or juggling new plant combinations makes keeping a current list difficult, though. Plant tags have been tried and have walked out the gate with someone desperate to remember the name of that particular treasure! An interesting option is to join NPA and volunteer some time to work in the border.

DRIVING DIRECTIONS:
Leaving the Bellevue Botanical Garden turn right onto Main St. Turn left onto 124th Ave. NE. Turn left onto NE 12th St. Turn right onto Bellevue Way NE, then left onto NE 124th St.
Driving distance: 4.5 miles; *Estimated driving time*: 15 minutes

▨ Wells Medina Nursery

8300 NE 24th St., Medina, WA 98039; (425) 454-1853. Open Daylight Savings hours Monday-Saturday 9 a.m.-6 p.m., Sunday 10 a.m.-5 p.m.; winter hours Monday-Saturday 9 a.m.-5 p.m., Sunday 10 a.m.-5 p.m.
❖ ♀ ✳ RR
For over twenty five years Ned Wells and family have consistently presented what is commonly agreed to be the area's premier selection of top notch plants. At the core of this nursery's success is Ned Wells and his relentless dedication to seeking out and providing for his loyal patrons plants he finds that show remarkable qualities yet are not popularly known in the trade. He travels widely in search of quality growers who have recognized the potential of rare species or new varieties from the vast store of plants yet unknown to the gardening public. A man of vision, he has invited the bodacious design team of Glenn Withey and Charles Price to create and maintain a wildly imaginative display border at the nursery (and one that grows on for a period of a few years then receives a major overhaul to remain fresh, as new ideas evolve and exciting plants come to their attention).

At the nursery you will find a focus on plants over products, though they offer a handsome selection of pots, large and small, and some subsidiary plant care supplies. There is a well-stocked reference library where savvy shoppers can double check details about planned purchases to avoid the disappointment of the wrong plant in the wrong place syndrome. The five-acre nursery is packed with the full range of plants from the obvious seasonal stars like *Primula* and *Pelargoniums* to landscape-sized species *Rhododendrons* and exquisitely formed specimen *Styrax obassias*. If this is your first visit then I suspect this will become a familiar destination on future days of exploration and serious plant hunting expeditions.

(Wells Medina Nursery is also on the **Tree and Shrub Enthusiast's** Tour, as woody plants are a long-time spcialty. Read there about their collection of rare Chinese trees offered to adventurous gardeners).

Dʀɪᴠɪɴɢ Dɪʀᴇᴄᴛɪᴏɴs, Eɴᴅ ᴏꜰ ᴛʜᴇ Tᴏᴜʀ:
Go east on NE 24th St. Turn left onto 84th Ave. NE which takes you to Hwy. 520. Take the westbound on-ramp, cross the Evergreen Floating Bridge, follow signs onto I-5 for Seattle City Center.
Driving distance: 7 miles; *Estimated driving time*: 15 minutes.

Fᴜʀᴛʜᴇʀ Rᴇsᴏᴜʀᴄᴇs
Food
Azaleas Fountain Court: 22 103rd Ave. NE, Bellevue, WA 980004; (425) 451-0426. $$$, L Tuesday-Friday, D Monday-Saturday. One of my favorite romantic hang-outs in the Seattle area. Warm ambiance, professional service and an inventive menu (try their exquisite house made raviolis and baked brie in a feather light puff pastry) make this 1920s cottage a memorable destination. A word of warning – you may be inspired to linger!

Il Bacio: 16564 Cleveland St., Redmond, WA 98052; $$, L Monday-Friday, D Monday-Saturday. It is the skill from the kitchen that is the attraction here so don't be put off by the strip mall brick facade. Perfect traditional pastas (tagliolini with artichoke, fresh diced tomato, basil and parmesan), herby lamb and succulent seafood are all highly recommended.

Larry's Market: 699 120th Ave. NE, Bellevue, WA 98055; (425) 435-0600. Open daily, year-round. This up-scale grocery/food emporium has many choices for picnic packers in search of the full array from creative sandwiches to a fabulous deli case filled with imaginative fare. You can also call ahead to have them prepare box lunches. The catering number is (425) 8646.

Lᴏᴅɢɪɴɢ
A Cottage Creek Inn: 12525 Avondale Rd., Redmond, WA 98052; (425) 881-5606. This is a secluded Tudor-style Bed and Breakfast Inn set in park-like grounds surrounded by gardens, a romantic gazebo, woodland walk, koi and goldfish pond and a creek running alongside the front of the property. Reasonable rates. See photos on their site www.brigadoon.com/~cotcreek/

Pacific Guest Suites: 411 108th Ave. NE, Bellevue, WA 98004; (800) 962-6620. This company handles several properties on the Eastside. So if your stay will be 3 days or longer call for information.

For Further Information:

Bellevue Chamber of Commerce: 10500 NE 8th St., Suite 212, Bellevue, WA 98004; (425) 425-454-2464.

Bellevue Historical Society: Winters House, Mercer Slough Nature Park, 1625 118th Ave. SE, Bellevue, WA 98004; (425) 450-1046. The Society office is open Monday- Wednesday 10 a.m.-3 p.m. The Winters House, on the National Historic Register, was built in the 1930's and has historical displays including a notebook on Mr. Winters' prosperous bulb business. The 320-acre wetland park has extensive boardwalk and canoe/kayak trails,

East King County Convention and Visitors Bureau: 520 112th Ave. NE, Bellevue, WA 98004; (425) 455-1926, (800) 252-1926.

More Resources for Gardeners

Request information from these two non-profit organizations about membership opportunities and benefits:

Bellevue Botanical Garden Society: P.O. Box 40536, Bellevue, WA 98015-4536. (425) 451-3755.

Northwest Perennial Alliance: P.O. Box 45574, Seattle, WA 98145-0574.

Three more top quality nurseries (for Gardeners on the Go spending a couple of days in this area):

Hayes Nursery: 12504 Issaquah-Hobart Rd. SE Issaquah, WA 98027; (425) 391-4166. Open April-December 9 a.m.-6 p.m., January-March 9 a.m.-5:30 p.m. Beautiful display garden, very nice, full-service nursery.

Herbfarm: 32804 Issaquah-Fall City Rd., Fall City WA 98024; (800) 866-HERB. Open daily, April-September 9 a.m.-6 p.m. and daily October-March 10 a.m.-5 p.m. Request a copy of their extensive class and workshop catalog.

Squak Mt. Greenhouse: 7600 Renton Issaquah Rd. SE, Issaquah, WA 98027; (425) 643-0601. Beautiful nursery; ask about special events.

Two major garden centers on the Eastside are profiled in the "Glorious Garden Centers" itinerary: **Molbak's** and **Furney's**
.

Smith and Hawken: 12200 Northrup Way, Bellevue, WA 98005; (425) 881-6775. Up-scale home and garden shop offering durable, attractive gardening duds, high quality imported tools, handsome teak garden benches and other essential details for the elegantly accessorized garden.

Specialty Nursery Guide: 1220 NE 90th, Seattle, WA 98115. There are two free guides with excellent profiles and directions to just over one hundred small specialty nurseries in the greater Seattle and Puget Sound area. Send a SASE with two first class stamps.

VASHON ISLAND IDYLL

―――――――――― Itinerary Highlights ――――――――――
welcoming little shop grows a big crop of garden books
creative nursery also features fantastic garden art
old-fashioned mercantile specializes in goods for gardeners

Idyll is such an appropriate word to capture the essence of this rustic Puget Sound spot. To drive the back-roads of the island is to step back in time, as though the razzle-dazzle 80's and 90's made it as far as the mainland ferry dock and never bothered to venture out to Vashon. Here is a haven for artists (including a nationally acclaimed botanical illustrator) and a number of highly respected wholesale nursery growers call the island home. Roadside farmstands laden with fresh produce are a common sight in summer. To me this is a fascinating phenomenon, with Seattle (to the northeast) and Tacoma (to the southeast) – each mere minutes away by ferry.

Vashon offers Northwest Gardeners on the Go diverse enticements well worth this pleasant Puget Sound island excursion.

THE ITINERARY IN BRIEF

❶ Books by the Way

If the vast selection of books one finds available to gardeners is any indication, gardeners are avid readers. So here is an inviting little bookshop that has a particularly nice selection dedicated to our passionate and horticultural hobby.

❷ DIG

This little nursery will charm the socks off creative gardeners, from the moment you turn off the highway and make your way down a 150' display border packed with exuberant color, tantalizing texture, bold foliage and daring plant combinations. As much a gallery of garden art (snazzy trellises and beauteous bird baths) as an emporium of intriguing plants, DIG visitors linger and linger to soak in all that has been skillfully packed into so modest a site. There is genius and humor at work here, so come to enjoy.

❸ Country Store and Gardens

This old-fashioned general store/garden center is quintessential Vashon. Locals come here to stock up on garden supplies and buy their rubber boots; in spring they find vegetable seeds on the shelf and starts in the nursery; and mid-summer they stop here for natural fiber clothing and, of course, perennials, herbs, vines, trees and shrubs, the majority of which are field grown by the Country Store proprietor and long-time Vashon gardener, Vy Biel.

This itinerary features three MUST DO destinations, but there are *many options* that will appeal to resourceful Gardeners on the Go. Peruse "Tour Timing and Tips" and "More Resources for Gardeners" to customize your expedition to Vashon Island based on season, your own proclivities and the ambition level of the moment.

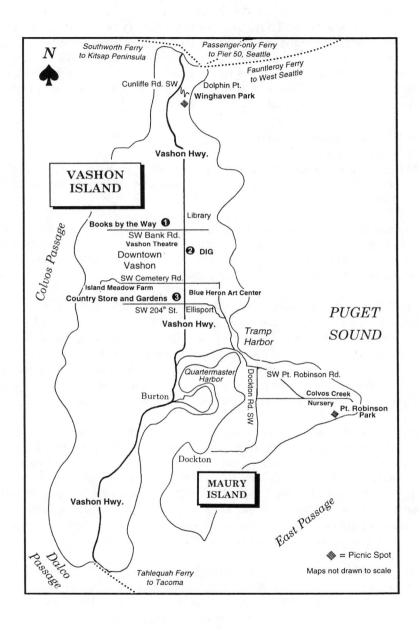

TOUR TIMING AND TIPS

🍎 Vashon Island is synonymous with art and agriculture. A number of activities revolve around the opening of working studios of the Island's many artists. There are likewise country farmstands and the Saturday Market that provide locals and visitors alike with the freshest produce, dairy products, fruit, nuts and cut flowers of the season. Avoid the shoulder-to-shoulder weekend crowds of Pike Place Market and meet these entrepreneurs on their home turf, enjoying a pleasant day or week-end in the country to boot!

🍎 Here are some special annual events around which to plan your Vashon get-away:

Gallery Open Tour: The island is home to a wealth of artists and artisans. This annual tour is scheduled the first two weekends in May and December.

Annual Garden Tour: in 1998 the dates are May 30-31, when five private gardens are open to the public. The event is sponsored by the Blue Heron Art Center. Concurrently, there is a tea at the Center with an art show and live music; (206) 463-5131.

Land Trust Plant Sale: Held annually 9 a.m.-2 p.m. the first Saturday in May in the lot adjacent to the Island Theater on the main route through the center of the island. Organized to help the Island Trust protect sensitive land, the cause draws several top wholesale growers who bring everything from ornamental grasses to heather and heaths, the latest introductions in perennials and unique vegetable starts to fruit trees and hybrid rhododendrons.

Saturday Market: This open-air public market has served residents and visitors since 1965. Set up at Vashon Village (look for the John L. Scott Real Estate office on Vashon Hwy.), vendors are ready to greet you Saturdays, 10 a.m.-3 p.m., May through September. You can expect activity to be seasonally dictated, with an abundance of fresh farm goods at the height of the season. Arts represented include pottery, clothing, jewelry, woodworking, painting, fiber arts, glass and Vashon's own hand-crafted brooms. (206) 463-3010.

Strawberry Festival: This annual, mid-July event draws crowds of locals and off-islanders alike in search of a genuine slice of mid-century Americana. The noontime parade is the highlight, with the likes of the Thriftway grocery cart drill team . Make an early start if you are coming by ferry to avoid the predictable lines of traffic.

SETTING THE SCENE

While given separate names, Vashon and Maury Islands are actually joined by a narrow neck of land (augmented later by a great deal of fill material). Capt. George Vancouver named the larger island for his Naval compatriot James Vashon in 1792. It wasn't until 1841 that smaller Maury Island was named by a member of the Wilkes expedition. Vashon Island was first settled when four families from Tacoma took up homesteads on Quartermaster Harbor in 1877. The Bleeker family arrived in 1880 with machinery in tow to start the first brickyard, of which there were eventually several on Vashon-Maury Island, along with a number of sand and gravel pits that supplied the material for major building projects in Seattle.

Regular steamboat service to Vashon Island commenced in 1885. By 1908 there was daily service, primarily to serve farmers involved in fruit production but also early working commuters. The first auto ferry, the *Vashon Island*, began operation at Portage in 1918. If you have seen or ridden on the *Virginia V* she is the last remaining member of the Mosquito Fleet. She served Puget Sound commuters from 1922 until 1940, replaced by better roads, bridges and the advent of car ferries. Today horses and bicycles remain popular modes of transport on the island and two island beaches provide campsites along the 150-mile Cascadia Marine Trail, the route for human-powered craft stretching from Olympia to the San Juan Islands. While Vashon harvested its timber resources, operating several sawmills, and the harbor attracted major shipbuilding and dry dock businesses, farming remained an enduring occupation until WWII. Even during the Depression the residents of Vashon report having lived a pretty good life by comparison to those living elsewhere in the country. The mainstay crops grown on the Island were currants, strawberries, pears, peaches, apples and gooseberries.

FERRY ACCESS

There are four ways to get to Vashon-Maury Islands using public transportation. Below I have described the most direct route for someone who wants to have a car to drive around the island, leaving from the center of Seattle (via I-5). If you are coming from Tacoma or south, from I-5 take exit 132 going west on Hwy. 16 and follow the signs 8.4 miles to the Point Defiance/Tahlequah Ferry. (This crossing takes 15 minutes). From the Kitsap Peninsula there is a ferry that leaves from Southworth, southeast of Bremerton, taking SE Sedgwick Rd. east from Hwy. 16. (This crossing takes 15 minutes.) There is also a passenger-only ferry that leaves from downtown Seattle, Pier 50. You can take bicycles on board as well. (This crossing takes 25 minutes. There is bus service on Vashon Island, daily except Sunday.)

DRIVING DIRECTIONS:
Drive southbound on I-5 from downtown Seattle, following signs for Tacoma/Portland. Take the West Seattle Freeway exit 163A and follow it west across the Duamish Waterway to West Seattle. Follow signs for the Fauntleroy Ferry to Vashon Island as the West Seattle Freeway turns into Fauntleroy Way SW. It is about 8 miles to the ferry landing and takes about 20 minutes to drive. When you disembark, drive south on Vashon Hwy. SW., a route that takes you down the center of the island, and through the central business district of Vashon (the town). At Vashon (town) turn right on SW Bank Rd. one block.

Driving distance: 13 miles; *Estimated driving time:* 20 minutes to the Fauntleroy ferry from downtown Seattle, 15 minutes' ferry crossing and 15 minutes from the Vashon Island ferry terminal to Books By the Way. (This does not account for the time you will wait in line to catch a ferry.)

Books by the Way

9928 SW Bank Rd., (mailing address P.O. Box 367, Vashon, WA 98070); (206) 463-2696. Open Monday-Saturday 10 a.m.-6 p.m., (open Fridays until 7 p.m.), Sunday 11 a.m.-4 p.m.

Insider Tip: BBTW offers author readings and book signings on Friday evenings. They organize an occasional event around a gardening theme.

❖ 🍸 📖 ☆

Any gardener who loves books will appreciate the wonderful selection in this welcoming little bookshop and, once there, will immediately realize that a gardener must surely be involved in putting the collection together. Owner Susan Montoya does find some time in her busy Books By the Way schedule to relax at her gardening tasks but she readily admits that she is helped enormously in building the gardening book section by a knowledgeable employee who keeps her hand in the horticultural profession in additional to her tasks caring for patrons of the shop. With a well-informed staff member on hand, you should feel free to seek advice on book selection and if you don't see something you've sought, they will special order it for you at no extra cost (other than shipping to you if you are from out of town).

TOUR TIP:
Before leaving this building, look next door at **Frame of Mind** (fine art prints and posters) to see the glorious botanical illustration work depicting Washington State native plants by nationally known Vashon artists Michael Lee (conifers, broadleaf evergreens and herbs) and Jean Emmons (wildflowers).

DRIVING DIRECTIONS:
From Books by the Way, turn right from SW Bank Rd. back onto Vashon Hwy. SW. Turn left at the sign for DIG.
Driving distance: 1 mile; *Estimated driving time:* 2 minutes.

❋ DIG

19028 SW Vashon Hwy., Vashon, WA 98070; (206) 463-5096. Open April-August, Tuesday-Sunday 9 a.m.-6 p.m. (open later in summer)
Insider's Tip: Request to have your name added to the mailing list to receive notice of classes, events and sales.

❖ ⍭ 📖 ☆ ❋ (there is a sweet itty-bitty shop)

This wonderful little nursery is incentive enough for me to make the trip from Bellingham with a carload of enthusiasts. The energized dynamo at the helm, Sylvia Matlock, puts together destination-quality events, sales and classes, not to mention a splendid selection of top-notch plants. She has great connections with local leading edge wholesale growers who provide her with the latest hot plants that are new introductions to Northwest retail nurseries. Her display border houses perennials and annuals that are just being tested for performance characteristics, so you'll get a sneak preview of some snappy newcomers. She has gone in for "trees with attitude" (featuring those with pendulous and contorted forms).

The artist in Ms. Matlock expresses herself in many ways here – through her skillful collection and intermingling of functional and ornamental hand-crafted garden art to the careful thought put into her assembly of handsome planting containers. And she orchestrates some excursion-worthy events and classes. A few examples: evenings in the garden with live jazz or a classical string quartet, a wildly popular bird bath show, a class on creative container gardening, one on gardening to attract butterflies, and a series on bog and native plants that supports the concept of land stewardship.

Lunch: If this is a Saturday or Sunday excursion I would head directly for the historic community of Burton and the **Back Bay Inn** for their scrumptious weekend brunch (currently the only meal they serve, 8:30 a.m.-1 p.m.). **Emily's Café** offers an excellent health-conscious menu and **Sound Food Restaurant and Bakery** is an enduring favorite, especially if you can sit back and relax over lunch (vegetarian selections offered) on "island time". Or try **Mary Martha's** (offering their own strudels and pot pies, freshly made soups, interesting sandwiches like "Kate's Club" which is a BLT plus turkey and avocado on sourdough, and take-out deli fare—be sure to try Grandpa Fred's Macaroons). Otherwise put together a picnic from Thriftway Market (with a well-stocked deli, also). **Wingehaven Park** and **Point Robinson** both offer spectacular views and quiet waterfront locations with beach access. (The former requires more of a walk, including a rigorous return trip uphill to your car. See notes at the end of this chapter about this historic property.)

DRIVING DIRECTIONS:
Country Store and Gardens is located pretty much right in the middle of the island on the main Vashon Hwy. SW at SW 204th St.

 Country Store and Gardens

20211 Vashon Hwy. SW, Vashon, WA 980070; (206) 463-3655. Open Monday-Saturday 9:30 a.m.-5:30 p.m., Sunday noon-5 p.m.

❖ 🌱 📖 ☆ ❋

Vy Biel has been in business selling plants and providing for the general store needs of local residents for 35 years. Her 1910-style building reflects the shop's old-fashioned character. This is a terrific place to shop for hard-wearing work clothes, warm socks and a large selection of rubber footwear. The garden center carries organic fertilizers and pest controls, quality tools, gardening books, seeds and sundry garden supplies. The nursery offers display beds that represent a variety of growing conditions: a dry bed for drought-tolerant plants, a wet bed for plants that thrive with moisture at their "feet," a shady bed for plants that don't require much sun, etc. Vy specializes in unusual perennials (*Euphorbia charocias ssp. wulfenii, Romneya coulteri, Ligularia dentata* 'Othello'), herbs (*Verbascum* olympicum and V. *bombyciferum*), trees (that glorious little Redbud *Cercis canadensis* 'Forest Pansy' and a collection of nice maples) and shrubs (especially hydrangeas like the oak leaf variety H. *quercifolia* and several viburnums).

DRIVING DIRECTIONS, ENd OF THE TOUR
Return to Vashon Hwy. SW and head north to the ferry terminal at Dolphin Point. At the West Seattle terminal, turn left from the docking area and follow signs along Fauntleroy Way SW. for I-5 and Seattle.

FURTHER RESOURCES

Food

Back Bay Inn: 24007 Vashon Hwy. SW, Vashon Island, WA 98070. (206) 463-5355. $$, B weekends. The likes of Challah French Toast, Cheese and Spinach Strada and Dungeness Crab Cakes and Eggs come from a talented kitchen in this Victorian era Inn.
Emily's Café: Vashon Landing Building, 17530 Vashon Hwy. SW, Vashon, WA 98070; (206) 463-6404. $$,B,L until 4 p.m. daily.
Mary Martha's: 17520 Vashon Hwy. SW, Vashon, WA 98070; (206) 463-3702. $$, B,L,D. Really good sandwiches, freshly made soups, a deli counter offering picnic fixings.

LodGING

Vashon Lodging **Reservation Service**: (206) 463-5491.
Artist's Studio Loft: 16529 91st Ave. SW, Vashon Island, WA 98070; (206) 463-2583. $-$$, open year-round. The peaceful setting here is quintessential

farm country Vashon, complete with flower gardens and pond. My favorite of the three accommodation options is the Aerial Suite in the Carriage House. There is a fireplace, stained glass windows, unique artsy decor and a kitchenette.

Betty MacDonald Farm Guest Cottage: 12000 99th Ave. SW, Vashon Island, WA 98070; (206) 567-4227. $$. Judith Lawrence is a gracious hostess who welcomes you to the former Vashon home of Betty MacDonald, the famous creator of *The Egg and I* (Ma and Pa Kettle), the Mrs. Piggle Wiggle Books and the story of her life on Vashon Island, *Onions in the Stew*. The rustic, fun accommodation for two is located in the spacious loft of an old barn, and provides a retreat for an adventurous Gardener on the Go. There is a fully stocked kitchen, small library, wood stove and a deck to take in the stunning Mt. Rainier/water view. There are gardens and a greenhouse to visit, six wooded acres to explore and beach access.

Harbor Inn Bed and Breakfast: 9118 SW Harbor Dr., (mailing address P.O. Box 741, Vashon Island, WA 98070; (206) 463-6794. $$-$$$. Gracious hostess Kathy Casper warmly welcomes guests to her elegant English Tudor-style home, which sits on a bluff overlooking Quartermaster Harbor in a quiet neighborhood not far from Burton Acres Park.

Tramp Harbor Inn: 8518 SW Ellisport Rd. (mailing address and telephone same as Harbor Inn). $$. This lovely house would make a great nest for friends and relations on a special island get-away. The house, handsomely constructed with turn-of-the-century craftsmanship, has been restored with great historical sensitivity and sits among rolling lawns and a trout-stocked pond looking over a quiet harbor on the eastern shore of the island. The house is rented to a single party at a time, and features three bedrooms, a cheery stone fireplace, a Steinway grand piano, elegant antique furnishings and a kitchen outfitted for your use.

FURTHER INFORMATION

Vashon Metro Bus Service: (800) 542-7876. Frequent buses serve most of the main island highway to and from Seattle and Tacoma. Call for schedules. No service on Sundays.

Vashon-Maury Island Chamber of Commerce: P.O. Box 1035, Vashon Island, WA 98070; street address, 17633 Vashon Hwy. SW; (206) 463-6217. Open Monday-Wednesday 10 a.m.-4 p.m., Friday noon-4 p.m. www.vashonisland.com/chamber

Vashon-Maury Island Parks and Recreation District: (206) 463-9602

MORE RESOURCES FOR GARDENERS

The Bookmonger: 17600 Vashon Hwy. SW, Vashon, WA 98070; (206) 463) 5896. Open daily. This cozy used book shop has a small but worthy selection of gardening books and a revolving cat-door (Vashon Island Pet Protectors adoption service—come for a used book, leave with a used cat). If you are yearning to find a long out-of-print book, they offer a free computer search service.

Colvos Creek Nursery: Pt. Robinson Rd. at SW 240th on Maury Island (mailing address: P.O. Box 1512, Vashon Island, WA 98070); (206) 749-9508. Michael Lee has nurtured a tree and shrub connoisseur's nursery, offering a vast list of rare and uncommon woody plants (and a smaller range of perennials). He is well-respected nationally as a mail-order source, with an emphasis on natives and drought-hardy plants. As the bulk of his business is geared to mail-order sales, and with an active landscape architectural practice to manage, the nursery is open by appointment and on Saturdays. Likewise, plant size is generally small, appropriate to shipping requirements. But for discerning gardeners who are on the prowl for the exceptional and noteworthy to add depth and interest to their garden landscape, this would be a "must" for the Vashon excursion. I suggest requesting a copy of the plant catalog in advance in order to prepare a list of what you are interested in pursuing. The selection at the nursery is actually best in fall and there is generally a very good sale at the end of the season.

Insider Tip: If you have a group of committed aficionados, Mike maintains a splendid display arboretum/garden on the opposite side of the island. He is willing to take appointments to visit the site for a guided tour, but in view of his busy schedule such requests are primarily appropriate for serious students of woody plants rather than the random browser.

Island Meadow Farm: 10301 SW Cemetery Rd., (mailing address: P.O. Box 2542, Vashon Island, WA 98070); (206) 463-9065. Open year-round, with the best selection depending on harvest availability by season. A stop at this self-serve farm stand will yield what many enthusiastic regulars describe as a cornucopia of creative organic salad greens—a melange of interesting colors, textural variety and subtle flavors. Throughout the year the stand offers fresh eggs and nuts, and in the peak of the season the farm produces an extensive array of produce, herbs and fruit ranging from shallots to sweet corn, tomatillos to tarragon and raspberries to rosemary. Bob and Bonnie Gregson "retired" to restore a run-down farm on Vashon in 1988. Since then, their business has gained wide-spread recognition through the book they wrote on their experience (*Rebirth of the Small Family Farm, A Handbook for Starting a Successful Organic Farm Based on the Community Agriculture Concept*, $9.95, WA res. add $.70 tax). For those who have an interest in this farming/marketing alternative as a career, Bob and Bonnie offer classes and tours of their operation. For more information call or write them. Theirs is an impressively productive, well-managed two-acre farm.

Landmark Tree Self-Guide Tour: This brochure profiles 60 island trees that are in the Vashon-Maury Landmark Tree Program, established in 1989 by the local chapter of the Audubon Society. Those listed are recognized for their special horticultural qualities, historical importance, whimsical value or purely as a nod to their unique size. **Road Trees List**: This brochure profiles 110 trees of merit to be found along Vashon Hwy. SW from the north end ferry terminal to Burton (since it was published a few of the trees have been cut down). An address is given for each tree, its botanical name is provided and its virtues or distinguishing characteristics are elaborated upon. Request these two free publications from the Vashon Public Library, (206) 463-2069.

Horticultural Archeology: Brief Snapshots of Three Gardens/Nurseries from Vashon's Past

Peter Erickson's Olympic Berry: As a boy, Peter Ericson immigrated with his family from Sweden in 1867. After settling in Nebraska where he became an eminent horticulturist, he moved to Vashon in 1907. There he developed an interesting cross of Luther Burbank's loganberry (used with his permission) and a tiny wild blackberry to produce the Olympic Berry. A story on the berry in "The Past Remembered" (a Vashon-Maury Island Student-Community Project from 1978) states: "The Bon Marche featured the berry in one of the large display windows. Seattle General Hospital said it was the only berry they could serve to their diabetics with no ill effects. Cecil Solly, Northwest garden expert, kept a box of Olympics on his desk for a week, and said the berries were just as good as the first day—no bleeding. Finally Frederick and Nelson department store made the best offer and the berries were contracted out to them almost entirely. Their tea room became known for its Olympic berry pies, Olympic Frango jellies and other delicacies." Business was booming when tragedy struck and son-in-law Hallack Greider, family stalwart behind the enterprise, died of a heart attack. The family could not keep up the demanding work and closed the operation. Progeny of the original canes survive on the island.

The L.C. Beall Orchid Greenhouses: Another remarkable horticultural venture were the Beall orchid greenhouses. Built in 1890, two glass houses provided a protected environment in which to grow salad greens and vegetables for markets in Alaska. In 1912 Hilen Harrington sold his operation to L.C. Beall, who moved production into orchids and roses. His orchids won many coveted awards from the American Orchid Society and over the decades the Beall fame spread. The business was split between Bogota, Columbia and Vashon Island. At their apex of success they sent out as many as ten thousand catalogs in a month and sold orchids to collectors all around the world, including South Africa, Viet Nam and in countries behind the iron curtain. The work day for packers and graders started at 3:30 a.m. in summer, timed to beat sun rise. They hunted orchids in the jungles of South America and their own greenhouses were used as a safe haven for British rarities during WWII. All the while they also grew roses and shipped cut flowers throughout the country. Five generations of Bealls were involved in the company. Ultimately, however, the Vashon greenhouses were not cost effective, with the high energy bills and greater competition. They are now derelict, weeds growing where once awe-inspiring rarities covered 10 acres under glass.

Wingehaven Park/ The Twickenham Estate and Mr. Moy's Tropical Fish Farm: If you harbor a spirit of adventure, I can recommend a bit of horticultural archeology, perhaps in conjunction with a beachside picnic lunch. About ¾ of a mile south of the Fauntleroy ferry dock, east off Vashon Hwy. on Cunliffe Rd. and on a lovely sandy beach, is Wingehaven Park. I read an account that indicated an estate with lavish gardens had existed here from the before the 1920s. I immediately called Vashon gardening friends, some of whom grew up on the island—they had never heard of it! This is the story I have unearthed with a bit of sleuthing: Twickenham was the name given to his estate by Capt. Cowley, for his English home. He bought the property on the eastern shore of Vashon Island, just south of Dolphin Point sometime after 1907 and proceeded to install a 200' seawall promenade, capped with an ornately detailed concrete balustrade (part of which still exists but in a state of deterioration). Capt. Cowley planted an elaborate garden likened to the extravagant Italian gardens at Tivoli. There were greenhouses, a vineyard, iris and lily pad-planted ponds, carefully manicured grounds including a rock garden, fanciful fountains, statuary, topiary and many specimen trees, shrubs and flower borders. The adjacent property was marketed as a development for summer bungalows (an enterprise that never materialized beyond the promotional brochures). Ernie J. Moy inherited and added to this botanical tapestry, installing many more concrete ponds with stone crocodiles and swans spouting water. He raised exotic fish he then sold all over the world. The Winges bought the property in the 1950s and commuted to the estate from Seattle as a summer/week-end escape. However, in 1969 the property (by then renamed "Wingehaven") was traded to the King County Parks Department. They installed a caretaker but ultimately decided to raze the house rather than try to keep up with expensive maintenance. Ultimately the property was purchased by the Vashon Island Parks Department who today maintain the lawn and are working to preserve the eroding bulkhead. There are mere remnants of the former gardens and estate left today as a landslide has buried most of the original landscaping and ponds. There is limited parking at the top of a steep roadway/trail, open to foot traffic only down to the park where you will find a porta-potty and picnic table. Very few people know this intriguing place exists, even the locals! (And now, a bunch of adventurous Gardeners on the Go!) Directions: from Vashon Highway turn east onto Cunliffe Rd. SW, 1 mile south of the ferry terminal or 4 miles north of Vashon town. Please respect private driveways, access and property of neighboring landowners.

BOTANICAL
BAINBRIDGE
ISLAND

Itinerary Highlights

an historic nursery with a poignant past
cozy shop specializes in rare and out-of-print garden books
water garden gallery features reflections of the spirit
60-acre estate melds native plants with European and
Japanese influences
a quintessential "horse and horticulture" country nursery

This lovely pastoral and forested island has that "so near and yet so far" aura for visitors who disembark from their refreshing ferry ride across Puget Sound, leaving behind the buzz of the busy city in favor of the buzz of bees busy in the island's many diverse gardens. A walk down main street Winslow reinforces a first impression of its gentrified but genuine village atmosphere. A drive through the meandering back roads yields a rich cache of commercial and private gardening activity – with opportunities to view some of this region's most exciting botanical wizardry.

🌿 **THE ITINERARY IN BRIEF** 🌿

❶ Bainbridge Gardens Nursery

Junkoh Harui follows in his father's footsteps to revive and restore this beautiful, well-stocked nursery, a peaceful destination to buy plants and horticultural supplies and linger over a latte or lunch in a garden courtyard.

❷ Fortner Books

This is the consummate book shop, so inviting you fantasize it is the library of a cozy country inn—and you are snowed in for a week! A terrier curled up on his favorite chair, the twitter of finches, classical music drifting through the room, warm wood book cases ... plus the best new gardening books and quality botanical literature of the past – ambrosia!

Lunch Mingle with locals at Café Nola, a much loved local bistro, savor good food overlooking the tranquil boat harbor or spread out a picnic feast.

❸ Little and Lewis Water Gardens

This dynamic duo, an archeologist and a sculptor, have joined forces to create a substantial collection of cast stone work that has put them on the cover of national magazines and featured their work in the latest color "coffee table" books. Set in a lush garden they have lovingly created, their pieces elicit responses of awe, delight, respect and amusement.

❹ Bloedel Reserve

A spirit of serenity envelops visitors to this 150-acre estate set in a varied landscape of second-growth hardwood and conifers, meadow and wetland, glens and gullies. There is subtle artistic expression throughout this sophisticated garden with the ultimate nod of respect paid to Mother Nature's own contributions.

❺ Bay Hay and Feed

Part of the fun of dropping in on this neighborhood enterprise is the feeling of stepping into the shoes of a local, stocking up on wild bird seed and puppy chow, hay for the horse and grain for the geese. There is a friendly, welcoming atmosphere, and on top of that for an adventurous gardener, there is a terrific little nursery that carries not only old favorites but a good selection of exciting uncommon plants.

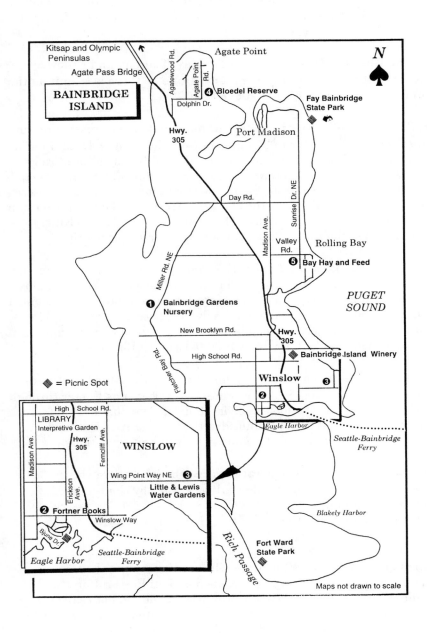

Tour Timing and Tips

🌿 This is a fairly ambitious itinerary, so I encourage you to consider making this a two-day excursion as the treat you undoubtedly need and deserve.

🌿 The **Bloedel Reserve**, closed Monday, Tuesday and Federal Holidays also, note, **requires reservations** as there is a limit on the number of visitors in a day; (206) 842-7631.

🌿 The **Seattle/Bainbridge Island** ferry makes the crossing of nine miles across Elliott Bay in 35 minutes from the Colman Dock, Pier 52, near Pioneer Square in downtown Seattle and lands on Bainbridge Island at Winslow. This route is also a major gateway to the Kitsap and Olympic Peninsulas for Seattleites and tourists anxious to leave the city behind and head to the country. Traffic can be a nightmare in summer, especially week-ends. The island connects to the Kitsap Peninsula via the Agate Pass bridge at the northwestern tip.

🌿 The annual **Bainbridge in Bloom** tour of private gardens in July includes subsidiary activities set in the various gardens: a speakers' series, plant and garden book sales, garden art exhibit and sales and a delectable luncheon is available. Early bird specials are available until May 15 (pay $18, instead of $20). This tour is very popular and tickets usually sell out. (206) 361-3890, tickets. Plan ahead.

🌿 A long history of agricultural enterprise on the island continues today. The Bainbridge Island **Farmer's Market** runs Easter through October, Saturdays 9 a.m.-1 p.m. on Madison Ave. just north of Winslow Way, next to the Bainbridge Performing Arts Cultural Center; call the Chamber of Commerce if you have questions.

🌿 The Island's largest celebration, the 4th of July Strawberry Festival, has been sponsored for half a century by the Filipino-American Community. Check with the Chamber of Commerce (telephone number at the end of this chapter) for details.

Setting the Scene

Bainbridge Island: While Capt. George Vancouver, the famous Pacific explorer and cartographer, anchored off Restoration Pt. at Bainbridge Island's southeastern tip in 1792, he did not realize this was an island. The Hudson Bay Company located Agate Pass at the northwestern tip in 1824 and visited what was to become Port Madison near-by, but it wasn't until 1841 that the American Wilkes

Expedition surveyors charted the island and named it for War of 1812 Naval hero, Commodore William Bainbridge. Thereafter, the first boat was loaded with lumber from the Port Blakely Mill, which was soon to become the world's largest sawmill, employing over 1,000 workers by 1888. Shipbuilding also developed as a major industry of national renown, and in 1871, at Port Madison, 3,000 people witnessed the launching of the clipper *Wildwood*, the largest ship to have been built on the West Coast. Throughout Puget Sound "paired" military forts were built on opposite shores to protect the region from invasion and on the southwestern shore of Bainbridge Island, Fort Ward was built in 1891, directly across Rich Passage from Fort Manchester (both are now State Parks). Although the fort was decommissioned in 1925, a mine field was maintained near there during WWII and underwater nets were strung across the waterway to snare enemy submarines threatening the Bremerton Naval Shipyard. In the early 1920s strawberries developed as a major commercial crop, drawing a large population of Japanese farmers to the island, and a cannery was built in Winslow in 1923. In 1950 the bridge at Agate Pass was opened, connecting the Island to the rest of Kitsap County and in that same year, ground was broken for the Seattle-Bainbridge Island ferry terminal at Winslow. The private "Mosquito Fleet" of Puget Sound ferries had neighborhood dock service all around the island. A car ferry had run from Seattle to Port Blakely from 1923-1937 (when it was moved to Eagle Harbor) and one from Pt. White to Bremerton transported vehicles from 1940-1950.

While joined politically to Kitsap County, Bainbridge Island is economically tied to Seattle. Forty percent of the Island's population commute to Seattle, with an additional 7% commuting off-island elsewhere. Those who remain are involved in home-based businesses, are active in the arts community, local government, the service industry and private enterprise. Two percent make their living farming, fishing or in forestry.

Winslow: Of the island's 18,500 inhabitants, the majority live in and around Winslow, the largest community on the island and the heart of commercial activity. There is a picturesque marina offering guest moorage and an appealing waterfront park overlooks the harbor. Originally called Madrone, the name Winslow became official in 1903. While a busy commercial harbor and growing community, Winslow did not incorporate until 1947. The 1950 Winslow ferry terminal was replaced in 1973 by the existing terminal. Small shopping enclaves are also found at **Lynnwood Center**, **Rolling Bay** and **Island Center**.

DRIVING DIRECTIONS:
This trip begins at Pier 52 on the Seattle waterfront where the ferry departs. From I-5 from the north take the 4th Ave. S. exit 164 and coming from the south take exit 164b. At 4th Ave. S. turn right (west), and then left onto Royal Brougham, move to the center lane, following signs to the ferry terminal. This route will take you along the elevated Alaskan Way Viaduct. The Ferry Terminal is located at Pier 52 (well marked.) (See the notes on "Taking the Ferry" in the Introduction for tips.) The crossing takes 35 minutes. From the ferry terminal at Winslow drive 1 mile north on Hwy. 305 to NE High School Rd. Turn left (west) and drive 2 miles to Fletcher Bay Rd. NE. Turn right. Fletcher Bay Rd. becomes Miller Rd. The nursery is .6 miles on the left.
Driving distance (from the ferry terminal): 4 miles; *Estimated driving time:* 10 minutes

⬡ Bainbridge Gardens Nursery

9415 Miller Rd. NE, Bainbridge Island, WA 98110; (206) 842-5888. Open Monday-Saturday 9 a.m.-5:30 p.m., Sunday 10 a.m.-4 p.m.
Insider's Tip: Owner and long-time Island gardener/nurseryman Junkoh Harui often teaches an informative class called "Gardening For Northwest Newcomers." Ask to be on their newsletter mailing list for event announcements, class schedules and nursery news.
❖ ☂ 📖 ☆ ✳ RR

In March of 1942, 278 Bainbridge Island residents of Japanese ancestry (49 families) were sent away to internment camps. Rather than face internment, the Zenhichi Harui family moved to Moses Lake, east of the Cascade Mountains. They had lived, gardened and worked on Bainbridge Island since their move from Japan in 1906. When they returned after the war, their property which had been described as "a miniature Butchart Gardens," was overgrown, they felt, beyond restoration. It was not until 1990 that one of Zenhichi's sons, Harui, and his wife, Chris, were able to embark on a life-long dream of reclaiming the property, gardens and nursery lost by his parents during World War II. The younger Haruis had begun a nursery of their own on the island in 1948, so were very experienced in the business. Their efforts on the original site resulted in the miraculous reclamation of a number of treasured plants from that earlier pre-war era, including Japanese Red Pines grown from seed brought from Japan. At the nursery, visit the Harui Memorial Garden to see an ancient pear Zenhichi Harui grafted and then pruned into an exquisite shape. Here you will also find several of his bonsai pines and an old wisteria that trails over a bamboo trellis.

One of the pleasures of visiting this nursery is the feeling that you are invited to relax, lingering awhile on one of the garden benches in a quiet rural, wooded setting or in the courtyard of the **New Rose Café** over a bowl of excellent soup or a wood-fired oven pizza. The nursery features such a large and varied selection of all kinds of quality plants, pots, statuary and tools, that it is easy to while away an enjoyable hour or two deciding what will make its way home with you. Discerning gardeners with a need for "instant gratification" will find many specimen-sized trees and shrubs. There is a large garden shop with botanically-themed gifts, garden books and the full range of horticultural supplies.

DRIVING DIRECTIONS:

From Bainbridge Gardens Nursery turn right on Miller Rd. and retrace your steps to Winslow turning left onto NE High School Rd. Turn right onto Madison Ave. (At this intersection you will pass the beautiful, newly remodeled and expanded library. A quick stop here will introduce you to the Japanese Interpretive Garden near the front entry—see "Resources" at the end of the chapter). Turn left onto Winslow Way E. and park (generally two hour parking, strictly enforced).
Driving distance:: 4 miles; *Estimated driving time:* 10 minutes.

🔲 Fortner Books

210 Winslow Way, Bainbridge Island, WA 98110; (206) 842-6577. Open Monday-Saturday, 10 a.m.-6 p.m., Sunday noon-5 p.m.
❖ ☂ 📖

For me it was love at first sight, and when on Bainbridge Island I still always find an excuse to make a beeline for Fortner Books. Would that all book lovers everywhere were blessed with such an inviting literary haven! It was here that I found my first *first edition* of a Beverley Nichols classic I'd searched high and low to get my mitts on! For it is the out-of-print rarities that move this shop from the category of a "delightful find" to "treasured resource." And for those not on the prowl for golden oldies, there is a wide but carefully selected collection (thanks to gardener-proprietress Nancy Fortner) of new gardening books, from the best "how-to's" to the most thoughtful of botanical essayists. If you happen to have a nautical spouse in tow, as I often do, that book lover will be pleased, as well. For book lovers, in general, a tour of all the inviting nooks is in order as there is a full complement of titles in all major categories represented.

Lunch: **Café Nola** is a European café (which means they take their pastries seriously, their extraordinary coffee is served in bowls as in France and the menu, though small, is innovative). **Sawatdy Thai Cuisine** attracts aficionados and culinary rave reviews from around the Sound. This is distinguished Thai cuisine. As an alternative, a walk to the boat harbor takes you to **Harbor Public House**, a Northwest brew pub with a welcoming fire in cool weather, a sunny deck with a view on a bright day—and great food. Or consider a picnic from the creative up-scale **Town and Country Market** deli, with the likes of crab cakes with red pepper aioli and tortellini. Picnic at tables provided on the lower level, in the park along the waterfront across from Eagle Harbor or (Wednesday-Sunday) try the picnic site at the Bainbridge Island Winery, .25 mile north of the ferry on Hwy. 305.

Driving Directions:
Leaving Winslow drive east on Winslow Way E. past Hwy. 305 to Ferncliff Ave. E. (.3 mile). Turn left onto Ferncliff then right onto Wing Point Way NE. *Driving distance*: 1.3 miles; *Estimated driving time:* 5 minutes.

❇ Little and Lewis Water Gardens

1940 Wing Point Way NE, Bainbridge Island, WA 98110; (206) 842-8327. Open <u>by appointment only</u>.
❖ ☂ (there is shelter from a shower in a glorious conservatory)
It is appropriate to find watermeisters George Little and David Lewis hidden unassumingly on a back road of an island. These aqueous Pied Pipers play their alluring tune of gently falling water and soon you fall under its magical spell. Throughout this small but lush garden gallery you feel the collaborative creations of an archeologist and an artist, most predominantly their signature columns, Tuscan, Doric or Egyptian, water oozing ever so gently from the cap, drip, drip, dripping to the little pool beneath. The elements of cast stone and water are set in the context of the garden, where unusual varieties of perennials and hardy tropicals vie for one's attention with the aquatic plants ensconced in garden vignettes—some as water gardens per se, some as focal pieces of garden art or "planted" among ornamental grasses or billowing perennials. The pieces range from mirror perfect reflecting basins to the fantastical cast leaves of the giant Gunnera. The *piece de resistance,* however, is the handsome conservatory dominated by a large pool and home to a multitude of exotic fish and water plants. If your timing is right, the lotus and several delicate water lilies may be in bloom. Tropical plants and orchids ring the pool, rising to a great height all around. Sit awhile and meditate, perhaps dreaming of a refuge from a less romantic world beyond.

Driving Directions:
Leaving Little and Lewis, drive west on Wing Point Way (the direction you came from). Turn right on Ferncliff Ave. NE then left onto High School Rd. Turn right onto Hwy. 305 and drive for 5.2 miles. Turn right onto Agatewood Rd. NE then right onto NE Dolfin Dr.
Driving distance: 7.3 miles; *Estimated driving time:* 15 minutes

✠ Bloedel Reserve

7571 NE Dolphin Dr., Bainbridge Island, WA 98110-1097; (206) 842-7631
voice in TTY. Open Wednesday-Sunday, 10 a.m.-4 p.m. except Federal
Holidays, by appointment only. No picnicking or pets allowed.
Insider Tip: The Reserve is now in the hands of the **Arbor Fund**, a non-
profit operating Foundation created by the Bloedels. Become a member ($35/
year) and you will receive an annual pass with unlimited visits admitting you
and up to three guests, as well as a newsletter and announcements of their
special events. As I write, general admission is $6, $4/seniors and children 5-
12. Children under 5 are admitted free.
Docent-led tours can be arranged with notice. There is a fascinating, well
illustrated book chronicling the history and development of the property by
Lawrence Kreisman called *The Bloedel Reserve, Gardens in the Forest.*

❖ ⚘ ✳ RR

From the time Prentice and Virginia Bloedel acquired this 150-acre
property and its impressive French Renaissance estate home in 1951,
they began implementing a design philosophy that marries the
designing hand of man with the natural attributes of the woodland
setting. Though noted for his leading role in the timber industry,
Prentice Bloedel was an ardent conservationist as well. Over a period
of 30 years, and with the commissioned partnerships of wisely selected
professionals—respected Seattle landscape designer Fujitaro Kubota,
for help with the Japanese Garden; and landscape architects Thomas
Church, Richard Haag and the Environmental Planning and Design
Group. He orchestrated the development of many garden rooms set in
the varied landscape of second-growth hardwood and conifers,
meadow and wetlands, glens and gullies. While incorporating the
traditions of Japanese and European garden design, a respect for the
natural attributes of the land pervaded. There are now about 84 acres
of second growth forest and 66 acres of altered landscapes: a native
woodland crisscrossed with shady paths, meadows and a broad
selection of formal and informal gardens. In the **Bird Refuge**, the
water and plantings both attract and display a wide range of birds:
red winged blackbirds, ducks, geese and **swans** are among the many
who find food, shelter and safety among the cattails, dogwood, spirea
and moosewood viburnum. In late spring and early summer vast
numbers of rhododendrons cast great drifts of color through the
understory of the forest. As they fade, the floral display is taken up by
thousands of wildflowers, perennials and bulbs, and most notably,
more than 15,000 cyclamen plants carpet the forest floor, one of the
largest plantings in the world. A unique and lush woodland **Moss
Garden** opens onto the **Reflection Pool**, a startling juxtaposition of
the soft, wild and almost brooding elements of the former with the
strict formality and reverent aura of the latter. Rosemary Verey
writes admiringly of her winter's day visit here accompanied by area

nurseryman, writer and teacher Dan Hinkley in the introduction to his book *Winter Ornamentals*. A visit in any season is rewarding, both botanically and spiritually.

DRIVING DIRECTIONS:
From the Bloedel Reserve go west on Dolphin Dr. Turn left onto Agatewood Rd. NE then left onto Hwy. 305, traveling south. Turn left onto Day Rd. East. Turn right onto Sunrise Dr. NE.
Driving distance: 6 miles; *Estimated driving time:* 15 minutes.

�֎ Bay Hay and Feed

10355 Sunrise Dr., Bainbridge Island, WA 98110; (206) 842-5274. Open Monday-Friday 9 a.m.-5:30 p.m., Saturday 9 a.m.-5 p.m., Sunday 10:30 a.m.-4 p.m. (winter hours vary).
❖ ☂ 📖 ☆ RR

Local farmers had long relied on Bay Hay and Feed to meet their feed store needs when Howard Block and his wife Ce-Ann Parker came along about 20 years ago and fell in love with this charming building in her favorite island neighborhood of Rolling Bay. Fortunately it was for sale, but with the proviso that the feed store was an integral part of the deal. They bought the operation lock, stock and barrel. Ce-Ann, with a horticultural degree in hand, developed a hankering to see the store expand into the nursery business and with recent experience as proprietors of a natural food store in New Hampshire, it is not surprising that organic pest controls and fertilizers have been offered from the beginning. Several of my personal botanical buttons are pushed at Bay Hay, including a special love of vines and unusual perennials, a sterling selection of attractive large pots (great candidates for water features) and, must I admit it yet again—an uncontrollable addiction to wonderful cards with an entire room devoted to my great weakness. If you happened to be on their Christmas mailing list you received a clever and lyrical message reminding you of their stock of "Meters for moisture, and gauges for rain, barometers to warn of the odd hurricane"; "Weeders and spreaders, and sprinklers and snippers, trowels and shovels, loppers and clippers."

DRIVING DIRECTIONS, END OF THE TOUR
From Bay Hay and Feed go west on Valley Rd. Turn left onto Madison Ave. NE. Turn left onto Hwy. 305 going south 2.2 miles to the ferry terminal at Winslow.
Driving distance: 3.5 miles; *Estimated driving time:* 10 minutes.

FURTHER RESOURCES

Food

Bainbridge Island Vineyards and Winery offers a place to picnic.
Café Nola: 101 Winslow Way East, Bainbridge Island, WA 98110; (206) 842-3822. $$, B,L Tuesday-Sunday. Fresh baked pastries, innovative menu, European bistro atmosphere, a few outside seats in good weather.
Harbor Public House: 231 Parfitt Way SW, Winslow, WA 98110; (206) 842-0969; $$, L,D daily. Daily specials join creative sandwich and burger combinations, excellent Brew Pub selection, snug setting with view of the pleasure boat harbor.
New Rose Café: Bainbridge Gardens Nursery, 9415 Miller Rd. NE, Bainbridge Island. $, B,L daily. This on-site café offers excellent espresso drinks, pastries, fresh sandwiches, hearty soups, wood-fired pizza and rustic breads.
Sawatdy Thai Cuisine: 8770 Fletcher Bay Rd., Banbridge Island, WA 98110; (206) 780-2429. $$, L Tuesday-Friday, D Tuesday-Sunday. This is a very popular spot so reservations are recommended. Great food!
Town and Country Thriftway Market: 343 Winslow Way, Winslow, WA 98101; (206) 842-7717. Open daily. This is a well-stocked, up-scale market with a particularly appealing deli department.
Winslow Way Café: 122 Winslow Way, Bainbridge Island, WA 98110; (206) 842-0517. $$, Sunday Brunch, D daily from 5 p.m. Excellent!

Lodging

Bombay House: 8490 Beck Rd. NE, bainbridge Island, WA 98110; (206) 842-3926; (800) 598-3926. This 1907 house was built by a master ship builder and sits on a rural half-acre hillside site overlooking Rich Passage. Bombay House exudes an inviting homey atmosphere of a traditional B & B, decorated with country antiques, offering a parlor with a cheery open hearth fireplace and five comfortable and reasonably priced rooms. Guests are treated to the talents of cookbook author and hostess Bunny Cameron's delicious country breakfast and gardeners will especially appreciate the luscious cottage gardens that surround the house.
The Herb Cottage Bed and Breakfast: Bainbridge Island, WA; (206) 842-2625. $, open year-round. Karen Day is crafting a garden lover's retreat, with a cozy and comfortable guest suite that opens onto a garden. The room is extravagantly stocked with many garden videos of interest to a Gardener on the Go. She has an enviable collection of gardening magazines and a library of books that takes up one wall of the room. She also features a delightful full breakfast, afternoon tea or late night snack. Pick up at the ferry can be arranged. (see below for class and tour information).
Island Country Inn: 920 Hildebrand Ln, Bainbridge Island, WA 98110; (206) 842-6861 or (800) 842-8429. There is only one hotel/motel on the Island. This pleasant facility offers 40 deluxe guest rooms and 6 suites (which have fireplaces). www.nwcountryinns.com (photos of rooms)
Summer Hill Farm Bed and Breakfast: (206) 842-0640. $$, open year-round. The guest room is located in a separate carriage house on this 12-acre working farm (Southdown sheep, Jersey cows, horse pastures, orchards and flower gardens populate this perfect pastoral setting). The decor is very

sophisticated *and fun*, though unusual with a "wild west" theme. A word of "warning": expect possible early morning farm music of roosters crowing and donkeys braying.

Camping / Fay-Bainbridge State Park, 17 acres, 36 beach and forested campsites, hot showers, beach walking (not extensive but sandy with lots of driftwood and fabulous views of the Seattle skyline). Open year-round for day-use and for overnight visits from late April to mid-October.

FOR MORE INFORMATION

Bainbridge Island Chamber of Commerce: 590 Winslow Way East, Bainbridge Island, WA 98110; (206) 842-3700. Among other brochures, they offer a listing of Island and near-by accommodations (B & Bs, Inns, motel).

MORE RESOURCES FOR GARDENERS

Bainbridge in Bloom Garden Tour: Bainbridge Island Arts and Humanities Council, 261 Madison Ave. S., Bainbridge Island, WA 98110; (206) 361-3890 (charge-by-phone ticket service). Generally six private gardens, always the weekend after the Fourth of July.

Bainbridge Public Library Interpretive Garden: 1270 Madison Avenue N., Bainbridge Island, WA 98110; (206) 842-4162. Installed in 1997, this public garden, a gift from the Japanese-American Community, is located near the entrance to the Library. The garden project, spearheaded and designed by islander Junkoh Harui, includes elements of traditional Japanese gardens and some that are Japanese-influenced American touches.

Bainbridge Island Vineyards and Winery: ¼ mile north of the Winslow ferry terminal on Hwy. 305; (206) 842-9463. Open Wednesday-Sunday noon-5 p.m. Grape plants and vine cuttings for sale and wine grape growers tours.

Eagledale Herb Gardens: 5276 Taylor Ave., Bainbridge Island, WA 98110; (206) 842-7284. Organic medicinal and culinary herbs and perennials at the Farmer's Market and with a call in advance, at the greenhouse.

The Herb Basket: (206) 842-2625. Karen Day offers herb related classes and "Gardener's Getaway Weekends" through her Bed and Breakfast (see above). Her enthusiasm is boundless, so consider a custom designed class/demonstration or tour to Bainbridge or Whidbey Island gardens.

Laughing Crow Farm: Roadside stand shared with Satyematsu's on Day Rd. East, Bainbridge Island; (206) 842-3516. Fragrant plants chosen specifically for this region. Also a specialty of organically grown onions, garlic and potatoes (many special varieties of each.)

Sequoia Center: Ann Lovejoy's Garden School, 9010 Miller Rd., Bainbridge Island, WA 98110; (206) 780-6783. Request a copy of the monthly newsletter ($15/12 issues) with commentary from Ann, resource recommendations, book reviews and class schedule.

Willow Brook Farm: (206) 842-8034 (voice mail recording provides dates, times and directions). This very popular family event welcomes visitors to the farm for a fabulous fall harvest celebration, most weekends in October. There are perennial, herb and vegetable gardens, pumpkin patches and orchards (including one that features antique varieties). Also come for Indian corn, corn stalks, dried flowers, apples, a huge array of winter squash, freshly packed flower seeds and certified organic produce.

A PLANT
COLLECTOR'S
EXPEDITION

Itinerary Highlights
an expansive labyrinth of gardens, packed with rare plants
a knowledgeable plantsman and a collector's Mecca
a skilled nurserywoman with vision and foresight
hosta nursery is a shade gardener's horticultural heaven

❧

Many familiar garden plants we take for granted today originated in far-off lands – in Nepal, China, Japan and Korea, in Turkey, in Chile and South Africa. The spellbinding tales of botanists and explorers recount great hardship and heartbreak, triumph and adventure, stunning discoveries and remarkable revelations. As the 21st century dawns there is a resurgence of interest and opportunity for modern day plant "hunters" to sally forth in search of rare and endangered species, glorious beauties, the medically significant and the horticulturally curious. A subculture of passionate gardeners who genuinely ache with lust in the pursuit and acquisition of the uncommon find northwest nurseries rich and satisfying "hunting" grounds.

❦ THE ITINERARY IN BRIEF ❦

❶ Heronswood Nursery and Gardens

A visit here is to enter the consummate collector's Garden of Eden. While assuredly grounded in a Northwest woodland setting, you'll find great diversity of unfamiliar plants, voluptuous borders spilling onto pathways, daring and dazzling plant combinations and unending sensual assaults of texture, form, color and scent. This may well require navigating immediately to a handsome garden bench for a moment of quiet contemplation, a gathering of one's wits.

Lunch Will probably be dictated by your time schedule. A swing over to Kingston for an innovative and memorable café lunch in a Hinkley/Jones designed courtyard garden or a picnic on the bluff overlooking Hood Canal are two choices.

❷ Reflective Gardens

Kelly Dodson's plant emporium harbors many extraordinary gems, some from his own wild-collected seeds, some from treasure hunting missions to England or from the expeditions of several of today's most respected plant-hunters. He is trusted with plants from historical gardens and the collections of many of the area's finest horticulturists. Be sure to draw on the savvy of this masterful propagator and knowledgeable plantsman.

❸ Woodside Gardens

Arriving at Woodside Gardens is like venturing into the picturesque countryside to visit your favorite aunt's farm which also happens to be a fabulous nursery packed with an exciting selection of best varieties and new introductions, with a keen focus on perennials. A talented Pam West has magically ferreted out, and beautifully grown on, many garden newcomers that collector's eyes zero in on with glee.

❹ Naylor Creek Nursery

Aficionados who bow to the goddess Hosta and those who seek out botanical bounty for shady places will thrill to the extravagant selection in this immaculate nursery, an esteemed destination for hosta fanatics from across the state, the country and even abroad. The mesmerizing sea of undulating texture is worth the visit alone!

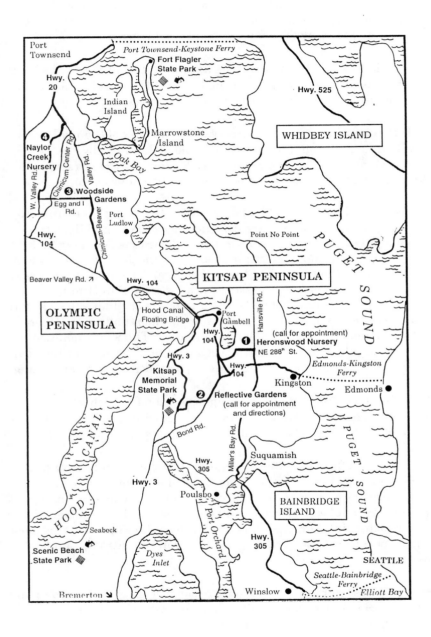

TOUR TIMING AND TIPS

❧ Two of the four nurseries listed on this tour ***require a call in advance*** as they are not open on a drop-in basis. This has to do with local zoning regulations or unpredictable and busy schedules.

❧ This is admittedly an ambitious itinerary. If it is at all possible to plan this as a special two-day outing that would be preferable so that you can fully explore the offerings of each nursery.

❧ **Heronswood** opens the nursery after the bulk of the mail-order rush has passed, from mid-May to the end of January, by appointment, 9 a.m.-2:00 p.m. Monday-Friday. As the nursery and gardens are extensive. Plan a minimum of two hours here.

❧ Open Garden Days, with no appointment necessary, are annually offered by **Heronswood Nursery and Gardens** to highlight the seasonal diversity of their world-renowned gardens (a Friday and Saturday in May, July and September – specific dates listed in their catalog and on the Cedarcroft Press Web site). Visitors have access to the extensive gardens, docents answer questions, Dan Hinkley provides slide presentations and the nursery is open for sales. In late February there is a Garden Open featuring the stunning Hellebore collection and other plants of winter interest. The $7.50 donation is collected as a benefit for a worthy organization. Throughout the year Seminars are offered, providing more opportunities for garden gazing.

❧ **Reflective Gardens** likewise opens seasonally each year, generally coinciding with the Heronswood openings in May, July and September. They are located about 20 minutes' drive apart.

❧ The most efficient routes to these destinations require crossing Puget Sound by boat to either Kingston or Bainbridge Island. The State Ferry System operates a fleet that makes the passage many times a day, but be forewarned, you will need to take a number of tour timing factors into consideration if you are not familiar with this mode of transportation. (See ***Taking the Ferry*** in the Introduction for more on travel planning details.)

❧ All of these nurseries participate in some or all of the region's plant sales associated with non-profit organizations (Arboretum Foundation, Northwest Horticultural Society, etc.)

Each of the nurseries on the Plant Collector's Tour is also a mail order source for rarities. Part of the reason their plants do not appear at your neighborhood garden center is that they are often too new to cultivation to have caught the attention of large wholesale growers. Alas, the plants may be very difficult to propagate and therefore too expensive to market to the masses. Not everything offered by these specialty nurseries will turn out to be the perfect specimen of your dreams, but you are given the *opportunity* to give these uncommon gems a try in your garden. I suggest you obtain plant catalogs in advance to scope out the nursery offerings. **Collection information** that will give you some background on plant origins.

Put together a good selection of **reference books** to pack along.

Labeling arrangements are less formalized in many specialty nurseries. You may be required to write out your own tag, and botanical Latin will be the *lingua franca* – and for good reason. Each name carries specific and valuable information about a unique plant. Consider it as important as your correct address, as opposed to just the name of the town you live in. Plants with even the same "street name" may be miles away (in terms of appearance and characteristics) from the one you are hunting for. While the uninitiated may find this approach initially intimidating, my advice is to go with the flow, be observant, realize that even the most knowledgeable plant buyers are probably giddy with the prospect of so many unfamiliar plants. Consider each visit a learning experience!

Many of the plants offered by these nurseries truly are new to cultivation. Based on collection data, nursery trials, experience growing similar plants and conservative educated "guesstimates" hardiness ratings and siting/cultural requirements are generally provided. If not, ASK! Assess intended plant purchases (if it looks a bit on the immature side then grow it on in a protected environment until there is more sustainable root development, or if this is not convenient then make this decision *before* buying the plant).

SETTING THE SCENE / GEOGRAPHIC

Kitsap claims more miles of coastline than any other county in continental America. The original residents, Native Americans of the Klallam, Twano and Suquamish tribes, were fishermen living off the abundance of salmon, shellfish and other sea life rather than turning to agrarian pursuits due to the poor quality of the soil. The legendary Puget Sound Indian leader Chief Sealth for whom Seattle is named

was buried June 7, 1866, in the town of Suquamish.
The dense timber stands, which the Native peoples revered, were a
major draw to the county's first white settlers. Capt. William Talbot
founded a sawmill at Port Gamble in 1853, modeling the architectural
style of the town he founded after his native East Machias, Maine.
Today this tidy traditional New England-esque community looks to
tourism, for its economy has suffered since the long lived Pope and
Talbot mill closed in 1995. The town has been preserved as an historic
district – with two museums and a genuine old time General Store, a
charming and nostalgic stop (listed under "Lunch" suggestions on the
itinerary).

Along the southerly reaches of the Peninsula at Bremerton the
Puget Sound Naval Yard was established in 1891. Primarily a repair
facility before WWI, some ship and submarine construction work has
also occupied the work force. The yard was very active repairing
damaged ships from the Pacific Theater in WWII. Near-by is the
Naval Submarine Base at Bangor.

The **Olympic Peninsula**, the dramatic body of land covering 6,500
square miles to the west of the Hood Canal, forms the State's western
boundary, fronting along the tempestuous Pacific Ocean. It is noted
for the lush rain forests of its 908,720-acre **Olympic National Park**,
for the rugged **Olympic Mountains** (with 160" of rain annually on
the eastern slopes), and the amazing rain shadow effect to the
northeast (with 17" of rain measured annually at Sequim!) Two of the
nursery destinations on this tour are favored by this phenomenon, and
are set in lovely pastoral valleys of rolling hills, small farms and
mixed species woodlands south of Port Townsend.

A word on "Plant-Collecting"

Lest the uninitiated take this phrase too literally, the term as it is
popularly and responsibly used today refers to the practice of seeking
wild species of plants in their native habitat with an intent to collect
seeds of those that look to be promising for study, rescue and/or
cultivation (and I might add here that this native habitat can be
virtually everywhere that plants grow – from the deep mountain
valleys of China to the "natural" urban ravines of inner city Seattle).
There is great concern voiced about this activity from a number of
corners, and not without some good cause for reflection.

Unethical, environmentally reckless collectors have decimated
native populations of untold numbers of species, sometimes for
financial gain, perhaps for fame and often out of pure ignorance. Yet
it is through educated and careful collection of seed, *where there is an
abundance*, that rare and endangered plants may be rescued and

hopefully reintroduced back to their native settings. Destruction of native habitat in the name of development and resource exploitation forever destroys plant species on a daily basis, to accommodate a dam project to the burning of tropical rain forests to clearing land for agricultural pursuits (to careless "land-scraping" of residential property right here in our own neighborhoods).

There are certainly horrific examples of introduced plants escaping into the environment as rampant thugs, a most notorious example being the smothering Kudzu vine brought to the Southern U.S. by an unsuspecting Department of Agriculture in hopes of using it for erosion control. The new breed of responsible growers test their collections in the ground under local growing conditions (and offer it around to like minded professionals and enthusiasts) for a period that may be a year or could be a matter of several years before introducing their stock to the retail market.

DRIVING DIRECTIONS:

Via Kingston Ferry: Drive north from downtown Seattle on I-5 to the Edmonds/Kingston Ferry exit #177 (11 miles) and proceed west on SW 244th St. which becomes Edmonds Way (Hwy. 104). Follow signs for the ferry, which docks near downtown Edmonds. Coming from the north, take the 196th St. (Hwy. 524) exit #181 and follow west. Approaching Edmonds follow signs for the ferry. Plan on taking a ferry that allows you to arrive closest to the nursery opening time of 9 a.m. My longest waits (up to three ferries!) have been Saturday mornings and holidays, so plan to arrive early on these days to avoid spoiled plans. After disembarking from the ferry drive up the hill, through the traffic signals and onto Hwy. 104. At Albertson's (approximately 3.5 miles from Kingston), turn right. At NE 288th Street (about 1 mile, not prominently marked) turn left and go about .3 mile watching for the unobtrusive Heronswood sign on the lefthand side of the road. Of the two driveways, take the one on the right. **Diving distance** from Seattle to the Edmonds ferry: 17 miles; **Estimated driving time**: 25 minutes; **ferry crossing**: 30 minutes; Kingston to Heronswood Nursery: 15 minutes.

Via Bainbridge Island: The ferry leaves from Pier 52, the Colman Dock near Pioneer Square in Seattle (see the "Book Lover's" Tour for step-by-step directions). The ferry crossing takes 35 minutes. From Winslow travel north on Hwy. 305 traversing the Island roughly south to north. Cross the Agate Pass Bridge and turn right at the traffic signal onto Suquamish Way, which becomes Miller Bay Rd. and then Hansville Rd. At the intersection at Albertson's proceed 1 mile to 288th, turn left .3 mile. **Driving distance** Winslow ferry to Heronswood Nursery: 17.5 miles; **Estimated driving time**: 25 minutes.

▓ Heronswood

7530 NE 288th St., Kingston, WA 98346-9502; (360) 297-4172. Open by
appointment mid-May through the following January, 9 a.m.-2:00 p.m.
Monday-Friday, with few exceptions, closed to visitors during the busy mail-
order season, February-mid-May.

The Gardens: Nursery patrons are invited to view the gardens, (the fifty cent
fee is donated to the Kitsap Regional Library horticultural reference section).
Borders closest to the house are likely to be closed to protect the privacy of the
owners (there is *much* else of horticultural interest, however, so fear not).

Garden Open Days (see the details under "Tour Timing") invite you to visit all
garden areas on a Friday or Saturday, 10 a.m.-4 p.m. in late May, mid-July
and early September with docents on hand to answer questions. The nursery
is open for sales, with many plants marked at special prices.

Garden Tours: Groups of six or more wishing to tour need to make an
appointment, a donation is required and a knowledgeable docent will be
happy to answer questions. In this botanical wonderland, visitors generally
have many questions about plant identification. (A large portion of your
donation is passed along, in your name, to the WildHaven Wildlife Center.)

∗ RR/ catalog $5

On a visit a few years ago to one of the most well-known and oft-
visited gardens in Britain, I was fortunate enough to meet and engage
the owner in conversation. Upon learning that I was from
Washington state. Her very enthusiastic response was simply, "Oh!
Are you anywhere near Heronswood?!" The national (and
international) notoriety of this nursery and garden is indeed
phenomenal. On seven-and-a-half-acres ensconced within a woodland
setting on the North Kitsap Peninsula, the gardens and nursery of
Dan Hinkley and his partner Robert Jones have captured the
imaginations of passionate plant lovers from far and wide. This is
evidenced through visits each year from thousands of plant pilgrims to
this rural outpost, most toting dog-eared copies of their botanically
correct, hysterically entertaining (yet slyly educational) 264-page
catalog, which lists and describes a staggering 2,500 separate plants.

So what is the hoopla all about? Extraordinary plants, many from
isolated locales, for an increasing market of gardeners who are
becoming more sophisticated in their tastes and more demanding of
their horticultural bounty. At the center of the Heronswood hurricane
is the key figure of Dan Hinkley who writes prolifically for the popular
gardening press (such as *Horticulture* magazine) and specialist
journals (*Pacific Horticulture*), maintains a rigorous local and national
lecture schedule including a Seminar series offered at the nursery,
makes a number of ambitious seed collection trips each year to the
likes of China, Nepal, South Korea, Japan, Chile and Great Britain,
conducts an enviable propagation program from his own travels and
from generous sharing within his impressive network of co-

conspirators AND orchestrates the planning and planting of an immense and distinguished garden. Not to take away from this remarkable feat, but as the operation has grown over the past decade there has been assembled an impressive team of horticulturally astute Heronistas who work their magic along with their mentor and friend. Robert has retired from his established career as an architect to provide not only managerial skills but guidance for the wildly successful Hinkley/Heronswood mystique.

Your visit to the nursery will no doubt be influenced by the plants you see in the gardens, as your first question of "What is THAT!" will be followed by "Do you have any available in the nursery?" What you *will* find in the two-and-a-half acre nursery, including 16 plant houses, is a breathtaking array of plants: coniferous, woody, perennial and "temperennial," viney, grassy and annual. It is difficult to call out noteworthy collections, because there are so many. But how could I not mention the outstanding selection of Acers (over 40), Buddleias (25), Hydrangeas (60! Including 4 climbers), Ilex (44), Viburnums (46), Clematis (69 species and hybrids), Coleus (29, a carefully considered selection of the cream of an enormous collection of named cultivars, the new fascination for adventurous and bold Northwesterners), Alliums (23), *Arisaemas* (a remarkable 24), Asters (48), Cardamine (8), *Epimediums* (17), *Euphorbias* (16), Fuchsias (21) Geraniums (the hardies – an even 100), *Hellebores* (30), species Lilies (16, not to mention 4 *Cardiocrinum* species), *Nepetas* (15), *Penstemons* (17), *Primulas* (35), *Pulmonarias* (25), *Ranunculus (14),* *Salvias* (22), *Tricyrtis* (11)...and so much more. A feature of the Heronswood catalog is to highlight strong collections with an introductory essay-esque paragraph (usually fashioned to tickle your funny bone or to help you bone up on some fascinating facts about the genus). Look for the vertical bar in the left margin.

Lunch: If you can take the time to relax (and catch your breath), my first choice would be to skip over to Kingston and the Old Kingston Hotel Café. Here you'll find a smashing Dan Hinkley/Robert Jones courtyard garden where you can settle in to study the innovative menu amid striking plant combinations. Restaurateur Judith Weinstock has created a brilliant marriage of a warm and friendly café with a sophisticated and talented kitchen. If on the other hand a quick picnic is in order, a bit of a detour 'round to Port Gamble provides a charming venue overlooking Hood Canal (DIY or pop into the circa 1914 General Store and make your way to the deli for an excellent sandwich and a generous hand dipped ice cream cone -- fuel for the rigorous afternoon of exploration ahead.)

189

DRIVING DIRECTIONS:

To Kingston: From Heronswood Nursery turn right on NE 288th St. and right onto Hansville Rd. At the traffic signal turn left onto Hwy. 104 and drive east into Kingston, about 3.5 miles, following the sign for "local traffic" in the far left lane. Turn left just before the entrance for the ferry onto Washington Blvd. The Old Kingston Hotel Café is on the left at the next intersection (with 1st St., the exit route for the ferry).

To Port Gamble: From Heronswood Nursery turn left on NE 288th St., which becomes Gambell Bay Rd. After 2 miles turn left at the intersection with Hwy. 104 and travel about 3.5 miles into Port Gambell. Follow the sign for the General Store.

From Kingston or Port Gamble: To reach Reflective Gardens, request directions when you make your appointment.

Reflective Gardens

24329 NE Snowhill Ln., Poulsbo, WA 98370-9101; (360) 598-4649. Open by appointment and for Open Garden Days in May, July and September (call or write for exact dates **and directions**). Catalog $2 refundable with order.

If you haunt this area's extraordinary array of plant sales (those organized by the Arboretum Foundation, Hardy Plant Society of Oregon and the Northwest Horticultural Society to name just a few) then you will surely have admired the handiwork of Kelly Dodson. His tables always beckon to serious plant collectors and avid gardeners in search of rarities and plants new to cultivation, mainly seed-grown herbaceous perennials and bulbous species. His offerings run from a strong showing of *Gentians* to an ever-expanding array of the ellusive *Aroids*. He caters to rock garden enthusiasts and those with an appetite for woodland natives. Those of us who garden in boggy soils find a gold mine of web-footed *Ranunculus* and the rare white skunk cabbage, *Lysichiton camtschatscensis*. If you are on the hunt for species Peonies (haling from eastern Europe and China as well as our own Northwest natives) to grace your spring garden, you'll find several to choose from. A number of outstanding plant collections have been entrusted to Kelly's hands as notable gardens have been disseminated due to a major move or the death of an avid plantsman.

While at the nursery you will no doubt be drawn to the work of wife and partner Sue Skelly, who custom crafts English-style wattle fences and trellises of western red cedar (a more *resilient* and weather resistant material than the traditional willow or hazel that have been the rage of late.)

DRIVING DIRECTIONS:

Receive directions from Reflective Gardens to the Hood Canal Bridge near-by. Cross over onto Hwy. 104 going west to the Port Townsend exit (Hwy. 19), turn right and go approximately 5 miles to Egg and I Rd. (yes, of Betty MacDonald fame). Turn left and drive 2.5 miles to the nursery.
Driving distance: 20 miles; *Estimated driving time:* 25 minutes.

✖ Woodside Gardens

1191 Egg and I Rd., Chimicum, WA 98325; (360) 732-4754. Open April through summer, Tuesday-Saturday, 10 a.m.- 5 p.m., fall hours are more casual so it is best to call. Catalog $2. There are many free roaming antique strains of Bantam chickens so it is best to leave dogs at home or at the very least, under control in your vehicle.

This nursery, located in a quiet pastoral valley on the eastern side of the Olympic Peninsula, is the farm and nursery of Pam West and her family. Besides the picturesque chickens that move about the place on slug and bug patrol, there are pygmy goats, sheep and the resident canine undergardeners. The winter of 1997-98 has brought expansion to this small nursery, so I hope by the time you plan a visit the new facilities will be in place for your shopping convenience. A transplant from her Oregon coast nursery, Pam has quickly established a reputation here for the quality of the perennials she grows and especially for her uncanny ability to seek out and offer uncommon, new varieties of old favorites. It was here that I saw my first *Ipomoea batatas* 'Blackie' and I.b. 'Pink Frost' a year before anyone else around the Northwest had them. She was an early advocate of the *Euphorbias*, hardy *Geraniums*, *Heucheras* and species *Lobelias* and has an excellent stock of irises (Japanese, Siberian and dwarf Bearded.) It is not easy to find such a wide selection of named English violas, many of historical significance and many that are strongly scented. Pam is also the *Dianthus* Queen (with 42 varieties on offer, you can imagine that all but the most absorbed collectors will need to familiarize themselves with what all this choice represents!) In addition to a commendable offering of perennials, she specializes in herbs with generous selections of Lavender (30), Mint (15), Oregano (14), Rosemary (32) and Thyme (27). While the range of vines is not extensive, I always find myself drawn to her choice selection, which includes *Vitis Vinifera* 'Purpurea' and several *Clematis* viticellas.

DRIVING DIRECTIONS:
Turn right on Egg and I Rd. and drive west. Cross Chimicum Center Rd. and proceed to W. Valley Rd. Turn right and travel north 2.5 miles. Naylor Creek Nursery is on the left.
Driving distance: 4.5 miles; *Estimated driving time:* 10 minutes.

✖ Naylor Creek Nursery

2610 West Valley Rd., Chimicum, WA 98325; (360) 732-4983. Open May-September 15; Thursday-Sunday, 9 a.m.-5 p.m. and by appointment. ⊤ ✱ (display garden open April-September). Catalog $1.

If you garden in a shady site, then this nursery will win your heart as you cross the lawn and find spread before you waves of lush, textural hosta foliage interplanted with sophisticated companions who likewise relish the dappled light of a woodland setting. Jack Hirsch and Gary Lindheimer are well known nationally, and internationally, among hosta "maniacs" for their overwhelming collection (their 1998 catalog lists over 700 varieties). They also have made a strong showing in the Northwest through their popular vendor booth at the Northwest Flower and Garden Show and all major plant sales throughout the region. A visit to the nursery provides a dramatic introduction to the seemingly infinite variety of foliar color and texture, shape and form that has been achieved in breeding these showy plants. What will strike you immediately is how exquisitely these beauties have been grown by two utterly devoted enthusiasts, who carefully protect their hostas in shade houses, in raised beds and in containers There are row upon row of undulating greens and grey-greens and limey greens and creamy-greens and blue-greens and silvery-greens, from deepest dark green to the softest whisper of green. Then there are those with gold centers, honey-colored accents, intense yellow leaves and chartreuse variegation. There are ones with thick fleshy leaves and those that are shiny, some are immense and some teeny tiny, some are lightly ruffled, some twisted like a corkscrew and some are corrugated. They are mesmerizing in their rhythm as you march up and down the aisles, transfixed by the vast variety. It is in the display garden that the talented companion planting brings to the spotlight the many other shade tolerant performers offered at Naylor Creek: frothy *Astilbes*, stately *Cimicifugas*, fascinating *Pulminarias*, hard-working Epimediums, eye-catching *Filipendulas* and bold *Ligularias*, to name a few. Be sure to ask about the luscious Tree Peonies that have been imported from China, with names like "Green Dragon in Deep Pond" and "Snow Kissed Peach."

Driving Directions, End of the Tour:

As I mentioned under "Tour Tips" this has been an ambitious itinerary. I hope you have been able to make this a two-day event, either by splitting your visits to nurseries into two leisurely days or by making a decision to relax after an exhilarating day of exploration in one of the many tempting accommodation opportunities this area provides. If not, then I shall direct you back to I-5 by three routes.

Via Whidbey Island: At Naylor Creek Nursery you are about 20 minutes south of Port Townsend, where you can catch the Keystone ferry to Whidbey Island (the crossing takes 30 minutes). This route would be most expeditious for those whose final destination is north of Everett (or those who will carry on with the itineraries for Whidbey Island, Skagit Valley or Bellingham). You will find yourself mid-Island on the western shore. You can follow Hwy. 20 northward to cross Deception Pass Bridge to I-5 (from the ferry this takes about 45 minutes). At Burlington, you can head north toward Bellingham (30 minutes) or Vancouver, British Columbia (90 minutes) or South toward Seattle (60 minutes).

Via Kingston / Edmonds: From Naylor Creek Nursery turn left onto W. Valley Rd. At the Chimicum-Beaver Valley Rd. turn right. At Hwy.104 turn left and follow across the Hood Canal Bridge. Keep following 104 all the way to the Kingston ferry (30 minutes). The ferry crossing is 30 minutes. Disembark and turn right at the first traffic signal, then follow the signs to I-5 (driving time is 15 minutes to I-5). For Seattle take the southbound on-ramp (approximately 25 minutes to downtown.)

Via Bainbridge Island / Winslow Ferry: Follow above directions until Hwy. 104 diverts to the left south of Port Gamble. Instead, take the Port Gamble-Suquamish Rd. and follow it to Suquamish. Turn right onto Suquamish Way. At the traffic signal turn left onto Hwy. 305 to cross the Agate Pass Bridge onto Bainbridge Island. Follow Hwy. 305 directly to the ferry (approximate total driving time is 45 minutes). The ferry crossing takes another 35 minutes and brings you to downtown Seattle.

FURTHER RESOURCES

Food

The Old Kingston Hotel Café: 25931 Washington Blvd., Kingston, WA 98346; (360) 297-8100. $$, B,L,D. Open with seasonal hours, daily in summer and Thursday-Sunday in winter. Generous portions with creative presentations that are as tasty as they are beautiful to look at.

Port Gamble General Store: 1 Rainier Ave., Port Gamble, WA 98346; (360) 297-7636. $, L. Picnic fixings from the grocery or order a generous sandwich from the deli to eat in or from the site near-by above Hood Canal.

Lodging / Kitsap Peninsula

Manor Farm Inn: 26069 Big Valley Rd. NE, Poulsbo, WA 98370; (360) 779-4628. $$$. Of the lodgings in this area, the Manor Farm has garnered the most national attention. It is an up-scale inn set on a picturesque "gentleman's" farm about 30 minutes east of Kingston. Much ado is made of the delicious breakfast; dinner is available Friday-Saturday or Wednesday-Thursday, seasonally (to guests and non-guests).

Scenic Beach State Park/ camping: fabulous views of the Olympics and masses of species rhododendrons grow wild, blooming in May (purported to have more rhododendrons than any other State park). Adjacent is the Emel House, built in 1912, surrounded by lovely gardens and gazebo; located near Seabeck, on the Hood Canal, northwest of Bremerton. (360) 830-5079.

Willcox House: 2390 Tekiu Rd. NW, Seabeck, WA 98380; (360) 830-4492, (800) 725-2600. $$-$$$ If what you are looking for is a memorable experience, along the lines of a splendid manor house in the British countryside, then this historic and elegant mansion and its equally wonderful gardens and grounds should be perfect. On Hood Canal with many pleasant diversions and excellent food, this a tour destination in itself. www.willcoxhouse.com

Lodging / Olympic Peninsula

Fort Warden Accommodations: www.olympus.net/ftworden/wordens.html or call (360) 385-4730 (Officer's Quarters houses, campsites, hostel). If you are traveling with a car full of friends and looking for something unique, consider the **Officer's Quarters** at Fort Warden, 1 mile west of Port Townsend. While not fancy they are spacious, clean, comfortable, have kitchens and an interesting location (the summer months are filled with cultural events on the grounds of the old Fort). A 6-bedroom house goes for around $230. Reservations are a must for summer..

Olympic Peninsula Bed and Breakfast Association: P.O. Box 1741, Port Angeles, WA 98362.   www.olympus.net/opbb

The Nantucket Manor: 941 Shine Rd., Port Ludlow, WA 98365. $$$. Located just west of the Hood Canal Bridge overlooking Squamish Harbor and is a very handsome bed and breakfast. I couldn't help asking Peggy Conrardy if she was a professional interior decorator as each of the spacious rooms is exquisitely inviting. The gardens that surround the home are a passion the owners love to share with their guests.

Port Townsend is Bed and Breakfast Mecca! There are *many* excellent choices. My personal picks would be romantic rose gardens and the walkable beach of **Bay Cottages**, 4346 S. Discovery Rd., Port Townsend, WA 98368, (360) 385-2035, $$; the lovely gardens and Victorian elegance of the **James House**, 1238 Washington St., Port Townsend, WA 98368, (800) 385-1238, $$; or the more contemporary welcome of **Ravenscroft Inn**, 533 Quincy St., Port Townsend, WA 98368, (360) 385-2784, $$.

Fort Flagler State Park / Camping:: located near Naylor Creek Nursery and Woodside Gardens on the northern tip of Marrowstone Island, 116 beachside campsites (as well as two Vacation Houses, once part of the fort's staffing quarters, a four bedroom and a two bedroom, call (360) 902-8600 for information). Listed on the National Register of Historic Places the Fort provides miles of wooded hiking trails, meadows and beach walking.

For More Information

Kitsap Peninsula Visitors and Convention Bureau: (360) 698-7411
Port Townsend Chamber of Commerce: Tourist Information Center, 2437 E. Sims Way, Port Townsend, WA 98368; (800) 499-0047.

More Resources for Gardeners

Abundant Life Seed Foundation: 930 Lawrence St., (mail to P.O. Box 772), Port Townsend, WA 98368; (360) 385-5660. ALSF acquires, preserves and distributes open-pollinated seeds, emphasizing rare heirloom vegetables, medicinal herbs and Northwest natives. They are responsible for the World Seed Fund, which has distributed thousands of packets of free seeds around the world to relieve hunger and help develop self-sufficiency. They are a commercial seed company but also a non-profit foundation and your purchase not only helps in the scheme to help preserve biodiversity but it also helps this Foundation in its work. Tours by appointment. Catalog $2 donation.
Peninsula and South Sound Specialty Nursery Guide: 1220 NE 90th, Seattle, WA 98115. Profiles small, specialty nurseries. SASE, 2 stamps.

WHIDBEY ISLAND RETREAT- NORTH

As the longest island in the continental U.S., Whidbey Island offers two distinctly different touring territories. Gardeners on the Go have two itineraries featuring the horticultural highlights from each region.

———— Itinerary Highlights / NORTH ————
shop draws raves for eclectic, exquisitely detailed dried flora
jaunty display gardens exude artistic flare, love of plants
erudite rosarian generously shares opulent garden
keen gardener tends grand floral labyrinth, great nursery
estate features vast collection of rhododendrons

🍂

A central highway meanders along the spine of this long, slender island. It is tempting to let the route dictate your perspective and enjoyment of this historically rich, agrarian island, often taking in the more obvious highlights but sadly missing the heart and character of the place. One hundred fifty years ago this fertile northern half of Whidbey was settled by farmers and sea captains. Their heritage is evident to those who travel the back roads to discover that early spirit lives on today in an ethic of preservation and protection.

195

🦃 **THE ITINERARY IN BRIEF** 🦃

❶ Lavender Heart Botanicals

An artist/designer's "gallery" of elegant and sophisticated decorative pieces for interior landscapes. The use of traditional and uncommon dried botanicals in unconventional creations is a visual delight that will surely stimulate your imagination.

❷ Hummingbird Farm

The display gardens here have attracted much more than the hummingbirds—having been photographed for the cover and story in a national gardening magazine and a national television program on gardening. Fortunately, this charming little nursery offers for sale many of the plants that gardner so much attention from the display gardens and strives to offer exciting new introductions.

❸ Crescent Moon Rose Garden

Rose fanatics and those who appreciate a lush garden with the focus on roses, grown beautifully, will find Crescent Moon Rose Garden heavenly. Whether you are seeking out a fellow aficionado to "talk roses", are a novice in search of inspiration or are visiting for the pure purpose of an enjoyable tour, you are warmly welcomed.

Lunch This is great picnic on the beach country but also offers a satisfying meal at a picturesque inn or in an hitoric waterfron town.

❹ Paris Gardens

A one-acre display garden is at the heart of this wonderful nursery. An extravagant planting of old garden roses and lushly planted drifts of perennials skillfully capture plays of color, texture and form. The nursery offers many seed-grown treasures gleaned from England's premier seed house for the keen gardener in search of the uncommon.

❺ Meerkerk Rhododendron Gardens

This estate garden on 54 forested acres features over 2,000 varieties of rhododendrons spectacular at the height of bloom in mid-April. Many trails take visitors through the beautiful woodland where rhododendrons and azaleas are planted among glorious companion plants and noteworthy specimen trees.

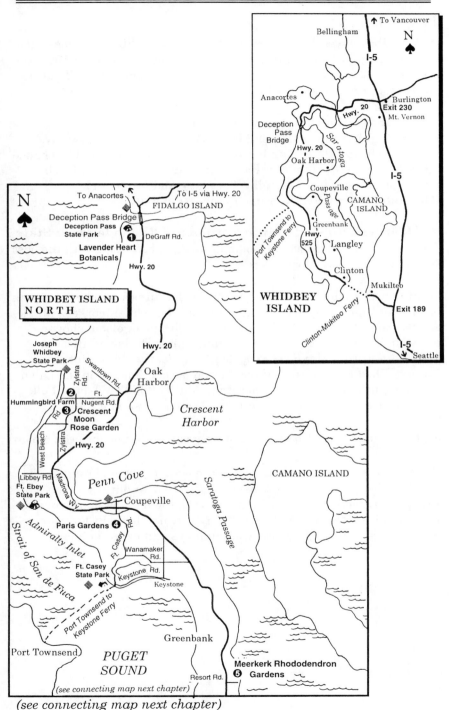

Tour Timing and Tips

🌺 **Whidbey Island Garden Tour** is offered at different times each year to feature what is best in the participating gardens. In 1998, the tour is slated for Saturday, **August 1**. Tickets generally sell out in advance, so order yours early: (360) 321-0358.

🌺 **Lavender Heart** is open year round (closed Sunday); **Hummingbird Farm** is open March-December (closed Tuesdays); **Crescent Moon Rose Garden** is open by appointment and by chance most days April-September; **Paris Gardens** is open mid-March to mid-September, (closed Monday-Tuesday); and **Meerkerk Rhododendron Garden** is open year-round daily.

🌺 **Meerkerk Rhododendron Garden** and **Rhododendron State Park** both feature masses of bloom in woodland settings, with the best "show" in April and May.

🌺 **Meerkerk Rhododendron Gardens** features a number of events each year: Spring Opening Plant Sale (late March); Meerkerk Magic, A Festival of Flowers, Fairies and Music with peak bloom showing over 2,000 types of rhododendrons (mid-April); Birds and Blossoms Gala (late April); Mayflower Garden Party (early May); Purple Passion Rhodie Sale (early May); Mother's Day Concert on the Lawn; Garden Party Benefit for Hospice (mid-May); Whidbey Island Folk Festival (early August). Call or check their Web site for dates.

🌺 **Crescent Moon Rose Garden** suggests mid-June for *peak* bloom.

🌺 If you are up for an adventure in innovative travel planning, Whidbey Island offers an extensive bus system, and it is entirely FREE. It travels the island from tip to tip, town to town and covers many roads off the beaten track. There are bicycle racks for your convenience as well. No service on Sundays and major holidays.

SETTING THE SCENE

Whidbey Island lies at the northern extremity of Washington's Puget Sound, at the mouth of the Straight of Juan de Fuca. Officially the longest island in the continental U.S., the island measures 45 miles from the northern tip at Deception Pass to the southern tip at Possession Point, a short distance from the community of Clinton. A slender strip of land, it is no more than 5 miles wide at any point.

To understand the character of the land that shaped the history and development of this place it is necessary to go back over 14,000 years to the time when Whidbey Island was covered by a sheet of ice more than a mile thick. For 30,000 to 40,000 years glaciers had advanced and receded over the area we now know as Puget Sound. In the last Ice Age, Vashon Glacier finally receded and left rich deposits of fertile soil, some of which settled out of shallow lakes and small streams as they dried up over time. The landscape is characterized by naturally occurring wide open prairies, gently rolling uplands, densely forested woodland ridges and narrow sandy beaches. The highest point on the island is at an elevation of 200'.

Records dating from 1790 reveal a population on the island of over 1,500 Salish Indians, one of the greatest concentrations of people found anywhere in the region. They fished, hunted and cultivated the land, periodically burning the prairies to encourage their favored root crops of bracken ferns and camas, to encourage fiber plants and provide forage for game. When British explorer Capt. George Vancouver came to Puget Sound in 1792, he named the island for Joseph Whidbey, master of his flagship the *Discovery* and the man responsible for actually locating and exploring the island. At the time, however, he did not recognize that Whidbey and Fidalgo Island were not a single land mass. This discovery fell, in 1841, to Capt. Wilkes, an American explorer. He also sailed into Penn Cove and recognized it as a valuable deep water harbor.

Later that decade droves of settlers were drawn west by the California Gold Rush and the Donation Land Claim Law of 1850, which offered free land in the Oregon Territory (of which Washington was included) to any citizen who would homestead it for four years. The first permanent settler to arrive was Isaac Neff Ebey, who landed on October 15, 1850, followed two years later by his family. They recognized the great value of their land for farming and were very successful growing wheat and potatoes. In time they produced record crops due to the tremendously fertile soil and the favorable climate. (Whidbey Island is on the rainshadow, or lee, side of the Olympic Mountains, resulting in a dry region along the coast claimed by Ebey that even supports several species of cactus!)

COMMUNITY PROFILES

Coupeville: Thomas Coupe, a New England sea captain, claimed land in 1852 along the shore of Penn Cove, recognizing the commercial value of the property as a port from which produce could be shipped to market. Coupeville grew up at the water's edge, the second oldest settlement in the region. Within only three years all the best land had been claimed—largely the prairie land of central and northern Whidbey—and new settlers moved upland to log the old growth forests of Douglas Fir and Western Red Cedar, a great deal of which was destined for San Francisco. Coupeville has retained a great deal of its late 19th century character as evidenced by the historic false-fronted buildings that line the main street along the waterfront. Many elaborate Victorian-style houses have survived, a testament to the prosperity of the early residents and now several can be enjoyed by visitors as Bed and Breakfast Inns. Coupeville remained a busy and important port until 1935 when the bridge at Deception Pass linked the island by road to the mainland. Boat traffic had essentially been the lifeline for all who lived anywhere on Whidbey and the bridge changed the value of the port towns forever.

Ebey's Landing National Historical Reserve: Established by Congress in 1978 under the auspices of the National Park System, this 17,400-acre Reserve located in central Whidbey is unique as the first preserve of its kind in the country. It represents a means of protecting historically important land, held largely in private hands (90% in this case) "in essence rather than in substance." The basic patterns of land use in this area had remained agricultural since the original Land Claims in the 1850s. With pressures to develop this sensitive and beautiful land on the horizon, a plan to protect its legacy was forged through tax incentives, purchase of development rights to key sites, zoning, local design review, easements and land donations. The Reserve is administered and managed by a Trust Board. There is a 43.6-mile tour (driving, bicycling, walking) that begins in Coupeville with a brochure delineating important historical, cultural and environmental features, interpretive exhibits and wayside markers similar to those used on Britain's public footpath system set along the way. There is a bluff-top pathway and one that leads through the pastoral countryside to a well-tended historic cemetery, especially notable for its many trees and flowering shrubs and the distinguished pioneers who were laid to rest here. (See information at the end of this chapter on the Historical Museum, where you can pick up a map and other free materials on the Reserve.)

Oak Harbor: The name of this bustling community, the largest on the island with a population of 19,000, refers to stands of Garry Oak trees, an unusual arboreal phenomenon in Puget Sound. Originally settled in the late 1850s by Irish immigrants, attracted by this favored site on Crescent Harbor with its fishing and farming potentials, at the turn of the century there was a large influx of Dutch settlers who moved here from the American Midwest. Their heritage and influence remains strong in Oak Harbor today. In 1935 the Deception Pass Bridge (9 miles north) was built, irrevocably impacting the rural character of Whidbey Island and this small, insular community. In 1941 the Whidbey Island Naval Air Base was established near Oak Harbor because of favorable flying weather and the absence of electronic interference and commercial air traffic patterns.

Deception Pass Bridge: At the northern tip of Whidbey Island, this bridge draws an estimated 3.5 million visitors as year. That is because it spans a narrow, 182' deep cut between Fidalgo and Whidbey Islands, providing a spectacular view of the turbulent waterway beneath. The project was built in 1935 by the Civilian Conservation Corps, whose handiwork can also be appreciated at the adjacent Deception Pass Park.

ACCESS TO WHIdbEy IslANd

There are three approaches to Whidbey Island: via Highway 20 over the **Deception Pass Bridge** at the northern tip of the island; via the **Port Townsend/Keystone Ferry** from the Olympic Peninsula to the west coast of central Whidbey and via the **Mukilteo/Clinton Ferry** at the southern tip of the island. This Whidbey Island Retreat/North itinerary provides directions from Seattle and from the north (Vancouver, B.C. or Bellingham) via I-5 and Hwy. 20 at Burlington. The first destination, Lavender Heart, is very near the Deception Pass Bridge. (If you have chosen to come via the Mukilteo ferry, it takes at least one hour to transit the island south to north, from the ferry terminal at Clinton, the approach described in the Whidbey Island Retreat/South Tour.) For details on the Washington State Ferry system see the introductory chapter on "Taking the Ferry."

DRIVING DIRECTIONS:

From mid-town Seattle drive north (from Bellingham or Vancouver, B.C. you'll travel southbound) on I-5 to exit 230 at Burlington. Proceed west on Hwy. 20 toward Anacortes, following signs for Deception Pass, Oak Harbor/Whidbey Island and Keystone Ferry (from I-5 to Deception Pass Bridge is 18 miles taking 30 minutes). Two miles south of the Deception Pass Bridge turn right on DeGraff Rd., 1 block to Lavender Heart. *Driving distance:* 75 miles; *Estimated driving time:* 1 hour, 30 minutes.

TOUR TIP
There is a great little restaurant just south of the Deception Pass Bridge on Hwy. 20, **The Island Grille.** If you have gotten an early start without breakfast, stop in here for at least a latte and croissant.

 Lavender Heart Botanicals

4233 DeGraff Rd., Deception Pass, WA 98277; (360) 675-3987. Open daily (except Sunday) 9:30 a.m.-5:30 p.m.

❖ ☂ ▢ ☆ ✽

The most rewarding experiences I have as a horticultural resource sleuth are the days I walk through the door of a nursery or shop and find I have discovered a knock-your-socks-off kind of place when I was not expecting such a revelation. Lavender Heart fits into this category. Tucked off the main thoroughfare a mere two minutes, the charming but totally unprepossessing little shop is set on owner Holly Henderson's parent's 12-acre property, one of the oldest and loveliest holly farms in the Northwest. Bob (recently deceased) and Jean Henderson moved from Minnesota in 1949 to this Whidbey Island farm featuring English Blue Stem *Ilex* (holly) trees and fresh cut greens at Christmas. They continued the business and in the process became hooked on collecting a wide *and wild* (as in unusual) variety of *Ilex* species and cultivars that are available for you to peruse in a specimen bed near the shop. Today there are over 200, seventy-year-old holly trees on about 14 acres. But I digress, for while this is a story about Holly, it is their daughter of that name who is the genius behind Lavender Heart Botanicals.

Holly Henderson is a talented designer, and her primary artistic medium is dried botanical materials—using unconventional elements like pomegranates, artichokes, nuts, pods and birch twigs. She has an eye for sophisticated combinations of plants like the fantastical Pitcher Plant *Saracena,* plant materials like bark, lichen and spices and ironwork that clearly express her insight into the integrity of the elements she incorporates. In the shop you will find elegant displays of wreaths and frames, topiaries and hedges (the massing of usually something very textural like dried lavender or wheat) and big decadent "bouquets" that have an elegant European flare. The shop also offers Japanese and hand-dyed silk ribbon, French milled soaps, lotions, herbal bath salts and garden accessories like stakes, urns, topiary forms and lanterns. In summer this is a source for lavender plants, with a specialty in L. x *intermedia* 'Grosso' and 'Provence' (from a single pot to quantities for a hedge). If you have an interest in seeing an acre-long row of lavender (7 or 8 years old) growing as tall as you, then ask to see the growing fields, where you will also see the likes of the PeeGee hydrangeas and row upon row of perennials in the cutting gardens.

DRIVING DIRECTIONS:
Return to Hwy. 20. Turn right and follow signs for Oak Harbor, proceeding straight through Oak Harbor. The road ends at a "T" where there is a traffic signa, turn right to follow W. Hwy. 20. At the top of the hill, turn right onto Swantown Rd., then immediately left onto Ft. Nugent Rd. Follow for 3 miles to Zylstra Rd. Turn right to Hummingbird Farm. *Driving distance:* 11 miles; *Estimated driving time:* 15 minutes.

TOUR TIP
If you are planning a picnic, you can stop for fixings at the Safeway on the route you are taking through Oak Harbor. They have a deli counter for sandwiches, salads and the like.

❊ Hummingbird Farm

2319 Zylstra Rd., Oak Harbor, WA 98277; (360) 679-5044. Open March-September Monday-Saturday 9:30 a.m.-5:30 p.m., Sunday 11 a.m.-5 p.m., closed Tuesday; call for hours October-December.
🍴 ▣ ☆ ✳ RR

First-time visitors to Hummingbird Farm are quick to grab their cameras, as the gardens are works of art that are not shy about getting their pictures taken (having appeared on the cover of *Country Living Gardener*, in *Sunset* Magazine and on the Ed Hume "Gardening in America" television program). There are two primary display gardens. The front cottage garden is enclosed in a snazzy periwinkle blue fence and shows off lusty plant combinations that demonstrate luscious color combinations, architectural structure and tantalizing texture. Light-hearted accents characterize the smaller garden, from the honeysuckle draped obelisk to whimsically painted corner post birdhouses which contribute character and individuality. In this garden you'll find that separate beds feature hummingbird and butterfly plants, fragrance, and white flowers in the moon garden. On the north side of the nursery is a shade garden featuring a small water feature and appropriate plantings. There is also a rugosa rose display underplanted with lavender.

In the nursery you will find herbs (lots of lavenders), perennials (like a chocolatey colored foxglove with unusually fuzzy foliage and many *Salvias*, both the hardy and the more tender varieties) and annuals (you can count on them to always do a beautiful job with a wide array of cheerful sunflowers, potted and fresh cut). Each year they look to Britain's Thompson and Morgan as a seed source for exciting new introductions to grow and offer. I particularly appreciate the easy-to-read descriptive profiles they post near plants, many of which are uncommon varieties for which I need an introduction. Leslie Johnson and Ward Beebe are also expanding their offerings of ornamental grasses and small flowering shrubs, especially those appropriate for the small urban garden and for mixed perennial borders. Some examples are *Cotinus* 'Grace", a particularly elegant form of Smoke Tree, Barberries, shrubs with colorful and interesting foliage and ones that attract hummingbirds. Another new focus is old roses selected for hardiness, fragrance and floral color. Examples are 'Sally Holmes', 'Sombreuil' and the Rugosa hybrid 'Fimbriata'.

In the nursery shop you'll find their signature dried flowers, garden books, supplies (organic fertilizers, Felcos, Territorial and Shepherd Seeds), accessories (locally crafted rustic furniture and gift items). They have installed a reference library for their patrons' use and offer informational handouts to help them select plants for particular situations (shade, drought tolerance, deer resistance, etc.)

DRIVING DIRECTIONS:
Leaving Hummingbird Farm, turn right onto Zylstra Rd. and drive east. *Driving distance:* 1 mile; *Estimated driving time:* 3 minutes

✾ Crescent Moon Rose Garden

1911 Zylstra Rd., Oak Harbor, WA 98277; (360) 679-1799. Open by appointment and by chance most days April-September.

✳

Crescent Moon Rose Garden is the private home, garden and rose collection *extraordinaire* of Tina and Bruce Weakly. Visitors here can enjoy discovering and discussing over 700 varieties of roses set in graceful borders with many luxuriant companion plants—bulbs, perennials, annuals, vines and small shrubs. Major features of the garden include the sculptural pieces Bruce has skillfully crafted in steel, from a statuesque heron lording its presence over the pond garden to the pond's arched bridge to the many rose arbors that mark one's passage along the garden paths. Tina is justly proud that she has represented in her garden every variety of hybrid musk available in the U.S. and Canada, plus over fifty varieties of David Austin English roses grown as free-standing shrubs and climbers. She is a fount of information about roses, rose care and propagation. Tina has developed a passion for the companion plants that marry well with roses for their form, color, texture or seasonal interest and she searches far and wide to find seeds of intriguing (many little known) plants to try. Another new interest, the pond, was installed and planted over the winter of 1997-98. It has "settled in" remarkably quickly, adds another captivating feature and plant palette to the Weakly garden and presents an excellent example for visitors who have contemplated adding a medium-sized pond to their own garden.

Lunch: If you are interested in having a picnic I have listed two beachfront choices and also two restaurant suggestions. Each is within a 10-15 minute drive of Crescent Moon.

To reach **Joseph Whidbey State Park**, turn left on Zylstra Rd. heading back toward Hummingbird Farm. At Ft. Nugent Rd. turn left and drive .5 mile. Turn right onto West Beach Road and drive to the end, about one mile. This lovely isolated (day-use only) beach offers glorious views across Admiralty Inlet. There are picnic tables upland from the beach. For Hwy. 20, follow West Beach Rd. to Libbey Rd. Turn left one mile.

The other picnic option is to head to **Ft. Ebey State Park**, an abandoned military base (as are many coastal Washington State Parks) set on a wooded bluff also looking out over Admiralty Inlet. This is a fairly secluded location and offers a wonderful beach to walk along. There are very nice camping spots here as well if you are casting about for a place to nest for the night. Leave Crescent Moon turning right on Zylstra Rd. After .5 mile turn right onto Hastie Lk. Rd. At West Beach Rd. turn left. At the "T" intersection turn right onto Libbey Rd. and follow the signs to Ft. Ebey State Park. To reach Hwy. 20 follow Libbey Rd. one mile east.

If you are interested in a restaurant lunch here are two choices:

Captain Whidbey Inn: This is a picturesque, rustic Inn on Penn Cove. I enjoy sitting out on the deck under the Madrona trees overlooking the peaceful waterfront enjoying a big bowl of the mussels the Inn and the cove are famous for. There is a sweet little kitchen garden to visit tucked alongside the Inn.

Christopher's: The most sophisticated restaurant in the area is Rosi's Garden Restaurant (open for dinner only, at the time I write). However, the same owners offer delicious, though not quite as ambitious, fare at this charming spot on the historic front street of Coupeville. I had a beautifully presented Cioppino soup that featured a perfectly spiced broth and a succulent mix of fresh seafood.

Leaving Crescent Moon Rose Garden turn right onto Zylstra Rd. At Hwy. 20 turn right and follow around Penn Cove. Take the first left turn, onto Madrona Way. Watch for the Captain Whidbey Inn on the left or continue on this road to Coupeville, two miles beyond. To return to Hwy. 20 follow N. Main St. about one mile west.

DRIVING DIRECTIONS:

From the Hwy. 20 and N. Main St. intersection in Coupeville (at the pedestrian overpass) turn right (west). At the turn signal at Terry Rd. turn left and drive 1.5 miles. Turn right onto Ft. Casey Rd. and drive .75 mile.

❋ Paris Gardens

338 S. Ft. Casey Rd., Coupeville, WA 98239; (360) 678-3577. Open mid-March to mid-September, Wednesday-Sunday, 9 a.m.-5 p.m.

🌱 📖 ☆ ✳

I met Maryanne Paris in the summer of 1996 as she put the finishing touches on the foundation display garden for her new nursery. I was very impressed with how knowledgeable this young woman is about plants. Having grown up the daughter of a lily breeder probably had something to do with an early love of that genus and their fine representation, including many of his, in the substantial one-acre display garden she has developed. The nursery offers a wonderful array of unusual perennials, lilies, grasses, roses and ornamental shrubs, most of which have been propagated at the nursery, with the British seed house Chilterns as favorite source for uncommon varieties. The garden features old and hardy roses (Damask, Alba, Gallica, Moss, Centifolia, Bourbon, rambler, hybrid musk, species and some modern hardy roses). There are trellises, arbors and fences placed throughout the garden to create vertical elements and to show off the roses, which are planted among massed plantings of perennials. Shrubs and ornamental grasses add structural integrity to the vignettes created to display and demonstrate various kinds of plants or to emphasize the season—a hot border of fiery reds, oranges and yellows, for example, the blue garden and Juliet's garden, which is heart-shaped and features purple, lavender and red flowers and foliage, and a formal kitchen garden (Potager) that mixes edibles and ornamentals in a pleasing tableau. From a wonderful early show of the bulbs emerging, through the irises, roses and lilies, to the grasses, asters, mums and fall foliage there is something of focal interest throughout the seasons. Another feature here is the integration of garden art, utilitarian and ornamental, from several talented local craftsmen including John Dewitt's glasswork, troughs and planters from Frontier Garden Art and metal work from Mary Taylor of Rosebar. Paris Gardens provides a handsome gallery venue for such excellent work. With the nursery there is a small shop offering trough gardens, fountains, garden-related gear, art and gifts.

DRIVING DIRECTIONS:
Leaving Paris Gardens turn left onto Ft. Casey Rd. At Terry Rd. intersection turn right. Three roads intersect here, so be sure to take the road that forks to the left. Turn right onto Hwy. 20 and follow it south. The highway becomes Hwy. 525. 1.5 miles south of Greenbank look for the highway sign for Meerkerk Gardens and turn left onto Resort Rd. The turn to the gardens is .5 mile off Hwy. 525.

Meerkerk Rhododendron Gardens

Mail/Tel: P.O. Box 154, Greenbank, WA 98253; (360) 321-6682; 3531 S. Meerkerk Ln, Whidbey Island. http://whidbey.net/~kabowers/Meerkerk.html
Open: Daily year round with an emphasis on spring bloom, 9 a.m.-4 p.m.
Entry Fee: $2 adults, children under 12 free
Insider Tips: Guided tours are available with advance scheduling. Meerkerk offers a number of festive events in the garden each year. See the "Tour Timing" for more specifics.

❖ ✳ RR

This 53-acre site originates from the estate of Max and Ann Meerkerk. Created as a private garden in 1963, the present preserve rests in the hands of the Seattle Rhododendron Society as an endowed gift from Ann Meerkerk. Plantings showcase more than 1,800 rhododendron varieties (species and hybrid) and include examples from many well-respected local breeders, as well as English and Dutch hybrids. In the 10-acre display garden, large-leafed species and hybrids of the Grande and Falconeri series grow well in this woodland setting alongside many plants from the American Rhododendron Seed Exchange, the University of Washington Arboretum Foundation and several of Ann Meerkerk's own unnamed hybrids. Their International Hybrid Rhododendron Test Garden is expanding to be the largest collection on the West Coast. It was established to "give an impartial and consistent rating to hybrids grown here", under carefully controlled garden conditions. Highly respected plant collector Warren Berg has been hard at work planting an Asian garden to show his rare species rhododendrons, many propagated from seed he collected in China, Tibet and Bhutan. The peak bloom period for the rhododendrons is mid-April through May, so there are many activities planned during that time for visitors. In addition to rhododendrons, however, many companion plants enhance the collection. You'll find Magnolia, Dogwood, Katsura and Beech trees along with many unique specimens of Diamond Bark Maple, *Davidia involucrata* (Dove Tree), *Paulownia tomentosa* (Empress Tree), *Araucaria araucana* (Monkey Puzzle Tree), and Sequoias. A stately 43-acre evergreen forest of cedar, hemlock and Douglas fir shelters the display garden and a five-mile nature trail wends its way through the forest past wildflowers, huckleberries, ferns, salal and other Northwest native woodland plants. There is a mix of accessibility on paving, grass, mulch and gravel.

DRIVING DIRECTIONS, END OF THE TOUR:

To return to Seattle: Drive south on Hwy. 525 17 miles to Clinton. Follow road signs directly to the ferry. After disembarking from the ferry in Mukilteo, follow signs for I-5/Seattle.

Estimated driving time: (including 20 minute ferry crossing): 1 hour 30 minutes

FURTHER RESOURCES
Food

Captain Whidbey Inn: 2072 W. Captain Whidbey Inn Rd., Coupeville, WA 98239; (800) 366-4097, (360) 678-4097. $$; B,L,D daily, call for winter service. A romantic spot for its authentic rusticity and setting among Madrona trees overlooking peaceful Penn Cove. Food can range from very good to ho-hum. I have returned more than once, however, for their special preparation of mussels in a spicy ginger-laced broth, and deck seating.

Christopher's: 23 Front St., Coupeville, WA 98239. $$, L,D brunch weekends. The talented chef here features creative contemporary cuisine with specials like lamb stew and grilled ahi. There is a pleasant ambiance among book cases that form room dividers.

Island Grille: Hwy. 20 just south of Deception Pass Bridge; (360) 679-3194. $-$$, B,L,D daily. A consistently good bet offering a range from an excellent burger to more ambitious and sophisticated offerings.

Lodging

Colonel Crockett Farm Inn, 1012 South Ft. Casey Rd., Coupeville, WA 98239; (360) 678-3711, $-$$. Three acres of gardens and grounds, antique apples, old-fashioned decor. **Compass Rose**, 508 S. Main St., Coupeville, WA 98239; (800) 237-3881, (360) 678-5318, $$. A Queen Anne Victorian on the Historic Register, lots of antiques, elegant full breakfast.

Guest House Cottages Bed and Breakfast, 3366 South Hwy. 525, Greenbank, WA 98253; (360) 678-3115. $$$. Placed for seclusion and privacy on a 25-acre woodland and meadow, five individualistic, charmingly decorated cottages and a much-photographed log lodge overlook a pond. Each accommodates a maximum of two adults.

Old Morris Farm, 105 W. Morris Rd., Coupeville, WA 98239; (800) 936-6586; (360) 678-6586. $$. Just a hop off Hwy. 20 and tucked back into a woodland setting is this very stylish Colonial-style B & B, with gardens and small gift shop. Rooms are comfortable and tastefully furnished, the welcome warm. In the evening relax in front of the fire or on the sunporch with hors d'oeuvres.

Camping:

Deception Pass State Park, the most popular State Park in Washington, has a fabulous location with great beach to walk, forested campsites that look out to the water and a spellbinding view of the dramatic bridge spanning the gap between Whidbey and Fidalgo Islands 182' above. Photographers love this place, too.

Fort Casey State Park, located adjacent to the Keystone/Port Townsend ferry on one side and the historic military fortification with WWI-era bluff-top bunkers and (restored) gun-emplacements. Beachside campsites, fabulous cross-Sound views, terrific place for history buffs and for kids to play.

Fort Ebey State Park, Former WWII fortification. Wonderful beach to walk, campsites under the forest canopy, great views to the Olympic Mountains, marine traffic and sea life.

For More Information

Central Whidbey Visitor Information Center, 302 Main St., Coupeville, WA 98239; (360) 678-5434.

Island Transit, (800) 240-8747, (360) 321-6688 or visit their Web site: www.islandtransit.org/bus

Island County Historical Museum, 908 NW Alexander St., Coupeville, WA 98239; (360) 678-3310. Open May-September, 10 a.m.-5 p.m. daily, October-April 11 a.m.-4 p.m. Friday-Monday. Small fee. There is a very nice Herb and Drought Tolerant Plant Demonstration Garden along the front of the Museum.

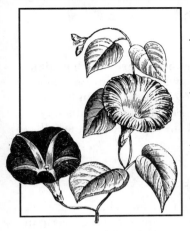

WHIDBEY ISLAND RETREAT- SOUTH

As the longest island in the continental U.S., Whidbey Island offers two distinctly different touring territories. Gardeners on the Go have two itineraries featuring the horticultural highlights from each region.

─────────── Itinerary Highlights / SOUTH ───────────
romantic Victorian farmhouse sets tone for special nursery
native plants provide focus for two passionate plantsmen
garden center balances old-fashioned favorites with the new
landscape professional offers uncommon woody plants
──────────── ⁊ ────────────

For several years I toured Whidbey Island in much the way a majority of visitors do: up and down the main highway, in and out of the island towns and on a beeline for the little cadre of special nurseries that I had come to know and love. Then, one glorious Sunday, with two good friends in tow, I slowed my pace to wander the private gardens of the generous folks who participated in the first (now annual) Whidbey Island Garden Tour. The experience gave me a greater appreciation for the people who make this island their home, for the land they cultivate and for the historical context that colors their lives.

209

🌿 THE ITINERARY IN BRIEF 🌿

❶ Cultus Bay Nursery

This is just the kind of small specialty nursery experience that plant lovers dream about. There is a long, narrow tree-lined drive that leads to open fields, where sits a lovely Victorian-style farm house—the home of the astute and talented Mary Fisher, her lush display gardens and her laudable nursery—one of the most exciting small specialty nurseries in the state.

❷ Maxwelton Valley Gardens

A specialty in natives with a focus on those that love shade and moisture reveals the origins of this nursery, as owners Ron Kerrigan and Bill Halstead sought plants to reclaim the habitat surrounding their home, destroyed by years of cattle grazing. Now salmon again spawn in the stream and a network of trails over the nine-acre property beckons visitors to explore.

Lunch A picnic on a pleasant beach or a memorable lunch in the seaside village of Langley, Gardeners on the Go are lucky to have a number of tempting options

❸ Bayview Farm and Garden

This splendid country garden center has an old-fashioned nursery ambiance, and they do offer a goodly selection of popular old time favorites, but they also offer many lovely surprises for avid gardeners on the look-out for something out of the ordinary.

❹ RainShadow Gardens

With many years of experience in landscape design work under his belt, John Holbron has turned to one of his greatest loves in life – growing and enthusing about special and unusual small trees (as in garden size) and even smaller trees (as in bonsai). John's wife Anne (Davenport) is a talented weaver and has her studio and informal shop open when the nursery is open.

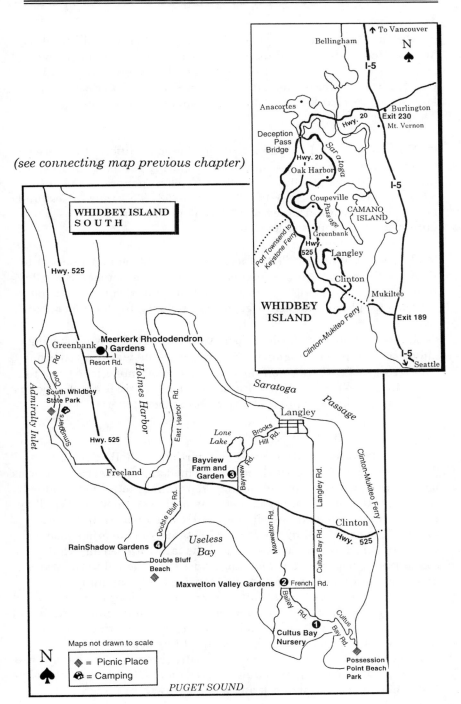

(see connecting map previous chapter)

To Vancouver

N

Bellingham

I-5

Anacortes

20
Exit 230
Burlington
Mt. Vernon

Deception
Pass
Bridge

Hwy. 20

Saratoga

Oak Harbor

I-5

Coupeville

CAMANO
ISLAND

Port Townsend to
Keystone Ferry

Pass age

Greenbank

Hwy.
525

Langley

Clinton

Mukilteo

WHIDBEY
ISLAND

Clinton-Mukilteo Ferry

Exit 189

I-5

Seattle

**WHIDBEY ISLAND
S O U T H**

Hwy. 525

Greenbank
Rd.

Meerkerk Rhododendron
Gardens

Resort Rd.

Holmes Harbor

Cove
Rd.

South Whidbey
State Park

Smuggler's

Admiralty Inlet

Hwy. 525

East Harbor Rd.

Freeland

Lone
Lake

Saratoga

Langley

Passage

Brooks
Hill Rd.

Bayview
Farm and
Garden ❸

Bayview Rd.

Langley Rd.

Clinton-Mukilteo Ferry

Double Bluff Rd.

RainShadow Gardens ❹

Double Bluff
Beach

*Useless
Bay*

Maxwelton Rd.

Clinton

Hwy. 525

Cultus Bay Rd.

Maxwelton Valley Gardens ❷ French Rd.

Bailey Rd.

Cultus Bay Rd.

❶
Cultus Bay
Nursery

Possession
Point Beach
Park

Maps not drawn to scale

N

🍂 = Picnic Place
🏕 = Camping

PUGET SOUND

211

TOUR TIMING

❧ **Cultus Bay Nursery** is open April-September (closed Tuesday); **Maxwelton Valley Gardens** is open year-round, daily in spring and summer (in fall and winter call for hours); **Bayview Farm and Garden** is open year-round, daily; **RainShadow Gardens** is open late-March to Thanksgiving, Friday- Monday (closed Tuesday-Thursday).

❧ **Whidbey Island Garden Tour** is offered at different times each year to feature what is best in the participating gardens. In 1998, the tour is slated for Saturday, **August 1**. Tickets generally sell out in advance, so order yours early: (360) 321-0358. This tour raises funds for "groups which work toward maintenance, restoration or improvement of common habitat."

❧ The South Whidbey **Tilth Farmers' Market** sets up adjacent to Bayview Farm and Garden from late May through October, Saturdays from 10 a.m. Along with produce fresh from the farm there are herbs, ornamental plants, flowers, eggs, berry products, fresh seafood, etc.

❧ Consider a mile-and-a-half loop walk through an awe-inspiring old-growth stand of Douglas fir, Sitka spruce and western red cedar. The **Wilbert Trail** starts on the eastern side of Smuggler's Cove Rd. at the **South Whidbey State Park** entrance. There is a rich tapestry of flora to quicken the pulse of any woodland gardener!

SETTING THE SCENE

From the 1850s onwards, central and northern Whidbey Island developed rapidly, as fertile land was farmed and coastal communities became commercial hubs for moving crops to market. This included trees from the active timber industry as well. But on south Whidbey Island, which was more heavily forested, timber was initially the name of the game and by the late 1870s there were over a dozen camps in this area and it wasn't until the late 19th century that communities began to develop. Logs were cut, skidded to the water and formed into floating rafts to be transported to sawmills by steamers. There was a great influx of workers for logging and sawmill work, including hundreds of Scandinavians. In time many settled and became farmers involved in tending orchards, cultivating food crops, raising livestock and establishing support businesses.

By the turn-of-the-century most of the first growth Douglas fir forest had been cut so logging companies moved on to Camano Island and/or began cutting cedar, hemlock and second growth fir.

COMMUNITY PROFILES

Clinton was first settled in 1870 (first named Phinney but later the name was changed to Clinton for a hometown in Michigan). Steamer traffic was an important business—all too important as it turns out, as the port closed with serious financial consequences in the early 1890s with the advent of rail developments on the mainland. Prosperity returned when the Clinton/Mukilteo ferry began operating in 1925 and the town began to take shape.

Freeland got its name as a socialist Free Land Association in the early 20th century. Five-acre sites were offered for $10 and the promise of labor towards a cooperative effort in building a town. They were able to build their first enterprise, a store, before the group disbanded. The name survived.

Greenbank claims fame as home to the largest loganberry farm in the world (circa 1946.) In the early 1900s 1,500 acres of land at this narrowest spot on Whidbey Island was purchased by Calvin Philips. He was a real estate agent who had been commissioned to come to the island to sell 10,000 acres. As the countryside was heavily forested, lumber and shingle mills were the first residents. A large migration of Finnish families to the area led to farming and the establishment of loganberry vineyards. The site of Calvin Philips' old dairy barn is now a Chateau Ste. Michelle property, Whidbeys Greenbank Berry Farm (still one of the largest loganberry growers in the U.S.) The berries are used in a distinctive liqueur.

Langley: In the early 1880s an enterprising German immigrant, Jacob Anthes (at age fifteen), purchased 120 acres on south Whidbey's eastern coast. He started a cordwood business to supply fuel for the steamers working on Puget Sound. At this time the boats were not very efficient, requiring up to 40 cords every 24 hours of running time! When he turned 21 he qualified for a homestead claim of an additional 160 acres. He built a post office and general store and joined with one of the investors in his company, Seattle Judge J. W. Langley, to plat the town of that name. Scandinavian immigrants had begun to arrive in large numbers to work as loggers.

Today Langley is the hub of commercial activity with several up-scale shops, inns and eateries. It retains its charming small-town ambiance, is a favored home and gallery venue for artists and has an excellent little bookshop, the **Moonraker**. Don't miss **Langley Village** a complex of intriguing shops that are a hidden (as in not very obvious) discovery (as in you'll be pleased to find them) nestled between Second and Third Streets. Gardeners on the Go will appreciate the climbing roses, wisteria and fountains along the bricked courtyard/passageway.

TOUR TIP

Ferry line-ups from Mukilteo headed for Whidbey Island are very long on summer Friday evenings and weekend mornings. Sunday afternoon line-ups are long in Clinton headed to Mukilteo.

DRIVING DIRECTIONS:

From mid-town Seattle drive north on I-5 to the Whidbey Island/Mukilteo Ferry exit #182. Drive north on Hwy. 525 to Mukilteo (26 miles from downtown Seattle) and follow signs for the ferry (20 minute ferry crossing). Disembarking in Clinton go north on Hwy. 525 for 2.7 miles. At the traffic signal at "Ken's Corner" (IGA Market) turn left onto Cultus Bay Rd., go 4 miles south. The nursery is at the intersection with Bailey Rd. Watch for the sign on your right.
Driving distance: 33 miles; *Estimated driving time:* 1 hour 15 minutes (including ferry crossing but not time waiting in line to catch the ferry)

TOUR TIP

If you are picnicking and in search of fixings, stop at the IGA Market deli at Ken's Corner. If you have arrived on Whidbey in need of sustenance, you'll find the excellent **Kiichli's Bagel Bakery** in the Ken's Corner shopping complex as well. For a pleasant breakfast, brunch or early lunch on the beach there is a waterfront park, **Possession Point**, a mile-and-a-half south of Cultus Bay Nursery. From Cultus Bay Rd. turn left onto Possession Rd. to the Park. Start your day of adventure on Whidbey with a lovely beach and great views, relaxing to the lap of the surf and the call of seabirds.

Cultus Bay Nursery

4000 E. Bailey Rd., Clinton, WA 98236; (360) 579-2329. Open April-September, daily, closed Tuesday, 9 a.m.-5 p.m.; after September by appointment
❖ ☂ ✳

The front path to Mary Fisher's inviting domain is flanked by mature lavender hedging. To the right a sumptuous perennial border is backed by a handsome Hemlock hedge. It is easy to gravitate immediately to the extravagant border, walking slowly along its face transfixed by the array of interesting plants that vie for your attention. It is a surprise, then, to realize that at the end of the border the Hemlock hedge forms an entry "gateway" to the nursery protected within. At the point of this revelation you have the serious decision to get right on with the business of poking through the pots of plants on offer or to continue around the house to view the additional display borders demonstrating the use of soft color combinations, hot color combinations, shade plantings, a kitchen garden and a terraced dry bank. When you do make your way into the nursery it is along a path bordered by espaliered apple trees. Within you will find well-described unusual perennials, herbs, vines (with delight I found an *Ampelopsis brevipedunculata,* the 'porcelain berry vine') and great shrubs for fall color (my current heart throb). Some examples are *Hippophae rhamnoides* (Sea Buckthorn, excellent seaside plant, great berries in fall/winter), *Medlars* (Crabapples), unusual hydrangeas and Mary's best ideas on deer-proof plants. My advice is to let Mary walk you through the collection to take advantage of her familiarity with less common plants. She has a genius for selecting hard-working varieties with outstanding features (fragrance, ornamental fruit, fall foliage, winter berry, elegant silhouette, hardiness, etc.) that may be totally foreign to most home gardeners. She continues to build an enviable vine collection: species clematis, *Loniceras* (honeysuckle), *Hobelia* and *Schisandra, Solanums* (Potato Vines) and the botanical treats she has brought back from England (as seeds or cuttings) have matured to good size.

Visitors are drawn to the hand-crafted English-style trugs, baskets, flower pots and cloches that give this nursery magical accents. By the way, did you see the snazzy write-up on Cultus Bay Nursery/Mary Fisher in the Early Spring 1996 issue of *Country Gardens* Magazine? The photos don't begin to do justice to the setting and I think you'll agree a visit in person is far more glorious. (See, also, *Sunset,* July 1995, *Pacific* Magazine, February 1998, *House and Garden,* March 1998).

Driving Directions:

From Cultus Bay Nursery return to Bailey Rd. at Cultus Bay Rd. Turn left onto Bailey Rd. and drive 1.25 miles to French Rd. Turn right .25 miles to Maxwelton Gardens.
Driving distance: 1.5 miles; *Estimated driving time:* 10 minutes.

❇ Maxwelton Valley Gardens

3443 E. French Rd., Clinton, WA 98236; (360) 579-1770.
www.whidbey.com/mvg
Open year-round, daily spring and summer 10 a.m.-6 p.m., but call ahead for fall and winter hours.
Insider Tip: If you are not on a big "plant hunting" expedition but more a "gardening" themed day of exploration, you will welcome the opportunity to walk the woodland trails at Maxwelton Gardens, especially for the many thoughtfully prepared informational signs that provide interesting horticultural and natural history notes.

❖ ✳

In 1985 Ron Kerrigan and his partner Bill Halstead bought this nine-acre property on Whidbey Island as their home and now, nursery, with a dream to reclaim the native habitat destroyed by years of cattle grazing. The plants they sought to reintroduce were not easily available, which led to developing a horticultural specialty in the plants they most avidly sought themselves, including ones for difficult conditions such as dry shade, wet soils, stream banks subject to drying sun and wind and aggressive browsing of deer and rabbits. (Sound familiar, anyone?) With a horticultural degree from Edmonds Community College and having former charge of the greenhouses at Seattle's Center for Urban Horticulture, Bill came armed with the expertise to direct their restoration plans. They now offer Northwest native plants; fragrant rhododendrons; woodland shade plants; plants for dry shade; drought-tolerant plants; unusual perennials; Pacific Coast, Japanese and Siberian irises and flowering shrubs and trees. They have put a tremendous effort into opening their extensive woodland, criss-crossed by two streams, with a nature trail system liberally marked with informational signage (wear appropriate foot gear). They have prepared excellent informational labeling on their plant stock, as well, and offer detailed plant lists organized by special conditions: "Plants to attract birds and butterflies", "Plants for seaside gardens", "Plants for general drought tolerance", "Plants for summer color", "Plants for fall/winter" and "Plants for shade", to name a few. A good time to visit for iris bloom is April-June and especially the week-ends before, during and after Memorial Day.

Lunch: If you are in a picnic mood return to Cultus Bay Rd. and drive one-and-a-half miles south to Possession Point Park (see note above). If what you want is a restaurant lunch then three *terrific* suggestions are **Trattoria Giuseppe** (a top favorite of locals, offering a glorious Italian menu) located at Ken's Corner or, in the town of Langley, the ever-popular **Café Langley** (for a memorable Mediterranean-influenced lunch) or just down the street and up the stairs, try **Star Bistro**, where you can enjoy delicious fare and a sunny day from their deck.

Driving Directions Lunch:
Leaving Maxwelton Valley Gardens continue along French Rd. traveling east .75 mile to Cultus Bay Rd. If you are going to Possession Point for a picnic turn right and continue as per the directions given above. Otherwise, turn left onto Cultus Bay Rd. At the traffic signal at the intersection with Hwy. 525 you will find Trattoria Giuseppe straight across the highway in the Ken's Corner complex. If you are continuing on to Langley, go straight through the traffic signal where Cultus Bay Rd. becomes Langley Rd. and follow for 1.5 miles to Langley.
Driving distance: 5 miles; *Estimated driving time:* 15 minutes.

DRIVING DIRECTIONS:

To reach Bayview Farm and Garden, continue north on Hwy. 525 from Ken's Corner two miles. Turn right onto Bayview Rd. then left onto Marshview Ave. The nursery is behind the big red barn on the left. If you are coming from Langley, travel west on 3rd St. which becomes Brooks Hill Rd. and then becomes Bayview Rd. Turn right onto Marshview Ave. *Driving distance:* 2 miles; *Estimated driving time:* 10 minutes

❈ Bayview Farm and Garden

2780 Marshview Ave., Langley, WA 98260; (360) 321-7161, FAX 321-0959
Open: Monday-Saturday 9 a.m.-6 p.m., Sunday 10 a.m.-5 p.m.

❖ ⚲ 📖 ☆ ✳ RR

This great little garden center was a happy discovery one summer as I poked around the back roads on Whidbey Island. The serious greenhouse was my first clue, particularly one nestled amid lots of handsome trees, shrubs and perennials. Closer inspection revealed the selection included lots of tasty surprises—the unusual varieties that make a "plant hunter's" pulse quicken. Maureen and Jim Rowley have grown plants for other nurseries throughout this region since 1988, and opened their own retail nursery in January, 1993. Maureen comes from a family business of manufacturing an excellent line of greenhouses. It is especially gratifying to see the effort put into a super selection of seeds (Shepherd, Solly's Choice, Seeds of Change, Territorial, Burpee, Ed Hume), customer education/support, and lots of organic supplies with a strictly non-toxic approach to pest control. This year-round garden center has on-hand a good selection of quality English gardening tools and Wellies, bulk soil amendments, books, pots, houseplants . . .

DRIVING DIRECTIONS:

Leaving Bayview Farm and Garden, return to Hwy. 525. Turn right and drive north three miles. Turn left onto Double Bluff Rd. Drive two miles and turn right up the steep driveway to RainShadow Gardens.

TOUR TIP:

The beach of Double Bluff Park is directly beyond the turn for RainShadow Gardens if a sandy beach walk is in order.

❈ RainShadow Gardens

6298 So. Double Bluff Rd., Freeland, WA 98249; (360) 321-8003
Open: late March through Thanksgiving, Friday-Monday 11 a.m.-5 p.m. and by appointment

✳

Anne Davenport and John Holbron offer an enthusiastic welcome to their nursery, which has risen from the richly enhanced soil of a former dairy farm. There is a spectacular view west from their setting atop a bluff overlooking the Strait of Juan de Fuca with the Olympic Mountains beyond. I first met Anne Davenport a few years ago as we bumped heads over a flamboyant pot of ornamental grass at Bayview Farm and Garden. We left exchanging cards; the one she gave me was for a "dream nursery" she and partner John Holbron had for a place specializing in the plants they love, primarily unusual trees and shrubs with a smattering of uncommon perennials. Skip forward a few years and there I was snooping around a nursery I'd been directed to explore when along came a vaguely familiar face and simultaneous recognition dawned. Hours later we emerged (John had joined us) from a distinguished display garden collection of "woodies" which had engaged our undivided attention. From the *Stewartia monadelpha* to the handsome *Paulownia tomentosa* (Empress Tree) and from the *Xanthoceras sorbifolium* (Yellowhorn) to the *Viburnum setigerum* (Tea Viburnum), I had much to learn and they to share. There are a number of display garden areas (including an extensive collection of ornamental grasses, a large display of shade-loving plants and an impressive bonsai collection). In the nursery look for *Prunus mume* (Japanese Flowering Apricot noted for late winter flower and superior fragrance), *Idesia polycarpa* (noted for its large leaves and later in life fall berries), *Betulas* (they offer birches noted for pest and disease resistance), and several Japanese maples (a particularly outstanding cultivar is *Acer palmatum* 'Ukigomo', the Floating Cloud maple).

Driving Directions, End of the Tour

If you are headed for Seattle, return to Hwy. 525 proceeding east on Double Bluff Rd. Turn right onto Hwy. 525 and drive south eight miles to Clinton. Follow the signs for the ferry. Disembark at Mukilteo, and follow signs for Seattle along Hwy. 525, turning left onto Hwy. 525 (84th St. SW) 4.5 miles to I-5, take the southbound on-ramp for Seattle (26 miles). *Driving distance:* 39 miles; *Estimated driving time:* 1 hour 20 minutes (including the ferry crossing but not time in the ferry line at Clinton).

Further Resources

Food

Café Langley, 113 1st St., Langley, WA 98260; (360) 221-3090. L Wednesday-Monday, D daily, reservations recommended week-ends (closed Tuesday in winter). $$. I've enjoyed many memorable meals here over the years. There is a Mediterranean/Greek specialty but Northwest seafood features prominently as well. Lamb is succulent, served as a kebob sandwich; Moussaka is deliciously spicy, and their pastas (artichoke heart, roasted red pepper, feta or one with seafood) are consistently well prepared.

Island Bakery, 1625 E. Main, Freeland, WA 98249; (360) 331-6282. $-$$, B,L and until 5 p.m. (except Sunday until 3 p.m.) A bustling bakery that offers sit-down café fare as well—delicious quiche, substantial sandwiches, homemade soups, and a couple of pastry cases packed with temptation

Kiichli's Bagel Bakery, at Ken's Corner Mall Hwy. 525 at Cultus Bay Rd., Clinton; (360) 341-4302. Fabulous New York style bagels made in-house with great variety: Cranberry, Onion Dill, Sundried Tomato, Jalapeño, Pesto. Order yours with lox and cream cheese, scrambled egg and salsa, etc.

Sfoglia, 1594 Main St., Freeland, WA 98249; (360) 331-4080. $. Open Monday-Saturday, 10:30 a.m.- 6:30 p.m., gourmet fresh pasta take-out or enjoy outdoor seating in the garden in summer. The deli counter features fresh greens from the garden, luscious pasta sauces and fresh pasta, many cheeses, sliced meats and rustic breads. If you are picnicking or self-catering this makes an inspiring culinary resource.

Star Bistro, 201½ 1st St., Langley, WA 98260; (360) 221-2627. $-$$, L,D daily. Busy hot spot and a favorite lunch spot for locals. Jazzy decor, view of Saratoga Passage, deck for sunny summer days. Good burgers, sandwiches, and pasta dishes with specials that are a bit fancier.

Trattoria Giuseppe, 4141 E. Hwy. 525, Langley, WA 98260; (360) 341-3454. $$, L Monday-Friday, D daily. The romantic ambiance within belies the strip mall facade of this traditional and sophisticated Italian restaurant. The talent in the kitchen wins rave reviews and a loyal local following.

LodGiNG

There are around 50 Bed and Breakfast Inns on Whidbey Island—this represents 25% of the total registered in the State of Washington! Look to the "Introduction" chapter for books I recommend that specifically review accommodations in the Pacific Northwest, as they do quite a good job reviewing the possibilities in this area. There are many wonderful choices I just don't have room to list here!

Island County Bed and Breakfast Page: www.whidbey.net/islandco/b_and_b.html

Bed & Breakfast Association, P.O. Box 259, Langley, Washington 98260; www.whidbey.com/bandb

French Road Farm Cottage, (360) 321-2964 or (360) 321-4378; $$$ www.frenchroadfarm.com A beautifully restored and decorated farmhouse cottage on ten acres is surrounded by perennial, rose, herb and kitchen gardens, a vineyard and a trail that leads across the hayfield to the woodland. The reading room features antique and modern books to delight literary gardeners. The cottage is available for up to four persons who have the entire farm and its wonderful gardens to themselves.

Froggwell Garden, same telephone contacts as French Road Farm Cottage; $$$ www.froggwell.com The home and garden of Ralph Hastings and the late Holly Turner (see note at the end of this chapter) is available on selected dates to accommodate up to four persons who will have the entire "Estate" to themselves to roam and enjoy. Enveloped by a Douglas fir and hemlock forest, the extensive and varied gardens surround a remarkable, creatively designed home built by Ralph. Respect for the talented Holly Turner is evidenced in the 1998 *House and Garden* magazine feature on Froggwell and praise from Rosemary Verey in her book *Secret Gardens*. This makes a particularly special restorative retreat because of the peaceful setting, inspirational surroundings and the wheelchair accessibility of the house and grounds.

Camping: see the recommendations in **Whidbey Island Retreat/North**.

For More Information

Langley Chamber of Commerce, 124 ¾ 2nd St., Langley, WA 98260; (360) 221-6765.
South Whidbey Historical Museum, 312 2nd St., Langley, WA 98260. Open Saturday-Sunday, 1-4 p.m.

More Resources for Gardeners

North Cascades Institute, 2105 State Route 20, Sedro-Woolley, WA 98284-9394; (360) 856-5700, ext. 209. The NCI offers a class annually in May, "Nature's Intimate Details, Botanical Drawing with Pen and Pencil", with skilled artist, Ramona Hammerly. The course takes place at a retreat on south Whidbey over a three-day week-end. Request their catalog which lists many, many courses (offered throughout Western Washington) of interest to gardeners from the perspective of the naturalist (many wildflower-related hikes, kayak trips; illustrated journal keeping; ethnobotany by kayak; wild edibles; alpine ecology; forest ecology).

❧ Tribute to Holly Turner ❧

If a garden is the reflection of the garden maker, then the sophisticated, vibrant and dignified garden at Froggwell provides a semblance of the creative hand that shaped it from a wilderness woodland. I regret that I did not know Holly Turner during the time she shared her great knowledge, wise insights and deep love of gardening through classes offered at the garden. I am most fortunate, though, to have visited Froggwell several times during the last two years of Holly's life, because from the moment that I emerged from the surrounding forest on that first visit, this magical masterpiece had a profound influence on me that has forever changed the way I see a garden. Holly was a talented visionary, who orchestrated the artistic interplay of the horticultural context and constituent parts brilliantly and was anxious to invite others in for a look.

When you see something as strong and vital as Froggwell it is hard to think of it also as fragile. Holly's death to Lou Gehrig's disease on December 1, 1997 leads one to reflect on the vulnerability and ephemeral qualities of gardens and garden makers. It is a tribute to Holly that throughout her two-year illness she remained firmly in control of her work of art, although from her scooter and through the hands of many faithful and admiring friends who volunteered untold hours to fine tune a demanding, labor-intensive garden to one pared down to a more manageable scale.

This is the kind of garden that begs for the time to wander and absorb the whole and all its integral elements. Happily, the garden legacy of Holly Turner, and the glorious home she and partner Ralph Hastings built, lives on with the opening of Froggwell for overnight accommodations. Revenues will provide up-keep funding for the garden while offering a restorative retreat for visitors who will appreciate the opportunity to intimately experience this outstanding garden. It is a fitting tribute to Holly's memory.

PASTORAL SKAGIT VALLEY

—————————— Itinerary Highlights ——————————
world renowned commercial tulip fields
an English style stroll garden
rustic barns and romantic farmhouses
shops featuring elegant and eclectic garden ornaments
award-winning "destination" nursery

———————————— ❧ ————————————

For decades this valley has drawn many thousands of visitors each spring to meander the country backroads soaking in vast carpets of brilliantly-hued tulips, commercial bulb fields planted in wide swaths from here to the horizon. Where flowers don't grace the landscape, the more subtle foliage of a multitude of crops clothes the countryside, punctuated by picturesque wooden barns, sturdy farmhouses and evocative country churches. It is no surprise that Gardeners on the Go find an affinity for those who make their home in this rich agrarian valley.

❦ THE ITINERARY IN BRIEF ❦

❶ Christianson's Nursery

The ambiance of this "destination" nursery, noted for its extensive selection of roses, reflects the heart and soul of the surrounding countryside. Resident beasties (llamas, rabbits, cats) draw praise from children who have brought their parents along on the tour.

❷ La Conner Flats English Garden

Now here is a genuine *secret* garden. Amazingly, this gem was planted in 1987, though you will swear it must date back decades. It is very possible to have haunted the nursery adjacent for years and never dreamed the essence of an English garden lay tucked but a few paces away.

❸ Through the Garden Gate

Wendy Bott confesses to being a "new gardener" but the display garden she has planted for her visitors bursts with vitality and imagination, belying her modest assertion! Her shop is an eclectic mingling of decorative and functional accessories for home and garden with an emphasis on arbors and trellises, topiaries and pots.

Lunch La Conner has a number of inviting restaurants or you may plan a picnic.

❹ Inside Out

This distinctive shop, fanciful and fun, offers a vast inventory of garden statuary from the classical to the whimsical, from elegant cast sandstone pots to the ever popular piglets that populate the shop's showroom and extend out into the surrounding garden.

❺ Go Outside

The sophisticated selection here will appeal to home and garden enthusiasts who have a taste for elegance, an eye for quality in design and craftsmanship and an appreciation for the unique.

❻ Larkspur Farm

Fields of glorious color and texture surround Jan Johnson's fresh cut and dried flower shop, where festive seasonal events feature special antique treasures along with hand-crafted garden art, garden-related products and a buffet lunch under a gala party tent.

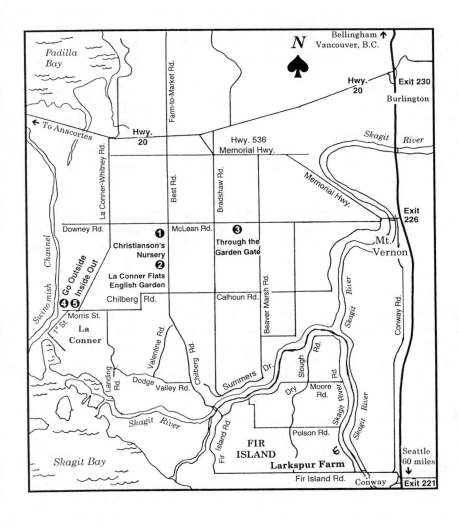

TOUR TIMING

❧ If you plan a visit to coincide with the **Tulip Festival** (late March to mid-April, with peak bloom time dependent on the weather) I suggest you consider scheduling the *Gardeners on the Go* Tour for another time! The roads are quite congested and restaurants and accommodations draw overflowing crowds. If the lure of the event draws you inexorably, try mid-week if you can, and get an early start! I personally love the vision at early dawn, but was once skunked by a heavy fog and found solace in a good breakfast at the *Calico Cupboard* (Mt. Vernon) until the sun shone through.

❧ While famed for its stupendous April tulips, this Valley is also justly famous for fields featuring daffodils (March), iris (May), summer lilies and crops of peas, cabbage, cauliflower, broccoli, cucumbers, carrots, corn, wheat, strawberries, raspberries and blueberries, a number of seed crops, and in the fall, potatoes, apples, squash, pumpkins and dahlias. A total of 70 commercially significant crops grow in this area.

❧ In winter's solitude, the farm fields draw flocks of Trumpeter swans and snow geese, feeding on the stubble of summer's crops or on winter barley planted under a program, "Barley for Birds", which pays farmers a stipend to provide this nutritious crop.

SETTING THE SCENE

The Skagit Valley stretches from the North Cascade Mountain Range westward to the salt marsh shores of Puget Sound, 60 miles north of Seattle and 90 miles south of Vancouver, British Columbia. Snaking its way along the spine of the valley, and central to its history, development and character is the mighty Skagit River, second largest river (after the Columbia) in the western continental U.S.

Early pioneers of the mid-1800s logged the valley floor and years of flooding brought annual deposits of fertile alluvial soil. In the 1880s the arduous task of building dikes began throughout the Skagit flats, now the province of diverse and productive farms. The character of the small communities that dot the countryside is flavored by the nationality of settlers drawn to build their lives here: Swedes in La Conner, Croatians and Scandinavians in Anacortes, Norwegians in Edison and Conway, the Dutch in Mt. Vernon, Finns near Lake Murray, Italians and Greeks in Concrete and people of the North Carolina Smoky Mountains settled "up-Valley"—from Lyman to Marblemount. One of the charms of this area is the legacy of turn-of-the-century architecture spared the eraser of progress. The towns of

La Conner, Anacortes and Mt. Vernon, along with farmhouses throughout the Valley, reflect their heritage in the elegant brick facades and fanciful wood detailing of the late-1880s to the 1940s. Watch for murals, plaques and historic descriptions.

The history of the valley's most widely admired crops, tulip and daffodil bulbs, goes back to 1906, when Mary Brown Stewart planted the first recorded commercial bulb crop. A 1926 embargo on imported bulbs brought Dutch growers to Washington in search of business opportunities here. It wasn't until after WWII (in spite of the lifting of the embargo) that a viable, competitive commercial industry had established itself in this most hospitable climate. While tulips tend to be the star performers, drawing hundreds of thousands of admirers early in April, in fact, for every acre of tulips planted there are two acres of daffodils. Their bloom period is in March. The largest bulb grower in the United States, the Washington Bulb Company, is located here with hundreds of acres in daffodils, tulips and irises. All told, there are 2,200 acres in these crops throughout the Skagit Valley, amounting to about $12 million in revenue and representing 73% of Washington State's bulb-planted acreage. Gardens far and wide are enriched by over 41 million bulbs sold from this productive region in one year! Orders for bulbs are taken during the Tulip Festival when visitors can make their discerning decision first hand while touring labeled display gardens and the dazzling fields in bloom. Sale of freshly dug (dormant) bulbs is in September and October, and makes a compelling excuse for Gardeners on the Go to plan a trip to **Pastoral Skagit Valley** at this time.

COMMUNITY PROFILES

Mt. Vernon: This community of 21,820 developed along the shores of the Skagit River around 1890 as a natural commercial port with access to settlers arriving from Puget Sound downstream and traders with products to get to market from upstream forests, mines and farms. The commercial district in the heart of town prides itself on the many turn-of-the-century buildings that have survived.

La Conner: This community of 780, with much of its original architecture intact, is on the National Historic Register. Sited near the confluence of the Skagit River and Puget Sound it was founded as a trading post shortly after the Civil War. From the 1930s it attracted artists and writers, many of whom have become prominent: Morris Graves, Guy Anderson, Richard Gilkey, Tom Robbins and frequent visitors from Seattle Mark Tobey and Kenneth Callahan. Many charming shops line First Street drawing crowds year-round.

225

DRIVING DIRECTIONS

From Seattle: from northbound I-5 take exit #212, go west through Conway on Fir Island Road, which becomes Chilberg Road and then intersects Best Road. **From Vancouver B.C. / Bellingham**: from southbound I-5 take the Hwy. 20 exit #230, and go 5 miles west to Best Road. Turn left crossing the highway and drive 2 miles. Christianson's is on the right, past McLean Road.

Driving distance (Seattle): 70 mi.; *Estimated driving time:* 1 hr. 20 min.

※ Christianson's Nursery:

1578 Best Road, Mt. Vernon, WA 98273-9294; (360) 466-3821, (800) 585-8200. Open year-round 9 a.m.-6 p.m., Sunday 11 a.m.-5 p.m.; in spring, daily 9 a.m.-6 p.m.

Insider Tip: if you are drawn by the vast collection of roses, write in late winter for the list, then call ahead to reserve your "must haves". Request the newsletter and you'll be able to plan for the monthly plant sale specials and perhaps fit one of their timely lectures into your schedule, too.

❖ ᛏ ▦ ☆ ✳ RR

Past visitors to the Northwest Flower and Garden Show will no doubt recognize this nursery for its award winning display gardens, the creative efforts of John and Toni Christianson. Their nursery embodies that same romantic ambiance in an appealing country setting. Some of the reasons this endures as a favorite spot for me are the well chosen plants (many unusual varieties), broad range of good-sized trees and shrubs and the pleasure of wandering through the large glass greenhouse, home to exuberant vines, exotic foliage plants and the musical murmuring of the resident (caged) doves and parakeets. The circa 1888 Lee Schoolhouse, an original one-roomer moved from across the valley, houses lectures, an annual Rose Show (in July) and other festive events. In 1998 the new display garden, featuring roses, establishes itself around this nostalgic building.

TOUR TIP

Flower lovers rejoice! This Valley has many seasonal roadside stands offering fat bouquets of fresh cut tulips, iris, daffodils, sunflowers, dahlias and the like. Rig a receptacle that won't slosh water all over the car to keep your bouquets in top shape for the ride home. Larkspur Farm offers a handy version for sale, adapted from this professional's own successful system. In Fall also find top quality, freshly dug bulbs ready for replanting: the selections at Roozengaarde and West Shore Acres are justly famous, and draw faithful customers back annually (see details in the **Resources** list at the end of this chapter.)

DRIVING DIRECTIONS

Leaving Christianson's parking area turn right onto Best Road. Watch for the sign and parking lot for the La Conner Flats Garden, 200 yards south, on the right.

🎌 La Conner Flats English Garden

1598 Best Road, Mt. Vernon, WA 98273; (360) 466-3190. Open: year-round, daily, dusk to dawn, entry by donation

Timing Tip: Of course, tulip time in April is wonderful, but there is an impressive show of roses in June, long borders of perennials through the summer and in fall the orchard puts on an enviable display.

The Granary: This restaurant in the garden was in transition at the time of printing. They intend to serve hot and cold beverages and light lunches.

❖ ✳

Long-time Gardeners on the Go visiting the Skagit Valley fondly remember Hart's Nursery. These days you will find Bill and Margery Hart still hard at work next door to their former passion, now Christianson's Nursery. Their traditional English garden is planted to provide interest over a span of eight months, with a rose garden, an orchard, a large pond, an extensive cutting garden, perennial borders and annual beds. Most of all, though, here is a rich tapestry of trees, shrubs and hedges—who could imagine they were planted in 1987! Not many of our gardens can accommodate the sheer scale of the long mixed shrub allée, and the many island beds mingling stately conifers and a glorious mix of deciduous trees. These gardens continue to thrill visitors with a sense of having left the Pacific Northwest for the horticultural heritage of the British Isles, if only for a brief stroll.

DRIVING DIRECTIONS

Turn left on Best Road and then right (at the first stop sign) onto McLean Road. Your destination is 2 miles on the right.

🎌 Through the Garden Gate

1374 McLean Road, Mt. Vernon, WA 98273; (360) 424-0195. Open: March through October, Tuesday-Saturday, 10 a.m.-5 p.m. (fall hours, call ahead)

Insider Tip: incredible strawberries available, in June; also call ahead if your visit is on a Sunday afternoon or Monday, as Wendy is most happy to open.

⛱ ☆ ✳

Wendy Bott, has assembled a snazzy collection of garden trellises and arbors (a specialty are the hand-forged iron pieces by Fir Island artist Mary Taylor), outdoor cedar and willow furniture and witty and whimsical garden ornaments. In the cozy shop you'll find an espresso bar (tea also offered) and freshly-made sweets to enjoy while perusing the outstanding work of local artists along with Wendy's own pieces of hand painted furniture and her excellent selection of appealing topiaries (my favorite is a very fat skulking cat but the cocky rooster is a close second). Be sure to stroll through the garden gate at the back of the shop into a melange of display gardens, where a pleasant patio beckons for you to rest awhile. You are also invited to bring a picnic and spread out in the shade of the majestic trees.

TOUR TIP:
Have you ever tried to guess what crop it is you are driving past when you are in farm country? In the Skagit Valley helpful signs along the roadside inform you that you are passing "Alfalfa (Cow Food)" or "Beet Seed" or "Potatoes".

DRIVING DIRECTIONS
Turn left onto McLean Road and proceed to the La Conner-Whitney Road. Turn left and drive into La Conner. Two of my favorite haunts here are on this main street, Morris, coming into town. Keep your eyes peeled on the right for a riotous row of gawking gargoyles signaling your arrival at Inside Out. Further along, at the intersection with 2nd Street you'll find Go Outside.
Driving distance: 5 miles; *Estimated driving time:* 10 minutes

Lunch: La Conner has a number of good places for lunch. If you are hungry NOW, proceed up Morris Street to the heart of town. For its splendid atmosphere and knockout hand-tossed, wood-fired pizzas go straight to the **La Conner Brewing Company**. For a more up-scale lunch plan on **Palmer's** or its sister **Andiamo**. For simpler deli fare, try the excellent **Hungry Moon** for eat-in, deck seating or consider take-out for a picnic. There is a place to sit along the Slough at Waterfront Park, across First Street and to the left two blocks.

❖ Inside Out

711 E. Morris Street; P.O. Box 1367, La Conner, WA 98257; (360) 466-3144
Open Summer, daily 11 a.m.-6 p.m., Winter, Monday-Wednesday by chance or appointment, Thursday-Sunday 11 a.m.-6 p.m

❖ ⚘ ☆ ✳ (garden art)

This is a terrific shop to find a wild conglomeration of cast sandstone garden ornaments, from stately statues to the ever popular piglets. Karen Hackett will invite you into the dazzling livingroom populated with architectural and garden statuary: pedestals for your parlor fern and pots for your patio petunias, urns and urchins—classical, historical, ornamental English, contemporary and whimsical. Something for every sensibility, and especially for Northwest gardens, summer *and* winter alike! Innovative as always, Karen has come to the rescue of garden creators who puzzle over the expense and hassle of acquiring (BIG, HEAVY) stone—she has perfected a very respectable look-alike, durable AND lightweight!

❊ Go Outside

111 E. Morris Street; P.O. Box 216, La Conner, WA 98257; (360) 466-4836.
Open year-round, daily 10 a.m.-6 p.m.
Insider Tip: Ask to be on their mailing list for the date of the annual sale
which brings loyal customers from afar for great bargains.

❖ ⵎ 🕮 ☆ ✳ (garden art)

This artfully assembled and masterfully arranged collection of
temptations offers serious English garden tools, handsome hand
painted serving bowls (perhaps from Provence or Tuscany), a library
of well-chosen horticultural books, rustic bee skeps and sophisticated
urns. At a time when everyone seems to offer designer bird houses,
the Epsteins have outdone themselves in seeking out *la creme de la
creme*, worth a visit in their own right. While essentially elegant and
upscale, this shop provides a good snoop for gardening types of all
persuasions. I turn to Go Outside for my (very reasonably priced)
authentic French rubber shoes and favorite waterproof, breathable
gardening gloves.

TOUR TIP:
In the Fall (September, especially) plan on stocking up on farm fresh
vegetables from road-side stands along the route: corn, cukes, potatoes,
pumpkins and squash, carrots and the like. I suggest one such diversion
on this next leg of the itinerary:

DRIVING DIRECTIONS
Leave La Conner backtracking along Morris Street. At the outskirts of
town take the right hand fork in the road onto Chilberg Road watching for
Dodge Valley Road. Turn right and follow it along through farm country
past Valentine to meet Chilberg Road again. Turn right, go over the
Skagit River onto Fir Island Road at the blinking light keeping to the right.
You'll pass, or if you are so inclined you'll stop to explore **Snow Goose
Produce**, a very good farm stand, where you may divert for the rich, hand
dipped ice cream cones, an espresso and a wide selection of the
season's bounty. Fortified, proceed. Just past the white church with the
wonderful steeple, turn left on Skagit City Road and go .3 miles.
Driving distance: 11 miles; *Estimated driving time:* 20 minutes.

❊ Larkspur Farm

2076 Skagit City Road, Conway, WA 98273; (360) 445-2292. Open April-
November, 11 a.m.-5 p.m. and by appointment
Timing Tip: Jan's field of flower bloom peaks mid-summer through fall.

ⵎ ☆ ✳ RR

Jan Johnson is a collector at heart—right down to small farm
buildings and large watering troughs, which she has salvaged and

miraculously moved to her charming enterprise. This effort includes, I might add, the jackhammered pieces of thick concrete milking barn floor she has transformed into curvaceous raised garden beds. What you'll come for are her beautiful flowers fresh from the garden or expertly dried, and irresistible. Her shop features garden art from enchanting trellises and gates to handsome hand-painted porcelain pins. Free for all visitors to relish are the imaginative details that reflect a creative spirit at work. Each year Jan stages several festive events when she invites some forty friends and artisans to offer their finest work (including lots of functional and ornamental garden art), antique treasures and garden-related products. A big tent is erected on the lawn and a buffet lunch is served. Hundreds of appreciative visitors come to see and shop. Call for a current schedule.

DRIViNG DIRECTIONS, ENd OF THE TOUR

To get to I-5, drive back along Skagit City Road to Fir Island Road (at the church). Turn left and proceed past Conway (a tiny town, lots of antique shops here nowadays), to the stop sign (.8 miles from Larkspur Farm.) Turn left and watch for the I-5 on-ramp of your choice (north or south). *Driving distance (Seattle):* 60 miles; *Estimated driving time:* 1 hour.

FURTHER RESOURCES

Skagit Valley is blessed with an excellent range of formal and casual restaurants, brew pubs and delis, many bed and breakfasts, small inns and motels. This is a sampling of my favorites.

Food

Andiamo Restaurant Italiano: 505 South First St., La Conner, (360) 466-9111; $$, L, D (daily). More casual at lunch with soups and salads, pizza, pasta, grinders and the like, the menu takes on the flavor of traditional dishes with contemporary interpretations for dinner. The atmosphere is intimate and inviting.

Calico Cupboard and Bakery: two locations—720 S. First St., La Conner (360) 466-4451; 121-B Freeway Dr., (next to Scott's Books) Mt. Vernon, (360) 336-3107; $$, B, L daily, D Thursday, Friday, Saturday
Mouthwatering freshly baked pasties and innovative fare (from "old-fashioned comfort foods" to health-wise selections) garner rave reviews. The ambiance in Mt. V is charming; in La C, while often crowded, it is worth the wait (generally you hang out in front of the bakery case—so plan on toting a bag full of goodies home, too!)

Hungry Moon Delicatessen: 110 North First St., La Conner. (360) 466-1602; $, B, L, early D (8 a.m.-5:30 p.m. daily) The best deli in town, great for a quick sandwich, soup and salad. Everything is made on-site from scratch or brought in from a couple of top-notch local bakeries. A few tables inside, a few more on the deck or plan a picnic take-out. (Wine and beer are available).

La Conner Brewing Company: 117 South First St., La Conner (360) 466-1123; $$, L, D daily. The handsome natural pine interior, a cheery fire and fabulous wood-fired pizzas make this brew pub a *very* popular hang out!

Palmer's Restaurant and Pub: 205 E. Washington, La Conner; (360) 466-4261; $$, spring, summer L, D daily; fall, winter, L Friday, Saturday, Sunday, D daily. Equally at home with Northwest specialties and European preparations, the upstairs restaurant is an excellent choice for a more formal meal, while the snug pub below offers a more casual menu (good burgers, sandwiches). Alas, the pub is not smoke-free if that is a concern.

Wildflowers: 2001 E. College Way, Mt. Vernon (360) 424-9724; $$$, D Tuesday-Saturday. An inspired kitchen and the cozy atmosphere have earned this excellent restaurant consistently high acclaim from regional restaurant reviewers and is considered by many the favored destination for a serious meal. The setting is a charming older home, a welcoming fire crackling on cool evenings.

LODGING

Benson Farmstead B & B: 1009 Avon-Allen Road, Bow, WA 98232; (800) 685-7239, (360) 757-0578. $$, open year-round (mid-September to the end of March on week-ends). Carefully restored in 1981, this romantic 17-room, 1914 farmhouse is filled with antiques and surrounded by gardens, the pride of Sharon and Jerry Benson, grandchildren of Norwegian farming pioneers. Four upstairs guest rooms, on garden themes, offer country views, antiques and handsome iron bedsteads. For kids there is a special playroom.

La Conner Channel Lodge: 205 N 1st Street, La Conner, WA 98257; (360) 466-1500. $$$, open year-round. Conveniently located just off the beaten track, this waterfront inn faces onto the Swinomish Channel. Decor throughout is Northwest up-scale comfy. I appreciate the nice touch of a (gas) fire lit, warmly inviting my arrival in their well-appointed rooms. While not on a garden theme, this is appealing and well-located accomodation.

White Swan Bed & Breakfast: 1388 Moore Road, Conway, WA 98273; (360) 445-2292; $$, open year-round. When I first met Peter Goldfarb he told me that he was noted for his gardens, four friendly dogs and his chocolate chip cookies. Now this is a man after my own heart! I suggest you reserve one of the three heavenly rooms in this 1890's Queen Anne farmhouse, then wander among the voluptuous gardens with a kindred spirit (Peter is most generous in filling rooms with lucious bouquets of flowers) or nestle by the parlor fire, gardening book in hand. There is a lovely one-bedroom guest house (children are welcome – there is a special sleeping nook provided), with a complete kitchen and deck overlooking the farmland beyond.

Samish Point by the Bay: 447 Samish Point Rd., Bow, WA 98232; (360) 766-6610, (800) 916-6161; $$-$$$, open year-round. Located on the 43-acre woodland and seaside home and grounds of Teresa and Herb Goldston, this charming, secluded guest house would be a delightful destination nest.

FOR MORE INFORMATION

La Conner Chamber of Commerce: 315 Morris St.; P.O. Box 1610, La Conner, WA 98257; (360) 466-4778. The Chamber has a photo album of most of the area's B & Bs, with brochures.

Mt. Vernon Chamber of Commerce: 1700 E. College Way, #A, Mt. Vernon, WA 98273; (360) 428-8547

Tulip Festival Office: P.O. Box 1784, Mt. Vernon, WA 98273; (360) 428-5959; Hotline (24 hours a day) 424-3228, ext. 2100. Free detailed color brochure with maps/events. Information kiosks during the Tulip Festival at I-5 exits #221 and #226. Tulip@SOS.net www.tulipfestival.org

More RESOURCES FOR GARDENERS

Specialty Nursery Guide: 1220 NE 90th, Seattle, WA 98115. Free, details of many small and out-of-the-mainstream nurseries.

Bunnies By the Bay: 617 Morris Street, La Conner; (360) 466-5040. This makes a memorable photo-op stop for the playful use of whimsical whirligigs along the colorful folk art fence and the detail-laden garden within. If time permits, pop into this most up-scale of bunny warrens.

Charley's Greenhouse Supply: 1599 Memorial Highway, Mt. Vernon, WA 98273; (800) 322-4707; closed Sunday. One of the country's most complete greenhouse supply sources. Greenhouses set up for your perusal, books, seed starting equipment and supplies.

Discovery Garden: 1468 Memorial Highway, Mt. Vernon, WA. A display garden developed by the Skagit County Master Gardeners now well underway. Find a display of Enabling Gardening techniques (for those less mobile or in wheelchairs), a Children's Garden, a Japanese Garden, an Herb garden, a Cottage-style Garden, Vegetable/Fruit/Test Gardens, composting demonstrations, a Naturescaping Garden. The Skagit Valley Rose Society has a display rose garden as well.

La Conner Dahlias: (360) 466-3622. The display garden (blooms in fall), where orders are also taken, is at the entrance to La Conner at the intersection of Chilberg Road and La Conner-Whitney Road.

Moon Rose: 1592-B Memorial Hwy., Mt. Vernon, WA 98273 (across from Charley's Greenhouse Supply); (360) 424-0870. As I go to press I have learned one of my *favorite* garden antique and what-not shops has found a new home (in a cheery if tiny house appropriately behind an Antique Emporium). Find lots of garden-worthy architectural details including wrought iron, old and new tools, books and *very creative* planted containers (e.g. a picturesque old hanging dust pan planted with succulents).

Pioneer Dahlias: (360) 855-1357. Display garden (blooms in fall), where orders can be placed, is on Hwy. 20, approximately ¾ mile west of I-5.

Roozengaarde: 1587 Beaver Marsh Rd., Mt. Vernon, WA 98273; (360) 434-8531, (800) 732-3266. Two-acre display garden, gift shop, fresh cut flower service year-round, fresh bulbs in fall (free mail-order catalog).

West Shore Acres: 956 Downy Rd., Mt. Vernon, WA 98273; (360) 466-3218; 1.5 acre display garden, fresh-cut flowers and small gift shop open in spring and for bulb sales early September to mid-October. Mail-order catalog.

Tillinghast Seed Co.: 623 Morris Street, La Conner. The oldest business in Skagit Valley, opened in 1885. Picturesque premises, gift shop, flower and vegetable seeds, wild bird supplies and a well-stocked general nursery.

Wells Nursery: 424 E. Section St., Mt. Vernon, WA 98273; (360) 336-6544. This wonderful little nursery is a great source for conifers (though they also offer an excellent range of trees, shrubs, vines, etc.) Best of all are their 50% off sales. Call or write to request a current schedule of sales (and plan roomy transport home for your bargains!)

BLOSSOMING BELLINGHAM BEST BETS

――――――――――― Itinerary Highlights ―――――――――――

friendly nursery features classics, the rare, what's new
nursery punster makes beds, builds beautiful borders
tiny nursery a beloved local favorite, a delightful discovery
stylish shop with unique antiques, eclectic plants, fine tools,
an art gallery has expanded to embrace garden art

―――――――――――――― 🐝 ――――――――――――――

*This is the community which embraced me as a
new gardener some ten years ago. Through the
unmitigated generosity of a few avid gardeners I
met and the limited but quality nursery resources
that nourished my early forays into garden
making, my interest in plants and thirst for
knowledge was given a healthy dose of passion
and high expectations. Reflecting on the past
decade I am surprised to see how much has been
accomplished in my garden, how many dozens of
lectures and garden tours I have attended and how
many opportunities vie for this gardener's time. I
look with equal amazement and delight at how my
community has blossomed – now offering many
excellent resources to a burgeoning enclave of
bright, ambitious and devoted gardeners.*

THE ITINERARY IN BRIEF

❶ Bear Creek Nursery

A plant aficionado's delight, Bear Creek makes an exciting, rewarding and romantic destination for gardeners in search of a superb range of plants, exuberant display gardens (with many rare and collector plants) and a stand-out staff of knowledgeable and amiable longtime gardeners.

❷ The Gardens at Padden Creek

A welcoming ambiance, choice plants, specialty display gardens and a marvelous array of unique arbors and trellises invite visitors to slowly saunter through this small but enticingly stocked nursery and garden shop. A colorful collection of exotic looking, feathery-footed fowl entertain the staff and captivate visiting junior gardeners.

❸ A Lot of Flowers

Tucked onto a tiny corner in the very heart of historic Fairhaven is one of this region's most charming little nursery/garden shops. Basking in the warm glow of the vintage, vine-covered red brick building adjacent, this is the kind of place one happily consults in pondering the perfect gift for a gardening host(ess), friend or relative or to pick up a special horticultural treat for oneself.

Lunch Enjoy a picnic in a park by a quiet woodland lake or seaside, a bookstore café or a charming courtyard restaurant.

❹ The Garden Room

This cozy and elegant shop offers sophisticated decor for home and garden, from one-of-a-kind antique chests and Chinese pots to exquisite foliage plants and fine Italian terra cotta from Sienna. An adjunct to the offices of a professional landscape design firm, you will find they stock the finest quality garden tools, as well.

❺ Chuckanut Bay Gallery

From the origins of a highly respected fine art gallery (adjacent) has sprung a marvelous shop specializing in things for the garden and gardener, many of which are from the skilled hands of regional artisans. Their outdoor garden gallery is a real charmer.

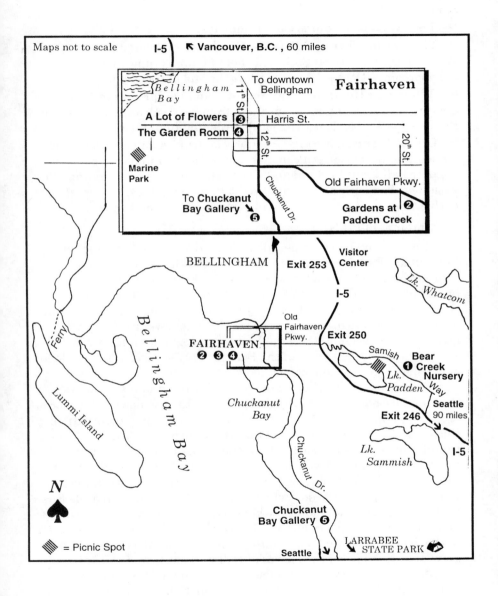

Maps not to scale   I-5 ↖ **Vancouver, B.C. , 60 miles**

Bellingham Bay

To downtown Bellingham   **Fairhaven**

11ᵗʰ St.

A Lot of Flowers ❸   Harris St.
The Garden Room ❹

12ᵗʰ St.

20ᵗʰ St.

Marine Park

To **Chuckanut Bay Gallery** ↘ ❺

Old Fairhaven Pkwy.

Gardens at ❷
Padden Creek

Chuckanut Dr.

BELLINGHAM   **Exit 253**   **Visitor Center**

I-5

Lk. Whatcom

Old Fairhaven Pkwy.   **Exit 250**

FAIRHAVEN ❷❸❹

Samish   **Bear** ❶ **Creek Nursery**

Lk. Padden   Way

Seattle 90 miles

Exit 246

I-5

Ferry

Bellingham Bay

Lummi Island

Chuckanut Bay

Lk. Sammish

Chuckanut Dr.

N ♠

Chuckanut Bay Gallery ❺

Seattle ↓

LARRABEE STATE PARK ⛏

▨ = Picnic Spot

TOUR TIMING AND TIPS

❧ **Bear Creek Nursery** is open from March through October and **The Gardens at Padden Creek** are open from March to mid-September.

❧ **The Garden Room** is closed Sundays.

❧ The **Annual Tour of Private Gardens**, sponsored by the Whatcom Horticultural Society, is held in June (June 13-14 in 1998). For more on WHS see "Resources" at the end of the chapter.

❧ **Whatcom Horticultural Society** offers a Spring and Fall Lecture Series drawing top speakers from Great Britain and around the U.S., as well as featuring local gardening luminaries.

❧ **Cloud Mountain Farm** (commercial fruit farm noted for their pioneering use of Belgian espaliered growing techniques) hosts a very popular Fall Fruit Festival and Celebration with fruit sampling (80 varieties offered) and rare fruit product tasting (jellies, sauces, etc.) in early October—date set in Fall to best time with the harvest.

SETTING THE SCENE

As with so many place names along coastal Western Washington, Bellingham Bay garnered its name from the British expedition of Captain George Vancouver when he made his way through Puget Sound in 1792. The bay had previously been named the Gulf of Gaston in 1791 by Spanish Naval Lt. Francisco Eliza, the first foreign explorer known to have visited here. The name we use today was given by Joseph Whidbey of the Vancouver expedition for Sir William Bellingham, the controller of the British Navy's stores responsible for outfitting Capt. Vancouver's ships.

In December, 1852 when Capt. Henry Roeder and his business partner Russell Peabody disembarked from their canoe on the shores of Bellingham Bay, they knew they'd found the magic combination: thick stands of virgin forest right down to the water's edge and the tumultuous waters of nearby Whatcom Creek to power a sawmill. Having suffered the first of several disastrous fires, the City of San Francisco, filled-to-bursting with new-found gold, wanted lumber at virtually any price. Roeder, who like many others had joined the Rush to the California goldfields, now knew there was more than one way to make a fortune from a goldrush. Today's Bellingham had its inception in the decision they made to locate their mill, and the town which grew up around it, on the shores of Bellingham Bay.

Within the next few decades four separate towns grew up on Bellingham Bay: Whatcom, New Whatcom, Sehome and Fairhaven. By 1904 these towns had consolidated (somewhat begrudgingly) into modern-day Bellingham.

Fairhaven, the site of the majority of this itinerary's destinations, retains much of its historic character and revels in its colorful past. The main street is named for "Dirty Dan" Harris, a character straight out of the legends of western Americana. An early settler on the Bay, he reputedly supported himself through a nefarious "importing business" centered on whiskey. In the early years Dan acquired his stock in trade by single-handedly rowing an open dory from Bellingham to Victoria, B.C. Over time Dan quietly acquired acres of property on the southern edge of the Bay and, in 1883, he platted this property as "Fairhaven". The impetus was a wave of immigration from the Midwest that had commenced the previous year and speculations concerning the western terminus of the Great Northern Railroad (an honor won in 1893 by Tacoma). Dan, who sold only on fixed prices and for cash, soon found himself the wealthiest man on Bellingham Bay, although, as often happened to such characters of American legend, Dan died in poverty, bilked of his fortune, before the end of the decade. Fairhaven continued to flourish in spite of the loss of the rail head and the ornate, red-brick buildings seen today are reminders of the prosperity of that fabulous decade. The area north of Fairhaven (imaginatively called South Hill) is a fascinating residential neighborhood to explore for the plethora of elegant Victorian architecture that has survived.

On Fairhaven's waterfront you'll find the **Bellingham Cruise Terminal**, southern homeport of the Alaska State Ferry system's marine highway to the Last Frontier. Adjacent is the old Pacific American Fisheries site, once the world's largest salmon cannery. **Chuckanut Drive**: South of Fairhaven is one of the most scenic drives in the state, fabled throughout the Northwest in much the same way as the drive along California's Big Sur. A winding two-lane road from Fairhaven to Bow of 11 miles, Chuckanut wends its way along the flanks of Chuckanut Mountain with fabulous vistas (and plenty of turnouts for appreciating them) across Samish Bay to the San Juan Islands and the snow-capped Canadian Coastal Range. Conceived in 1891 and paved in 1921, this route was a part of the Pacific Highway, from Olympia to Blaine. Built at a cost of $35,000/mile, much of the labor came from the convicts housed at a camp at Oyster Creek. **Western Washington University**: In 1893 the State Normal School opened its doors in Bellingham. The 189-acre campus of Western Washington University, made up of five colleges and two schools, today boasts a student body of something over 10,000. Western is recognized nationally for its award-winning architecture and its Outdoor Sculpture Collection with 22 pieces by such renowned artists as Isamu Noguchi, Robert Maki, Alice Aycock and Robert Morris. You can pick up a self-guided tour brochure at the Bellingham Con-Vis Bureau or WWU Visitor Information Center.

DRIVING DIRECTIONS:

From mid-town Seattle drive north on I-5 to the North Lake Samish exit #246. At the stop sign turn left onto Samish Way and drive 1 mile, watching for the nursery sign on the right.
Driving distance: 90 miles; *Estimated driving time:* 1 hour, 30 minutes.

�֍ Bear Creek Nursery

4999 Samish Way, Bellingham, WA 98226; (360) 733-1171. Open March-October, daily, 9 a.m.-6 p.m. and by appointment.
☂ ☆ ✳ RR

Jeanne Hager's history in the nursery business goes back to childhood when her parents operated a local nursery and specialized in bearded irises. In the 1960s her father purchased a collection of species rhododendron seedlings that had come from China, and many of those mature specimen plants now grow in the Hager's woodland display garden, the particular fascination of husband, Bill. For 12 years Bear Creek Nursery has offered choice plants to Bellingham gardeners—for the past three years as a retail nursery. Noted for its specialties in hostas, hardy ferns, native plants, hardy geraniums, iris, day lilies and succulents, you will also find a wide array of perennials, ornamental grasses, vines, peonies (including tree peonies) and shade loving woodland plants (like *Trilliums, Astilbes, Hellebores* and *Primulas.*) In the early season this is an excellent source for rarer bulbous plants like *Fritillaria persica* and *Erythroniums* (Dog Tooth Lilies) and a growing collection of trees (like the much sought-after Golden Acacia *Robinia pseudoacia* 'Frisia' and Lawson Cypresses) and shrubs like *Sambucus nigra laciniata*, an Elderberry with finely dissected leaves, and *Acanthopanax sieboldianus* 'Variegatus' (the variegated Five Leaf Aralia).

DRIVING DIRECTIONS:

From Bear Creek Nursery turn right onto Samish Way. (If you are picnicking at Lake Padden Park, it is one mile from Bear Creek Nursery on the left. Enter the East Entrance just past Yew St., which intersects from the right.) Continuing on Samish Way, turn left at 46th St. onto an angled street that follows alongside Lake Padden Park on Wilkens St. At the intersection with 40th St. turn right and begin a zig-zag route traversing and down the hillside to I-5: from 40th turn left onto Broad St., right onto 38th St., left onto Harrison St., right onto 37th St., left onto South Ave., right onto 36th St. then left onto Connelly Ave. You will be driving west toward I-5 and Bellingham Bay. At I-5 Connelly becomes Old Fairhaven Parkway. Drive 1 mile to 20th St. Turn left to the nursery.
Driving Distance: 5 miles; *Estimated driving time:* 10 minutes

✖ The Gardens at Padden Creek

2014 Old Fairhaven Parkway, Bellingham, WA 98225; (360) 671-0484. Open March to mid-September, 9 a.m.-6 p.m. daily.

🌱 📖 ☆ ✳

Mary Cragin, along with her nursery manager Wally Dunn, have built this charming little nursery's reputation on reliable service, high standards in plant selection (well-chosen annuals, perennials, ground covers and such), and on providing a real-life "we've got yucky soggy, clay soil, too" display beds—which are beautifully planted, by the way, and offer credibility and take-home inspiration. In 1995 the horse and llama pasture and barn on this Fairhaven/Happy Valley site gave way to a handsome new nursery that sensitively captured the character of the neighborhood. The barn has been remodeled as a classroom for workshops and lectures and a resident collection of distinctive poultry provide amusement and ambiance. The Gardens at Padden Creek featured the pieces of fine craftsmen and local artisans specializing in trellises and arbors at a time when this was a novel idea. They continue to seek out garden art, winter-hardy pottery and quality garden furniture not offered elsewhere. A specialty at the nursery is their notoriously creative container-planting service. Bring them anything from an old worn boot to an ornate Italian urn to see what magic they can perform for you to enjoy throughout the entire gardening season.

DRIVING DIRECTIONS:
Leaving the nursery, turn left from 20th onto Old Fairhaven Parkway and drive 1 mile to the traffic signal. Turn right onto 12th St. Drive three blocks and at the traffic signal turn left onto Harris St. A Lot of Flowers is on the next corner.
Driving distance: 1.25 miles; *Estimated driving time:* 5 minutes.

Lunch: You have a range of inviting options, from a Bellingham Bay-side picnic at Marine Park, to a bowl of exotic African Peanut soup at the Colophon Café (ensconced in the midst of our town's beloved Village Books) or lunch in a quiet little restaurant, Skylark's, nestled along the cobblestone courtyard/walkway of picturesque Fairhaven buildings (where even on a cool day you can sit out on a romantic little covered terrace next to a warming fire).

A Lot of Flowers

1212 11th St., Bellingham, WA 98225; (360) 647-0728. Open year-round (except January) spring-summer Tuesday-Saturday 10 a.m.-6 p.m., Sunday-Monday noon-5 p.m.; fall-winter Tuesday-Saturday 11 a.m.-6 p.m., Sunday-Monday noon-5 p.m.

❖ ☂ ☆ ✻

Penny Ferguson is the friendly familiar face that has remained consistently with A Lot of Flowers through the terms of four other owners. Now she has taken over the reins of this enchanting pocket nursery and shop that has been a fond destination of locals and visitors passing through Bellingham for over a decade.

In every season this cheerful stalwart welcomes patrons with appealing displays that spill out onto the sidewalk adjacent -- rustic willow plant stands overflow with terra cotta pots of lusty herbs in spring and buckets of fresh cut holly and aromatic greens are appealing finds at Christmas. Here is where you can head with confidence to find a thoughtful gift that goes beyond a handful of posies, but should a floral bouquet suit your needs, the flowers Penny stocks inspire creative and memorable matchmaking.

Plant specialties at A Lot of Flowers are vines (especially those that are out of the ordinary), topiaries, a wide range of unusual ornamental and culinary herbs, imaginatively planted containers and a very nice array of perennials. The shop has seeds, garden-inspired gift items, original artwork by local artists and lovely vases.

There have been flower borders flanking the nursery for many years. This favored gardening niche faithfully woos Bellingham's first sweet blossoms of *Clematis armandii* heralding the approach of spring and the tree-pruned lilac unfailingly blooms with the unforgettable fragrance of my childhood. There is one of the sweetest little courtyard ponds here, built flanked by brick, that may well inspire you to try this idea at home yourself.

WALKING DIRECTIONS:

The Garden Room is directly (south) across Harris St.

The Garden Room

1006 Harris St., Bellingham, WA 98225; (360) 734-9949. Open year-round, Monday-Saturday, 10 a.m.-6 p.m., open a few Sundays during the holidays.

❖ ☂ 🕮 ☆ ✻

This stunning little shop is the epitome of an elegant balance of tasteful, collector pieces (a fine showing of one-of-a-kind antiques) alongside the useful, everyday garden gear sought by everyday, down-on-your-knees gardeners. Susann Schwiesow has built her small but choice offering of quality horticultural tools (from Swiss-made Felco pruners to English imported Spear and Jackson stainless steel forks and spades) from her experience as a gifted gardener and a respected professional landscape designer. Evidence of her botanical skill is beautifully displayed in large planted pots on the streetscape in front of the shop. Each masterful mixed planting reflects seasonal interest, which, even in the heart of winter, provides the revelation of what can be accomplished in a tiny space with thought and imagination. Perhaps this is a clue to the success of the shop itself. While deceptively small, it warrants an unhurried and pensive look-around to soak up the carefully orchestrated details that make you feel good just being there—and perhaps you'll be enticed to take some of that "ambiance" home with you.

DRIVING DIRECTIONS:
Leaving Fairhaven, return to 12th St. and turn right. 12th St. becomes Chuckanut Dr. after crossing the bridge over Padden Creek, about 4 blocks south of Fairhaven. Follow the signs for Hwy. 11/Chuckanut Dr.
Driving distance: 1 mile; *Estimated driving time:* 5 minutes

Chuckanut Bay Gallery

700 Chuckanut Dr., Bellingham, WA 98226; (360) 734-4885. Open year-round, daily, 10 a.m.-5:30 p.m., Sundays noon-5:30 p.m.
Insider Tip: Groups can request a guided tour of the garden art gallery and a visit with Don in his studio as well.

❖ ☂ 🕮 ☆ * RR

For many years Don Salisbury has been admired in this region for his talent as a potter. In 1987 his studio was moved to a picturesque old gas station along Chuckanut Dr. (see details under "Setting the Scene") adjacent to the fine art gallery that housed his work. The gallery became a popular destination for visitors to the area who would stop for gifts and pieces to proudly display in their homes. As Don was not only an accomplished artist but an avid gardener, he and his wife Carol recognized the happy marriage of garden art with their current offerings and expanded the shop to encompass and feature horticulturally-inspired pieces as well. One of their first endeavors was to install an outdoor garden and gallery, which incorporated evocative water features, monumental forged steel sculptures and unique, hand-crafted outdoor lighting options. The key has been finding and showing the work of outstanding Northwest and Western craftsmen and artists.

Within the shop there are hundreds and hundreds of garden- and nature-related objects, from stately copper and brass weather vanes and classical cast iron lanterns to hand-carved water basins and whimsical wooden whirligigs. I have complete confidence that I can turn to Chuckanut Bay Gallery when searching out even the most creative of gifts for my husband, whom I know well, or a wedding gift for the daughter of a friend I hardly know at all (and the Gallery does a beautiful job gift wrapping and will take care of shipping as well).

DRIVING DIRECTIONS, END OF THE TOUR:
If you are not headed south toward Seattle and are not interested in this route to rejoin I-5 at Burlington (taking 20-25 minutes), turn left from the Gallery and return to Old Fairhaven Parkway at 12th St. Turn right and drive 1.5 miles to I-5. The drive from the Gallery to I-5 takes 10 minutes. If you are interested in taking advantage of the scenic route along the "Big Sur" of Washington State, from the Gallery proceed south, turning right onto Chuckanut Dr.
Driving distance (Seattle): 95 miles; *Estimated driving time:* 1 hour 40 minutes.

FURTHER RESOURCES
Food
Colophon Café: Located in Village Books, 12080 11th St., Bellingham, WA 98225; (360) 647-0092. $-$$, B,L,D daily. Quiche, hearty soups (the most famous being their African Peanut soup), generous sandwiches, decadent pastries and sweets ("life is short, eat dessert first") and lots of specialty drinks (hot and cold) are the standards at this perennial favorite. Year-round sidewalk (upstairs) and seasonal patio (downstairs) seating is offered, too.
European Bakery: 1307 11th St., Bellingham, WA 98225; (360) 671-7254. $,B,L closed Monday. Assemble a special picnic or decide to eat in.
Red Apple Market: 1401 12th St., Bellingham, WA 98225; (360) 733-4370. A quality super market with a good deli for picnic fixings.
Skylark's Fountain & Mercantile: 1308-B 11th St., Fairhaven, WA 98225; (360) 715-3642. From the downright 1950s Egg Salad Sandwich and authentic Banana Split to 1990s nouveau Butternut Lasagne (layered with roasted Buternut squash, parmesan and fresh rosemary served with a rich alfredo sauce), Skylark's is reliably delicious and offers a pleasant atmosphere tucked amid the turn-of-the-century-styled buildings.
Picnic:
Marine Park is located at the foot of Harris Street overlooking Bellingham Bay, 3 minutes from Fairhaven. There is a handsome shelter with a brick, raised fireplace and tables, as well as a grassy lawn on which to spread out a picnic. The beach is sandy and strewn with driftwood, and there are public restrooms available.

LODGING
A **new hotel** is slated to open in Fairhaven in the Fall of 1998. It will be in the classic idiom of the rejuvenation now underway in this historic neighborhood. Twenty two rooms ($85-135) will be available – those with a bay view will also have a fireplace and a balcony. For information call Ken or Brad Imus, (360) 671-5344.
Best Western **Heritage Inn**: 151 E. McLeod, Bellingham, WA 98226; (800) 528-1234, (360) 647-1912. $$, open year round. The rooms are very tastefully

and individually decorated in this cluster of Wedgewood Blue early American-styled structures. The elegant decor, thoughtful touches like an excellent free continental breakfast and reasonable rates are the reasons we have selected the Heritage Inn to house our out-of-town guests speaking to the Whatcom Horticultural Society. Located near Bellis Fair Mall and adjacent to I-5, I recommend you request a room away from the freeway.

Schnauzer Crossing: 4421 Lakeway Dr., Bellingham, WA 98226; (800) 562-2808, (360) 733-0055; http://members.aol.com/schnauzerx. $$$. Avid travelers themselves (both throughout Europe and to Japan), Monty and Donna McAllister are superb hosts, professional and personable to the core. Their home and B & B is exquisitely furnished, they provide a genuinely warm welcome, prepare a delicious and memorable breakfast and besides all that, are enthusiastic gardeners, too! Resident schnauzers on duty.

Lummi Island is a peaceful, rural island with virtually no commercial activity and no "town.". It is a great place for bicycling and long walks. The ferry is a 25 minute drive northbound from mid-town Bellingham via I-5 to exit #260, west on Slater Rd. to Haxton Way. The ferry departs hourly 7 a.m.-midnight and the crossing takes about 15 minutes.

Willows Inn Bed and Breakfast: 2579 West Shore Dr., Lummi Island, WA 98262; (360) 758-2620; www.pacificrim.net/~willows. $$$, open year round with two self-catering cottages. When we first moved to Bellingham we discovered this island gem and, though we live very near-by, have returned often for a romantic respite from our busy lifestyle. A plus are the glorious, award-winning gardens (ornamental and kitchen) and spectacular view that make this a popular wedding site.

Camping:

Larabee State Park is located on Chuckanut Drive (Hwy. 11) 5 miles south of Fairhaven. The camping sites are not right on the beach but close, and there is a marvelous network of trails near-by that meanders along the bluffs and driftwood-strewn beach. Trails depart from Larabee Park for Fragrance Lake on Chuckanut Mt. to the east.

FOR MORE INFORMATION:

Bellingham-Whatcom County Con-Vis Bureau: 904 Potter St., Bellingham, WA 98225; (360) 671-3990. www.bellingham.org Located one block east of I-5 at exit #253 and stocked with plentiful brochures for local B&Bs, restaurants, local events and attractions.

The Fairhaven Association: P.O. Box 4083, Fairhaven Station, Bellingham, WA 98227; (360) 738-1574. http://earthling1.com/nwcc/fv.html This merchant/neighborhood organization stages special events.

MORE RESOURCES FOR GARDENERS

Specialty Nursery Guide: 1220 NE 90th, Seattle, WA 98115. A free guide to small and specialty nurseries throughout the western region basically north of Tacoma to the Canadian border. Send SASE with 2 stamps.

Bakerview Nursery: 945 E. Bakerview Rd., Bellingham, WA 98226; (360) 676-0400. Open year-round, daily. In business for over a quarter century, this attractive *full-service* nursery, located on five acres, has the broadest range of gardening goods and plants (indoor/outdoor) in the area.

The Garden Spot: 900 Alabama St., Bellingham, WA 98225; (360) 676-225. Open year-round, daily. Lively display areas mingle garden art, sparkling planting combinations and the wide array of old favorites and "hot new" plants. Find everything from colorful basket stuffers to herbs to small specimen trees and shrubs for urban gardens. The shop is just as imaginatively stocked with gardening necessities and botanical gifts.

International Newstand: 111 E. Magnolia, Bellingham, WA 98225; (360) 676-7772. Open year-round, daily. This is a terrific source for garden periodicals from all over the world.

R.R. Henderson, Bookseller: 112 Grand Ave., Bellingham, WA 98225; (360) 734-6855. Open year-round, 5 days weekly, hours vary/call ahead. For locals and visitors alike, this uncommon mix of new and used books makes this shop a regular haunt as R.R. has a real commitment to building a substantive collection, including a noteworthy gardening book section.

Rosewood Nursery: 310 E. Magnolia, Bellingham, WA 98225; (360) 671-7078. This is a very savvy little nursery, right on top of the latest trends in great perennials, annuals, small woody plants, vines and roses. The tastefully stocked shop is worth a visit in its own right—this is a hidden resource in Bellingham and a great discovery for visitors and locals alike. Adventurous Kathy Anderson grows a variety of unusual annuals and perennials from seed she orders from around the world. Also, she is particularly gifted in assembling creative containers—she is happy to advise.

Village Books: 1210 11th St., Bellingham, WA 98225; (800) 392-BOOKS, (360) 671-2626; www.VillageBooks.com Open daily. If Bellingham has a favorite community gathering place it is Village Books. VB is not only a terrific bookstore with the warm ambiance of the historic building they occupy, they sponsor popular Literature Live author presentations and they share space with the Colophon Café. For gardeners there are thoughtfully assembled new, *used* (including bargain book) and magazine sections.

Whatcom Horticultural Society: P.O. Box 4443, Bellingham, WA 98227; (360) 738-6833. This non-profit, gardening education organization sponsors a terrific full-day Symposium in early Spring and a Spring and Fall Lecture Series (with notable horticultural speakers from abroad, around the country and Puget Sound luminaries, as well). They sponsor an annual Tour of Private Gardens, June 12-13 in 1998. Programs are open to the public.

Lily hybridizer, Scott Titus and plant collector/propagator Jennifer Titus, open their (otherwise wholesale) **Windy Meadows Nursery** 10 a.m.-6 p.m. the first weekend of May for a garden tour and sale of perennials and annuals and the first weekend of July, for lily (Asiatic and some Oriental) sales. 7020 Dahlberg Rd., Ferndale, WA 98248; (360) 384-5348.

❧ Index ❧

A

A & D Nursery 122, 124, 125, 128
A Garden of Distinction 75, 78, 82
A La Francaise 46, 48, 52, 70, 74
A Lot of Flowers 234, 240
Abundant Life Seed Foundation 194
Abutilons 26, 61
Access Seattle 7
Airport access 10
Alderwood Shopping Mall 125
Alexander, Emma 142
Alpine plants 130, 142, 152
American Bamboo Society 64, 139
American Horticultural Society A-Z Encyclopedia of Garden Plants, The 76
American Rhododendron Society 135
Andiamo 228, 230
Anna Clise Orchid Collection 51
Annuals for Connoisseurs 76
Anthiriums 62
Anthony's Homeport 63
Arboretum Adventures Program 97
Arboretum Foundation 93, 98, 120
　Gift Shop 52, 88
Artist's Studio Loft 164
Asia Grille 52
AW Pottery 86
Azaleas 45, 91, 113
Azaleas Fountain Court 146, 151, 155

B

Back Bay Inn 163, 164
Bainbridge Gardens Nursery 170, 174
Bainbridge in Bloom 172, 180
Bainbridge Island 69, 172
Bainbridge Island Chamber of Commerce 75, 180
Bainbridge Island Farmer's Market 172
Bainbridge Island Winery 176, 179, 180
Bainbridge Public Library Interpretive Garden 180
Baker and Chantry 64
Bakerview Nursery 243
Ballard 81, 110
Ballard Baking Company 116, 120
Bamboo 64
Bamboo Gardens of Washington 64, 146, 148, 151
Bamboo Society 125
Bananas 60
Barley for Birds Program 224
Basetti's Crooked Arbor Gardens 130
Bay Area Gardener, The 62
Bay Cottages 194
Bay Hay and Feed 170, 178
Bayview Farm and Garden 210, 217
Beall, L.C. 167
Bear Creek Nursery 234, 238
Becker, Carrie 153
Bed & Breakfast Association (Langley) 219
Bed and Breakfast Association of Seattle 9
Beebe, Ward 203
Begonias 62
Begoun, Paula 10
Bellevue 148, 151
Bellevue Botanical Garden 146, 148, 151
　Garden D'Lights 148, 152
Bellevue Botanical Garden Society 156
Bellevue Chamber of Commerce 156
Bellevue Historical Society 156
Bellevue Square 149
Bellingham 75
Bellingham-Whatcom County Con-Vis Bureau 243
Benson Farmstead B & B 231
Best Places to Kiss in the Northwest 10
Betty MacDonald Farm Guest Cottage 165
Bhy Kracke Park 40
Biel, Vy 158, 164
Bingo Ya Japanese Restaurant 20
Block, Howard 178
Bloedel Reserve 170, 172, 177
Bloedel Reserve, Gardens in the Forest, The 177
Bloedel, Elizabeth 136

Bloedel, Prentice and Virginia 177
Blue Canoe 42, 47
Blue Heron Art Center 160
Bombay House 179
Bonsai 38, 127, 139, 218
Bookmonger, The 165
Books by the Way 75, 158, 162
Bott, Wendy 222, 227
Boulangerie 104, 108
Bow Wow Meow Treatoria 108
Bowen, Betty 40
Brian O. Mulligan Sorbus Collection 113
Briazz 48
Brickell, Christopher 76
Bromeliads 51, 62, 94
Brugmansias 26, 62
Brydon, P.H. 135
Bunnies By the Bay 232
Burk's Café 117, 120
Burton 163
Bus Information 7
Butler, Fir and Merlin 114

C

Cacti 51, 64
Cactus and Succulent Society 125
Café Flora 17, 20
Café Lado 40
Café Langley 216, 218
Café Nola 70, 71, 74, 179
Caffé Appassionato 29
Calendula Books 75
Calico Cupboard and Bakery 224, 230
Camellias 113
Cameron, Bunny 179
Camping
　Deception Pass State Park 208
　Fay-Bainbridge State Park 180
　Fort Casey State Park 208
　Fort Ebey State Park 208
　Fort Flagler State Park 194
　Kopachuck State Park 144
　Larabee State Park 243
　Scenic Beach State Park 193
　U.S. Forest Service Campgrounds 6
　Washington State Parks 6
Cannas 60
Capitol Hill 81
Captain Whidbey Inn 205, 207
Carey, Jim 85
Carl S. English, Jr. Botanical Garden 110, 115
Carnivorous Plant Society 64, 125, 139
Carnivorous plants 36, 64, 95
Cascade Cactus and Succulent Society 63, 64
Cascade Heather Society 139
Casper, Kathy 165
Cats, Used 165
Cavanaugh House 115
Celebrations To Go 27, 29
Center for Urban Horticulture 42, 48, 52, 117
Center of the Universe 25
Cestrum 26
Chapman, Gail 82
Charley's Greenhouse Supply 232
Chateau Ste. Michelle Winery 59, 63
Cherries 45, 113
Chihuly, Dale 58
Chinaberry Hill 143
Chittenden, Hiram M. 115
Christianson's Nursery 222, 226
Christianson, John and Toni 226
Christopher's 208
Chuckanut Bay Gallery 241
Chuckanut Drive 237
Church, Thomas 132, 142, 177
Chutneys 106, 108
Cinnabuns 46
City People's Garden Store 12, 15, 18
City People's Mercantile 22, 28
Clemons Tree Farm 136
Clinton 213

❦ *Index* ❦

❦ *Index* ❦

❦ *Index* ❦

❧ *Index* ❧

CEDARCROFT PRESS

🍂 🍂 🍂 Order Form 🍂 🍂
🍂

DATE: _____

NAME: _____

STREET: _____

CITY: _____

STATE: _____   ZIP/POSTAL CODE: _____

TELEPHONE: (_____)_____

Quantity   **Price**

_____   *Gardeners On The Go: Seattle* @ $15.95   _____

S/H (Total for any number of books in U.S) $2.50

Washington State Residents add 7.8% tax   _____

_____   *Northwest Gardeners' Resource Directory*

1999-2000 Edition—Send Me Information

TOTAL   _____

☐   I have enclosed my check or Money Order
☐   Please bill my Visa/Mastercard:

Account # _____-_____-_____-_____

Expires: _____

Signature:_____

You may **ORDER TOLL-FREE: 1-888-828-8891**

or mail to: Cedarcroft Press, 59 Strawberry Pt., Bellingham, WA 98226